CLASSICAL C

CLASSICAL CATS

The rise and fall of the sacred cat

Donald Engels

London and New York

FOR MY MOTHER
ALICE F. ENGELS

First published 1999
by Routledge
11 New Fetter Lane, London EC4P 4EE

Simultaneously published in the USA and Canada
by Routledge
29 West 35th Street, New York, NY 10001

Routledge is an imprint of the Taylor & Francis Group

©1999 Donald Engels
The right of Donald Engels to be identified as the Author of this Work
has been asserted by him in accordance with the Copyright, Designs
and Patents Act 1988.

Typeset in Garamond by Routledge
Printed and bound in Great Britain by St Edmundsbury Press,
Bury St Edmunds, Suffolk

British Library Cataloging in Publication Data
A catalogue record for this book is available from the British Library.

Library of Congress Cataloguing in Publication Data
Engels, Donald W.
Classical cats: the rise and fall of the sacred cat/Donald Engels.
Includes bibliographical references and index.
1. Cats–history. 2. Cats–Religious aspects–History.
3. Cats–Greece–History. 4. Cats–Rome–History. I. Title.
SF442.6.E56   1999
398.24'529752'0901–dc21   99-25313

ISBN 0–415–21251–0

CONTENTS

CONTENTS

ILLUSTRATIONS

PREFACE

The cat has played a significant although underrated role in history, especially in public health, religion, art, and folklore. First domesticated in Egypt some 4,000 years ago, the animal has been the subject of several works covering its early history there until about 500 BC. The next millennium, though, 500 BC to AD 500, which saw the introduction of the cat into western Europe as a significant component in European culture, has not received much attention. This neglect has caused many misunderstandings about the history of the animal, especially its role in religion, and its unfortunate persecution between 1200 and 1700. It is hoped that the present book will help clarify the role of the cat in European life.

This work focuses on the history of the cat during the classical era and is based on original sources: literary references; artistic portrayals; and archeological remains. To help understand this history, the Introduction will explore basic biological and behavioral aspects of the cat. This will enable us to better comprehend the animal's responses to the challenges it faced through the millennia in its new home, the continent of Europe. The first chapter will be devoted to Egypt, since many aspects of the animal in later European art, religion, and folklore originate in that culture. Indeed, Egypt is where the cat was first domesticated. Hence the term "classical" is also used in its broader meaning, that is, a work of art or music, or an idea that sets the standard that later eras try to emulate. In the same way, the cultures of Egypt, Greece, and Rome set the standard for future concepts of the animal. The final two chapters will trace this influence through medieval Europe into the modern era.

The first task was to track down the ancient evidence relating to cats. As befits the nature of the animal, they often had to be coaxed from obscure and difficult hiding places. Yet every archeological report, compendia of ancient art, and obscure ancient author, that yielded a cat was a minor triumph. Sometimes they were hiding in plain sight, on inlaid Mycenaean daggers, savoring the rich smells at a long-forgotten Etruscan banquet, and even sitting beneath the seat of kings.

The *Thesaurus Linguae Graecae* and its editor, Theodore Brunner, were an invaluable help in my search for ancient literary references. The *TLG* brought many of them out of hiding and into the open. I am indebted to Michael MacKinnon of the University of Alberta for his helpful assistance with the archeological remains from western Europe. I would also like to thank Al Wesolowski, and David Reese of the Field Museum of Natural History for their help collecting archeological evidence. Richard Beal of the Oriental Institute provided welcome assistance for the cats in ancient Mesopotamia. I also wish to thank the selfless staff of the University of Arkansas libraries who provided all possible assistance to me, especially Beth Juhl. The college of Arts and Sciences of the University of Arkansas was helpful in providing me with a leave of absence in 1992 to do the preliminary research. As always, my department of history provided a sane, rational work environment.

Many individuals helped me during the writing of this work. I wish to thank Catherine Lux, Evan and Anita Bukey. I also wish to thank the members of my department, Suzanne Smith, Kimberly Chenault, Willard Gatewood, David Chappell, and Elliott West. Thanks are owed to Gary Shepard, Elias and Julie Saad, Robert Whalen, Deborah Peterson, Mary Hilt, Diana Delia, LeRoy and Helen Middleworth, Janie Penn, Julia Sheehan, and Errol Morris for their help and encouragement. Lynda Coon and John Arnold provided help for the medieval era.

I have also been assisted by various cats, past and present, that my family and I have owned over the last forty years, some of whom will appear in the notes on the following pages. Observing their behavior and interaction with other animals and humans has provided many insights. I have learned much from all of them.

I will use the names of the Egyptian pharaohs and the dates of their reigns given in Peter A. Clayton, *Chronicle of the Pharaohs*, New York, Thames and Hudson, 1994. For the citation of classical Greek sources, I will use those given in the *Thesaurus Linguae Graecae*. It is unfortunate that so many differences remain in the textual citations of Greek literature. Therefore common, alternative numerical citations will be added when needed in parentheses after the main citation.

A serious history of the cat in medieval Europe still awaits an author, despite the abundant literary, artistic, and archeological evidence for that important topic. In the discussion of medieval cats in the Epilogue, then, I had to rely on available secondary sources. For the eighteenth- and nine-teenth-century folklore concerning the cat discussed at the end of the Epilogue, I was once again able to rely on compendia of original sources concerning the animal.

Fayetteville, Arkansas

ACKNOWLEDGMENTS

I would like to thank the following organizations and individuals for permission to use their illustrations. The British Museum: 0.1, 1.2, 1.3, 1.5, 1.6, 1.7, 2.7, 3.3; Egyptian Expedition of the Metropolitan Museum of Art, New York City, Rogers Fund: 1.1, 1.4; National Museum, Athens, Greece: 2.1, 2.3, 2.9, 2.11; Thames and Hudson: 2.2; Yale University Press: 2.4; Bibliothèque Nationale, Paris: 2.8; Staatliche Museum zu Berlin: 2.6; Editions archéologiques de l'Université de Genève: 2.10; Ikuyo Tagawa Garber: 2.12, 2.13; Museum of Fine Arts, Boston, gift of Henry P. Kidder : 3.1; Soprintendenza Archeologica per L'Etruria Meridionale: 3.2; Musée d'Aquitaine, Bordeaux, France: 3.8; Musée Municipal Alise-Sainte-Reine, France: 3.9; Deutsches Archäologisches Institut, Rome: 3.10; Erich Lessing/Art Resource, N.Y.: 3.4; Alinari/Art Resource, N.Y.: 3.5, Scala/Art Resource, N. Y.: 3.11; Belgian Tourist Office: 4.1; British Library, Cott. Nero. D. IV: 4.3.

Figure 0.2 is taken from J. Anderson, *Zoology of Egypt: Mammalia*, London, H. Rees, 1902; 0.3 is from R.F. Scott, *Scott's Last Expedition*, London, John Murray, 1923; 2.5 is from G.H. Karo, *Die Schachtgräber von Mykenai*, Munich, F. Bruckman, 1930; 3.7 is from the *Corpus Inscriptionum Latinarum*, vol. 14, no. 2215; 4.2 is from M. Oldfield Howey, *The Cat in the Mysteries of Religion and Magic*, New York, Castle Books, 1956; 2.7, 3.6 and 3.7 are from O. Keller, *Die Antike Tierwelt*, Hildesheim, Georg Olms, 1963, reprint of 1909.

ABBREVIATIONS

Beadle   Beadle, M., *The Cat: History, Biology, Behavior*, New York,
                  Simon and Schuster, 1977
Briggs   Briggs, K.M., *Nine Lives: The Folklore of the Cat*, New York,
                  Pantheon Books, 1980
CIL   *Corpus Inscriptionum Latinarum*
Halm   *Fabulae Aesopicae*, ed. C. Halm, Leipzig, Teubner, 1901
IG   *Inscriptiones Graecae*
Malek   Malek, J., *The Cat in Ancient Egypt*, London, British
                  Museum Press, 1993
OED   *Oxford English Dictionary*
Perry   *Babrius and Phaedrus*, ed. and trans. B.E. Perry, Cambridge,
                  Mass., Harvard University Press, 1965
Perry, *Aesopica* *Aesopica*, vol. 1, ed. B.E. Perry, Urbana, Ill., University of
                  Illinois Press, 1952
RE   Pauly-Wissowa, *Real-Encyclopädie der Classischen
                  Altertumswissenschaft*
TLG   *Thesaurus Linguae Graecae*
TLL   *Thesaurus Linguae Latinae*
Van Vechten   Van Vechten, C., *The Tiger in the House*, New York, Knopf,
                  1936

INTRODUCTION
The cat in history

For I will consider my cat Jeoffrey.
For he is the servant of the Living God, duly and daily serving him …
For he keeps the Lord's watch in the night against the adversary.
For he counteracts the powers of darkness by his electrical skin and glaring eyes.
For he counteracts the Devil, who is death, by brisking about the life.
For in his morning orisons he loves the sun and the sun loves him.
For he is of the tribe of Tiger.

(Christopher Smart, "On Jeoffrey, My Cat")[1]

Today when we think of cats, we recall the familiar hearthside companion and the mischievous playmate. It is difficult to comprehend that in the past the animal has played a fundamental role in the development of European and indeed Western civilization.

Of all the domesticated animals, the relationship between man and cat has been among the most important for most of the last four millennia. In the past, this relationship was less visible than at present, but far more significant. In silence, in secret, and often at night, the ancient battle between the cat and the rodent, mankind's greatest natural enemy, has continued through the ages. Domesticated cats were the bulwark of Western societies' defense against the rodents and the thirty-five or so dangerous diseases they carry, including typhus and the bubonic plague. Furthermore, the presence of a barn cat often meant the difference between starvation and survival for many farm families through the millennia.

Although cats are far more visible today, their role as a major factor combating disease and starvation has been largely supplanted by modern medicine, public health policies, and the revolution in agricultural productivity. In earlier eras, cats were among mankind's greatest assets in this struggle.

It was not pampered house cats that led the fight, however, but the often shunned and neglected barn, village, and ship's cats. Recent studies have shown that well-fed house cats on average kill fourteen small animals, usually rodents, annually. Feral cats that must live on their own, however,

1

kill about 1,100 small animals, mainly rodents, per year to survive. In fact, so great are the hunting skills of this animal that they can decimate native species of small mammals.[2]

Nor was the native European wildcat (*Felis sylvestris sylvestris*) instrumental in the struggle against mice and rats. For the last 10,000 years, there has been a close connection between human settlements, grain production, and rodents. The European wildcat, however, shuns human association and lives in forests remote from human settlement, only making occasional raids on chicken houses, if no dog is present. It was only the Egyptian and Libyan wildcat (*Felis sylvestris libyca*) and its domesticated Egyptian progeny (*Felis sylvestris catus*) that from early times accepted a close connection with humans, attracted indeed by the abundant quantities of rodents that usually infested human settlements. Without these domesticated cats from Egypt, originally imported into the continent by the Greeks, European towns, villages, and farms would have been frequently overrun by mice and rats. As a consequence, European civilization would have been considerably poorer and sicker (not to mention less lively) over the past 2,500 years.

Nor was public health the only area where cats played an important role in European culture. For a thousand years, they were important religious symbols for the goddesses Artemis of the Greeks, Diana of the Romans, and the Greco-Egyptian goddess Isis. These divinities were worshiped, especially by women, throughout Greece and later the Roman Empire. Although the goddesses as well as other pagan divinities were later demonized by the Christians, they continued to be worshipped through the Middle Ages, especially in rural areas. In the eleventh century, secular and religious authorities began to crack down on the residual paganism of the countryside. This led to the infamous witch hunts and cat massacres of that era. Ironically, so far from reconciling God to humanity, the massacres of hundreds of thousands of women and cats resulted in plagues, famines, and population decline – events that have always been associated with divine vengeance rather than divine favor.

Finally, the cat has been an important element in European folklore and folktales over the centuries. Many of these simple tales had their origins in ancient Egypt, Greece, and the Roman Empire. As we shall see, the nursery rhyme that begins:

> Hey diddle diddle,
> The cat and the fiddle,
> The cow jumped over the moon ...

has its origins in the worship of the Egyptian cat goddess Bastet, who was identified with Artemis and Diana of the Greeks and Romans. Indeed, for no other animal has there been such a remarkable persistence of pagan associations surviving into modern European folklore and folk custom.

Despite the importance of the cat, very little has been done to study the animal during the classical era. This is despite the relatively large body of ancient evidence: literary sources, epigraphy, artistic portrayals, coinage (perhaps surprisingly), and excavated remains. Excellent studies of Egyptian cats have appeared for decades, but the millennium between its first widespread use in Greece to catch mice, and its spread throughout the entire continent of Europe by AD 400, has often been ignored.[3] This in turn has caused myths and misinformation about the animal to spread. The purpose of this work is to collect all this evidence in one place for the first time and analyze it, so that the role of the cat in our civilization may be better appreciated. It is to their story that we now turn.

Evolution, biology and behavior

The domestic cat experienced many vicissitudes, adaptations, and struggles for survival in the European continent, which was so different in climate, terrain, flora, and fauna from its Egyptian homeland. To understand why the cat was so successful in its new territory, some basic characteristics of its biology and behavior must be reviewed.

Our journey begins in the woodlands of North Africa some thirty-four million years ago (mya). In that region, there evolved from the order of *Carnivora* the lynx-like first ancestor to all modern felids, *Proailurus* of the Oligocene. Later, about 5 mya, several species of small wild cats, including the *Felis chaus*, *Felis margarita* (Sand cat), and the *Felis sylvestris* also evolved from the genus *Felis*.[4] It is this latter species that will be the center of our story.

Of all the carnivores, the felids and the related pantherines have the most specialized diets. Members of the Vulpavine family, for example, that includes foxes, dogs, bears, raccoons, and weasels, although essentially carnivores, have become omnivorous over time. When meat is scarce, they may eat fruits, legumes, insects, and plants. The panda indeed is an example of a Vulpavine carnivore that has become entirely vegetarian, with a diet limited to bamboo.

The Viverrine family that includes the cats and mongeese took a riskier path. They eat fewer plants than the Vulpavines and felids eat almost none. From time to time, a felid might eat the chyme that had been in its prey's stomach, chew a few leaves for vitamins, or swallow a few blades of grass as a purge. But their diets must consist of mainly animal proteins or they will decline and starve. They do not have the luxury of switching to berries if game becomes scarce; fresh meat killed by themselves or by their mothers is virtually the only item on their menu. They have chosen to live on the edge of survival.[5]

Thus the cats' survival depended solely on their hunting skills. Not for them are fruits and berries, waiting to be taken from bushes and trees. Their prey animals are intelligent, fast, brave, often well armed with horns and hooves (and sharp teeth in the case of the rat), and frequently larger than the cat. This is sometimes even the case for *catus* in relation to the black rat, which can grow to 18 inches in length, the size of a small cat, especially in the Middle Ages, fights in packs, and has a higher level of intelligence. The cat had to evolve speed, strength, intelligence, courage, and a formidable armament of its own to survive.

Since hunting is life for the cat, it preoccupies him from birth. Despite popular opinion, hunting is instinctual among cats, and does not necessarily have to be learned from the mother.[6] Mother cats may teach, but the basic instinctual behavior is already present at birth.

Members of the felid, pantherine (lion and tiger) and the related *Acinonyx* (cheetah) genera are among the fastest land animals. They are assisted by a remarkable, flexible spine, that enables them to fully extend their stride. Speed is useful for hunting, especially fast prey such as antelope, but also useful for evading capture or predation. Like other predators, even the lion on occasion, cats know when to run from danger, especially from malicious humans. This, however, indicates prudence in the face of overwhelming force. Pound for pound, the cat family contains some of the world's strongest animals. This is especially important for small felids, since it contributes to their speed and also to their ability to climb trees, both for hunting purposes and for escaping from predation.[7]

Courage is one of the domestic cat's greatest selective advantages. This can be seen most clearly in its successful defense against much larger animals, especially dogs and packs of large, fearsome rats. In Egypt and North Africa, the cats kill scorpions and poisonous snakes whose venom is powerful enough to kill humans. This ability also requires lightning-fast reflexes. Perhaps most admirable is the willingness of mother cats to sacrifice their own lives for the sake of their kittens. Mother cats that repeatedly enter burning buildings to rescue each of their kittens one by one provide an example of maternal concern matched by few other species.[8]

Felid bodies closely resemble each other and have remained essentially unchanged for millions of years, while those of herbivores and omnivores have altered dramatically. Specialized and efficient hunting capability has shaped the body of the cat. Dagger-like eye teeth fasten to the prey while triangular cheek teeth sever the victim's spine and shear flesh into bite-sized morsels. Binocular vision and effective night vision, some six times better than that of humans, has made all members of the genus effective nocturnal hunters. Since meat, unlike herbs and grasses, is easy to digest, felids have no need for large, heavy stomachs. This helps to further increase their speed and mobility.

Hunting and hunting alone accounts for a cat's sense of fun and play. The cat's only amusements are imitations of hunting, either with other willing (and sometimes unwilling) animals, humans, toys, hands, fingers, and especially tails (even their own will do in a pinch), or with live prey. It seems that felids have a sense of appreciation for their prey animals, even after their death.[9]

Coloration is another factor that has helped the wildcats to survive in many different environments, and human cultures, not all of them hospitable. Coloration helps the wildcat to escape predation, and camouflages it while stalking and striking. Wildcats in northern climates are soft colored and have greyish markings, since they must match the background during all four seasons, particularly in winter. This is true of the European wildcat (Fig. 0.1) who will later interbreed with the *libyca*, and produce the domesticated grey tabby.

Wildcats in warmer climates are often striped or spotted to match the dappled sunlight falling through the leaves of forests. This is true of the *libyca*, which has a tawny-golden color with darker stripes (Fig. 0.2). In its early history, North Africa was heavily forested, and the cats adapted well to the arboreal environment. Cats that live on the savannahs are generally tawny with little or no markings which match their surroundings. Nevertheless, they will blend in well even when the grasses are green.

Silence and undetectability are further advantages of the cat while hunting. Frequent grooming by the small cats removes much personal odor, and burial of its feces and urine performs the same function. In contrast to other animals, cats walk so quietly that they are often inaudible.

Figure 0.1   The European wildcat, *Felis sylvestris sylvestris*

Figure 0.2   The Libyan wildcat, *Felis sylvestris libyca*

> A cat lifts out each paw like a person offering to shake hands, then gently places the paw, outer edge first, very carefully on the ground before shifting any weight onto it.[10]

Indeed, the different steps of the dog and the cat represent two different hunting styles and approaches to life. The cats hold back and approach life with reserve and caution, while dogs are eager and more aggressive. Stealth, camouflage, and secrecy are of benefit for both hunting and escaping from predation themselves.

Effective hunters, feral (stray) cats (that is, domestic cats living in barns, or villages, or on their own in the wild), will kill about three small mammals, usually rodents, per day, or about 1,100 annually to survive.[11] In contrast, well-fed English house cats living in villages, kill only about fourteen prey animals annually.[12] When it is remembered, however, that there are at present some five million English house cats, the total number of their kills is quite large. The biologist Roger Tabor, though, has warned not to simply extrapolate the fourteen kills per animal to each of the five million domestic house cats.[13] Many English cats live in urban settings, remain indoors, have little opportunity to hunt, and have a more limited supply of prey animals. Indeed, most rodents living in large northern cities today (although not in the Greek and Roman eras) are large, fearsome brown rats, that many cats, especially well fed ones, would rather avoid.

Moreover, it has been shown that stray cats in urban settings often prefer garbage and refuse than prey animals for their diet.[14] Although such a diet lacks nutritional value for long-term survival, the life of urban strays is usually "solitary, nasty, brutish, and short," in any event. Still, such a diet would help deprive urban mice and rats of a major source of their food.

Finally, cat predation of birds has been frequently overestimated. One maxim often accepted on face value is that free-roaming cats are detrimental to wildlife populations in the United States, particularly songbirds. This perception of feline predation on birds persists despite the fact that many scientific studies from a variety of locations have refuted this assertion, or at least contradicted exaggerated numeric claims of bird mortality.[15]

Bird populations, indeed, especially ground feeders, may be under less pressure from cats than from disease and other natural predators. Many rats and mice prey on birds as well, especially their fledglings and eggs, and thus birds may in fact be more plentiful where there are cats who prey upon the rodents. Cats may also limit populations of hawks (when immature), cowbirds, blue jays, raccoons (when juvenile), and opossums, all of whom prey on songbirds and their eggs.

The senses of vision, hearing, and smell are acutely developed in the cat. It is the eyes, however, that have inspired the most attention over the millennia. Cats' night vision is six times better than our own and, relatively speaking, they have the largest eyes among the mammals, enabling them to gather 50 per cent more light than humans. The pupils of small cats expand and contract according to the amount of light as ours do, not into a smaller circle, however, but into a thin slit. This attribute has reminded many of the phases of the moon. Most notable of all, of course, is their reflective nature. This reflection is caused by an organic crystalline mirror-like structure, the *tapetum lucidum* at the rear of the eye. Photons that miss detection in the retina are reflected back from the rear of the eye to give the retina another opportunity.[16] To the ancient Egyptians, the cats' eyes shining on even in darkness symbolized their sun god Atum-Ra, who even after sunset still gleamed in the darkness of the underworld.

In addition to our five senses, they have at least seven and a possible eighth, and perhaps as many as ten. The cat's sixth sense is located in the vomeronasal organ, on the roof of the mouth, enabling it to detect the presence of certain chemicals in the environment, estrus pheromones for example. The seventh sense is the remarkable homing sense or instinct that allows cats to travel long distances, sometimes several hundred miles, back to their homes.

It has also been noted that cats have the ability to predict the weather, by sensing changes in humidity and barometric pressure. These changes are sensed in the cat's ear and when such changes occur, the cat will rub one of its ears with its paw.[17] The seventeenth-century English poet Robert Herrick noted local folklore concerning this aspect of the cat among the country people of Devon (where indeed the earliest remains of domesticated cats from the country were found):

> True calenders as Pusse's eare,
> Wash't o're to tell what change is neare.[18]

Roger Tabor has noted that this behavior can be readily observed in modern cats as well. Although this sense may have aided the farmer over the centuries, in the late Middle Ages it was regarded as yet more proof that the animal was a close ally of the Prince of the Air, that is Satan.

Finally, cats have also been known to predict earthquakes by their behavior immediately before the quake. Many cultures have observed too the animal's sense of death, the ability to sense and even predict the death of others.[19]

Cats have a phenomenal potential rate of fertility. Since earliest ages, the animal has been associated with this principle, which has often taken a religious form. Mating behavior resembles that of other species of solitary felids and pantherines, especially the tiger (*Panthera tigris*). A dominant male will have a territory that includes several females and their kittens. Dominance is determined by fights between males, the victor obtaining the territory. If a new male takes over a territory, he may kill the kittens that are present, if they are not his own, unless stoutly defended by the female. Specific aspects of mating behavior and its influence on folklore and religion will be discussed in following chapters.

Litters are usually four in number, and females can bear offspring at the age of only five months after their birth. The most fecund female cat ever recorded produced some 420 offspring, and the largest litter produced was thirteen.[20] The potential fertility of the cat is enormous, and can indeed be harmful for small mammals and birds if not controlled. Nevertheless, high potential fertility rates were one of the animal's greatest natural advantages over its enemies, both human and animal.

Let us take a breeding pair of adults with a litter of four kittens. Assuming that all the females will give birth starting in six months time and that they will have litters of four kittens – two males and two females – at six-month intervals thereafter, at the end of one year our original pair and four kittens will have expanded to a modest population of 54 cats. At the end of two years however, there will be 486 cats, in three years 4,374, at the end of four years, 39,366, and at the end of five, 354,294 cats.[21]

These high rates are never achieved in real life because of biological checks of limited food supply, diseases, predation, lack of a mate for a specific area and so on. Nevertheless, when cats expand to a virgin territory for their species, with abundant supplies of prey animals, and a specific ecological niche unique to themselves near human habitation, their initial numbers can be expected to dramatically increase.

Cats can carry diseases that can be transmitted to humans but these are fewer in number than those transmitted by dogs (which top the list), rodents, and monkeys. Furthermore, cats are far less likely to bite humans than dogs, thus reducing the risk of diseases such as rabies, the worst disease. Although it is not mentioned as an ancient disease in many modern works of reference, a passage in Dioscorides shows that it was present in the Mediterranean by at least the first century AD, and probably much earlier.[22]

Classification and terminology

In this work, we will use the most current terminology concerning the cat, given by J. Clutton-Brock, *Cats, Ancient and Modern*.[23] The species *Felis sylvestris* is divided into four varieties or races. The first is *F. sylvestris libyca*, the smaller, short-haired North African wildcat. (The varietal name of the cat, *libyca*, is almost invariably misspelled as *lybica* in most popular and semi-popular works!) This individual achieves a body size of some 25–30 inches (65–75 cm), and a tail length of 10–12 inches (25–30 cm). Its weight is between 8 and 14 lbs (3.5–6.5 kg). It has a tawny, golden-orange coat with somewhat darker, broken stripes (Fig. 0.1). The second is the *Felis sylvestris ornata*, the West Asian wildcat; the third, *Felis sylvestris sylvestris*, the larger, long-haired European wildcat; and, last, the domestic cat *Felis sylvestris catus*, which only dates from about 2000 BC.

Genetic and anatomical research has shown that all domesticated cats are descended primarily from the *libyca*, with some interbreeding occurring with *ornata* and *sylvestris*. Of the three subspecies, the *libyca* most closely resembles the *catus* genetically and anatomically. In fact, research has shown that many Asian breeds such as the Persian and Siamese are primarily descendants of the *libyca* with some interbreeding with the *ornata*. The *Felis sylvestris sylvestris* or European wildcat is itself incapable of domestication. Therefore it is not an ancestral form of the *catus*, and indeed is anatomically distinct from it. When the European wildcat is bred with a domestic cat, the result is a churlish, surly animal, that lacks the modicum of civil behavior necessary for human companionship. Nevertheless, over time, with continual interbreeding between hybrids of *catus* and *sylvestris*, an acceptable domestic cat can be produced.[24]

The word "cat" when used by itself in this work will almost always refer to the domesticated cat, *Felis sylvestris catus*. On occasion, the word "cat" will also be used to refer to members of the species *Felis sylvestris* in general, when the specific variety (*catus*, *libyca*, *ornata*, or *sylvestris*) of an individual cannot be determined because of limited evidence. The term "felid" will also be used to denote a member of the genus *Felis*. "Feline" will be used both as an adjective and a noun also denoting a member of the genus *Felis* (plural

Felidae, or the felids). In the past, the term "feline" was strictly an adjective,[25] but in more recent years the term has been used as both an adjective and a noun and will be so used here.

The term *libyca* will refer to the *Felis sylvestris libyca*, or North African wildcat; *ornata* will refer to the West Asian wildcat, *Felis sylvestris ornata*; and the term *sylvestris* when used by itself will denote the variety *Felis sylvestris sylvestris*, or European wildcat. On occasion, the term "wildcat" will also be used to denote the wild varieties of *F. sylvestris* in general, when the specific variety cannot be determined from the surviving evidence. Finally, the term *miu* will be used on occasion to denote specifically the Egyptian domesticated cat, since this was the concise, onomatopoeic word the Egyptians used themselves for the animal. Accuracy is the goal, but it cannot always be achieved because of the often limited nature of our ancient evidence.

Types of domestic cat

Felids and pantherines of various species and varieties have distinct cultures that are learned from the adults and shaped by their natural and human environments. These variables will also shape the cat's role in different circumstances.[26]

Our ancient sources portray the domestic cat in three distinct roles. The first and most familiar is the house cat, the human companion and terror of household mice and rats. The second role is the barn cat whose home is in the barnyard where he protects the farmer's grain supply from rodents and lives in an uneasy truce with roosters and chickens. The third role is the feral cat. A feral cat is a *Felis sylvestris catus* which, although its territory often includes human dwellings, has to adapt to a life on its own. Sometimes barn and village cats are lumped together in the feral category, but it is clear from our sources, both ancient and modern, that most of these have a degree of tameness and familiarity with humans that would exclude them from the feral category. Nevertheless, it is also true that some barn and village cats are intolerant of human presence, hiding at their approach. Our Greek and Latin sources used the same words for domesticated, feral, and wildcats (*Felis sylvestris catus* and *Felis sylvestris sylvestris*). In Greek, both the domestic cat and the wildcat are called *ailouros* (or *aielouros*, later *kattos*).[27] In Latin, both varieties are called *felis* (or *feles*, later *cattus*).[28] Some wildcats will therefore inevitably find their way into our discussion.

Cats play two other roles that, while not mentioned by our literary sources, can be deduced from other evidence. The first is the ship's cat. Cats are found throughout the world far from their North African homeland and may in fact be the most ubiquitous mammal on earth. They are found in every continent (even in Antarctica under human protection) and many uninhabited islands.[29] Almost all these cats were originally brought aboard ships, probably to protect their stores from rodent depradations, and jumped ship when the chance arose. Hence the cats found on Mediterranean islands and Britain, as will be discussed below.

The second is the village or town cat, a common sight throughout the Mediterranean today and in cities and towns the world over. This is another type of cat whose home is in settled environments, but which is essentially free from human protection and control. Because of their ability to destroy rodents, they are tolerated and sometimes encouraged with scraps of meat and fish.[30]

Barn and village cats

The difference between barn and village cats is often not distinct. Both are to some degree feral and were often in fact the same individuals, as can still be the case today. This is because of the nucleated rural settlement of much of the Mediterranean region both in the past and the present. Farmers often lived together in villages with their equipment, barns, barnyard animals (especially chickens), and grain storage facilities.[31] Thus a barn cat would frequently have been a member of village society.

The life of the barn cat has often been harsh. Elizabeth Marshall Thomas's description of such cats in rural New Hampshire is probably indicative of the life most have led since their introduction into Europe by at least the eighth century BC:

> Farm cats, after all, are neither pets nor livestock. They have no monetary value whatever and are tolerated with mild amusement as long as they intrude only by occasional visits to the dairy at milking time to beg for milk. Barn dwellers, these cats were traditionally the province of the men, not of the women, and few male farmers had much commitment to them … When the cat population got too high for the farmer's liking the cats were simply put into bags and gassed or drowned. To care for a group of animals for a time, and then to suddenly round them up and dispatch them without warning, is what farming is all about.[32]

The life of some village cats could be more fortunate. The best description and photographic essay on village cats is Hans Silvester's *Cats in the Sun*.[33] This work represents the fruit of a year of studying and photographing village cats of the Greek Cyclades islands. Here we see a range of social positions, some privileged, some marginal among the islands' cats.

> On one side are the privileged individuals who belong to someone. While they are not allowed inside the house, the doorstep is theirs: they are regularly fed, and may even receive extra rations on demand; sometimes they serve as living toys for the children of the

family. Fatter and less wild, these cats are easily spotted. They are no less free than the rest, but enjoy much better conditions. At the opposite extreme are those cats who are tramps by temperament and refuse to fit in, scavenging beyond the boundaries of any given neighborhood ... In fights, they always lose to their more established brethren. Their diet is irregular, feast one moment, famine the next, nearly always very poor in quality. They are often ill, and they die young.[34]

The village cats have an intimate knowledge of their neighborhood territory.

Within the district, they know every house, garden, roof, shrub, tree, and hiding-place. They also know every inhabitant, human or animal. They see a dog at a distance, and know at once how to behave towards that particular creature. People, too, hold no mysteries, and they know to the last detail every shift and nuance in the rhythm of village life: precisely when and in what house leftovers will be put out for them, when the fishermen come back to port – and a great deal more. In the same way, the village cats know who is fond of them, who tolerates them, and who hates them, and they adjust their manners accordingly. Their understanding of people is unerring, and their judgement acute. The slightest change in their world is cause for surprise: a new smell, no matter how faint, arouses their curiosity; at an unexpected sound they instantly awake.[35]

The homing ability of the cat combined with its intimate knowledge of its territory, makes it something of a *genius loci*, a "spirit of the place." Indeed, cats often seem far more attached to their place than to their "owners." Topsell, writing in 1607 noted:

The nature of this beast is to love the place of her breeding; neither will she tarry in any strange place, although carried far. She is never willing to forsake the house for love of any man, and this is contrary to the nature of the dog, who will travel abroad with his master. Although their masters forsake their houses, yet will not cats bear them company, and being carried forth in close baskets or sacks, they will return again or lose themselves.[36]

Ship's cats

Unfortunately, no direct ancient literary evidence exists for ancient ship's cats, although their presence can be inferred at least as early as the sixth millennium BC from their presence on islands such as Cyprus, and later from coins from Rhegion and Taras that depict their eighth-century BC Greek founders with pet cats.

Perhaps the most famous ship's cat was the (unnamed) one that accompanied Scott's ill-fated expedition to the South Pole in 1912 (Fig. 0.3). Edward Wilson, an explorer who accompanied Scott wrote that,

> He has a hammock of his own with the hands under the fo'c'sle. A real man o' war hammock with small blankets and a small pillow and the blankets over him. He has learned to jump into his hammock and creeps in under the blankets with his head on the tiny pillow.[37]

Unfortunately, he was swept overboard in a gale and lost. The British navy required ship's cats on all its vessels until 1975.[38] The sailors regarded the animals highly as good luck for their ships, as rodent killers, and as objects of amusement and affection. As we shall see, a ship's cat was seen as the guardian spirit of its vessel. It is likely that this belief dates to the Roman Empire, and perhaps even earlier. A ship without a cat was regarded as derelict, but as long as the cat remained on board, the ship was believed to be safe even in adverse conditions. Once the guardian spirit jumped ship, the ship was doomed.

Figure 0.3   The ship's cat that accompanied R.F. Scott on his Antarctic expedition, 1912

Mice and rats

Before we begin our study of the cat, two other animals must be discussed, the mouse (*Mus musculus*) and the black rat (*Rattus rattus*). These are two main prey animals of the cat, and the latter, when it fights in packs, can also be a predator if the cat is not wary. If rats and mice had played an insignificant role in human history, then indeed, the role of the cat would not be as important, but as the epidemiologist Hendrickson has noted, "any history of the rat is the history of human misery."[39]

Mice

In some ways the mouse (*Mus musculus*) is a greater threat to man than the rat, since its smaller size enables it to hide where its larger cousin cannot. It also carries the full complement of diseases and infections as the rat. The genus *Mus* contains some nine species, some of which have dwelt in Europe since the Neolithic period and the introduction of agriculture in that region. The most important is the common house mouse (*Mus musculus domesticus*). Members of this species have been found in Gussage All Saints in Devonshire, England dating to the third century BC.[40] If they had reached England by that date, it is probable they were already ubiquitous in the European continent by that time as well. This particular species is wholly dependent on human habitations for its survival, and is generally found west of the Elbe river in western Europe. Through Western expansion into Asia, the New World, and Oceania, this species is now found world-wide.

The house mouse consumes about four grams of food per day, but contaminates far more through its droppings and urine, rivaling the spoilage of the rat. It has many natural predators besides cats, including the owl, the weasel, snakes, and poisonous spiders. Unlike the rat, which can be aggressive, mice are generally timid creatures "meek as a mouse," or "mousey."

In addition to the house mouse, the field mouse (*Apodemus sylvaticus*), has been a major scourge throughout history. These mice tend to over-reproduce, and periodically to have more offspring than a local region can feed. This causes the "mouse plagues" that have been recorded since Biblical times. At present, such plagues of field mice, related to the European genus (*Apodemus sylvaticus*) can devour millions of tons of food in the affected region and leave behind thousands of tons of mice carcasses when the food runs out. As many as 17 mice per square yard have been recorded in such plagues, or 82,000 per acre. Such plagues of field mice were also mentioned frequently in Greek and Roman sources.

The related genera of field mice are the most abundant and fastest breeding of all the rodents. In ten months, a breeding pair of field mice will have produced three generations of 2,557 offspring. One species of field mouse in Britain (*Microtus agrestis*) can produce as many as 17 litters per year with 13 in each litter. Pregnancy among females can begin as early as 25 days after birth.[41] Fortunately, field mice have a great range of predators including cats, lynxes, weasels, badgers, skunks, wolves, dogs, foxes, bears, and many species of birds including owls, hawks, seagulls, snakes, frogs, and some species of fish.

Mice appear frequently in Aesop's fables, and subsequent European nursery rhymes and folklore. Many of those stories that contain cat protagonists will appear in the following pages. Greeks and Romans sometimes made pets of mice, but generally recognized their harmful nature. A pet mouse that is well fed and kept in a secure place is little threat to food supplies. One species was even domesticated and eaten, the dormouse (*Glis glis*), so called from its propensity for sleep. The sleepy dormouse appears in Lewis Carroll's *Alice in Wonderland* where Alice tries to keep it awake at the Mad Hatter's tea party. The name for the mouse genus is *Mus*, its name in both Greek and Latin. In the latter language the term can refer to the rat as well, while in Greek, the term *mus* can also be used for "muscle". As we will see in Chapter 2, there was no ancient Greek word for rat, although they were certainly present in the country from the first century AD. In Latin, another term for mouse is *musculus*, "little *mus*." This latter term may have been developed to differentiate the mouse from its larger cousin, the rat, when it became endemic to the Mediterranean region by the first century AD. The term "muscle" in Romance, English, German, and Scandinavian languages is also derived from the Latin word *musculus*, which also meant "muscle."[42] Apparently, the rippling effect of muscles on athlete's bodies reminded some Greek and Roman spectators of mice running and hiding. The term for marine mussel was also derived from Latin *musculus* because of its size and color.

Rats

The rat family has been the greatest enemy of the human race, killing perhaps billions through the spread of diseases and depredations on food supplies. Two major species of the genus *Rattus* that have played the greatest role in this respect are the black rat (roof rat, tree rat) *Rattus rattus*, and the brown rat *Rattus norvegicus*, both, despite the specific name of the latter, originating in Asia. There are in addition some 570 other species of Old World rats that have been so far recorded.

Fortunately for earlier eras of Europe and North Africa, the black rat did not become endemic to the Mediterranean region until the first century AD, despite its occasional appearance earlier.[43] The larger brown rat is not recorded in Europe until around 1600 AD, but probably appeared some decades earlier. It is critical to distinguish between the two species for the purposes of this study. While the black rat is no match for the cat under most circumstances, this is not the case of the larger, more ferocious brown rat, especially when it fights in packs. Only when a group of large toms works together can a pack of brown rats be defeated and killed.[44] Indeed, from the seventeenth century onwards, the two species of rats have been engaged in nothing less than total war against each other, with the brown rat having the upper hand in more temperate climates, while the black rat holds out in warmer, semi-tropical and tropical regions, despite the almost ubiquitous presence of its larger cousin. In subsequent pages, the brown rat will not be discussed, since it does not appear in Europe for many centuries after the end of the era under study.

The black rat originates in South and Southeast Asia. It is not a natural migrant but must be transported by man in trade goods (including food) over land or sea. Trees are its natural habitat and it tends to climb to roof areas of human habitations, hence its other name, roof rat. Black rats average 4 to 12 oz (110–340 gm) in weight and 13–17 inches (330–430 mm) in total length, the bodies usually 6–8 inches (150–200 mm) and tails from 7–10 inches (180–250 mm).[45]

The black rat is the main carrier of the flea, *Xenopsylla cheopis*, that in turn carries the infectious bacillum, *Yersinia pestis*, the organism that causes the bubonic plague. In addition, along with the mouse it carries many of the diseases present in antiquity – including murine typhus, Salmonellosis, trichinosis, leptospirosis, Rickettsia, and dysentery.[46] The roles that the cat and the rat have played in the public health of Roman cities will be discussed below in Chapter 3.

Rats are genuine omnivores, eating not only plants and animals, but paper, glue, plastic, rubber, leather, and so on. Their predation on other animals has led to the extinction of many New World and Oceanic species of birds, small mammals, and amphibians. Today, rats alone destroy 20 per cent of human food supplies by depredation and spoilage, enough to eliminate world hunger. Rats' teeth continuously grow as much as 4 inches per year, so they must continuously gnaw, or their lower incisor teeth will penetrate their brain. They can gnaw through many man-made substances and for this reason are responsible for enormous amounts of property damage every year. Millions of humans are bitten by rats each year and they attack, kill, and eat thousands of the infirm, elderly, and infants annually. After a body has been consumed by rats, nothing remains but the bones – every particle of soft material is eaten.

Rats are also capable of prodigious rates of reproduction. Potentially, in three years, a single breeding pair can produce 359 million offspring! The measured intelligence of rats places them just below that of dogs and considerably higher than that of cats. Rats can also cooperate effectively, often feeding and caring for their old and infirm. They can also form packs to coordinate attacks against aggressors, animal or human.

An adult mouse eats about 0.14 oz (4 grams) of food per day but spoils approximately five to ten times more through its droppings and urine, or a total of 0.85–1.5 oz (24–44 grams) per day. A 12-oz adult black rat consumes about 4 oz (115 grams) of food per day and also spoils about five to ten times more, a total of 24–44 oz (680–1,250 grams).[47] In one year, therefore, a mouse can potentially damage up to 34 lbs (15.4 kg) of food, and a rat up to 1000 lbs (453 kg), eating about 91 lbs (41 kg) and spoiling 910 lbs (412 kg). Thus, if a cat kills about 500 rats per annum, he can prevent the potential destruction of 250 tons (226 tonnes) of human food supplies per year. This does not count the potential diseases that he will prevent.

In our study of cats, it is important to remember that dogs were not bred as predators of rats in antiquity, nor was their skill in killing rats mentioned. Our ancient sources concerning the dog show that it was used to hunt large game animals, as guard animals, as sheep-herders, and as house pets.[48] Nor were their services as ratters appreciated in medieval and early modern eras, when there were more dog-catchers than rat-catchers. Indeed, forty thousand dogs were killed by humans in London after an outbreak of the plague in 1665. It was not until the nineteenth century when the skills of dogs, especially terriers, in killing rats were finally appreciated.[49]

The cat's main competitor in antiquity for killing mice and rats was the ferret or domesticated weasel. Nevertheless, as a human companion this animal presents grave problems that will be discussed fully in Chapter 2. Being a member of the Vulpavine family, it is omnivorous and competes with humans for food. It also has episodes of vicious temper and will frequently attack humans, especially infants.

Cats have thus had a difficult but important task fighting the mouse and the rat for the last two-and-a-half millennia. If it is indeed true that the rat has played a more important role in world history than emperors and kings,[50] then the cat too must have a significant claim.

1

EGYPT

I am one pure of mouth, pure of hands,
One to whom, "Welcome" is said by those who see him;
For I have heard the words spoken by the Donkey and the Cat,
In the house of Eternity.

(From the Book of the Dead)[1]

Egypt is the ultimate homeland of all domestic cats throughout the world, and so will always have a significant place in the history of the species. We are fortunate that a superb book has recently appeared on the topic, Jaromir Malek's *The Cat in Ancient Egypt*,[2] that treats all aspects of the animal. A chapter devoted to Egyptian cats may therefore seem redundant; nevertheless, it is important for a work devoted to Greek and Roman cats to include a section on Egypt, since many later characteristics of the animal in iconography, symbolism, religion, and folklore have their origins in that culture. Furthermore, it remains true that important descriptions of the Egyptian cat come from Greek authors, most notably Herodotus, Diodorus Siculus, and Claudius Aelian. Finally, we will emphasize the history of the animal in the later period of the country's history (1070 BC – 330 AD), not the earlier era.

The Libyan wildcat

The *Felis sylvestris libyca*, the direct ancestor of all domestic cats, is a feline opportunist that has not only survived but flourished in the drastically changing natural and human environments of North Africa for the last five million years. Its head and body length are some 30 inches (75 cm) and its tail, some 12 inches (30 cm). Its ears are not tufted as in other small African wildcats and it has proportionally longer legs than a domesticated individual. As in the case of *F. sylvestris sylvestris*, and indeed even more so here since the *libyca* is the direct ancestral form, there has probably been considerable interbreeding between it and the *catus*. This has led to a gradual reduction of its modern body size and other wild characteristics. This may be why an examination of many mummified ancient Egyptian cats shows

18

that they are larger than the modern *libyca* (Fig. 0.2). The ancient cats were more closely related to the larger, ancestral *libyca*, and the modern *libyca* itself has declined in size through interbreeding.

Its color is also variable depending on genetics and local environments. Generally, however, the body is a "pale sandy fawn ... with a rufous line on the back and multiple traverse stripes of the same colour, though paler, on the body."[3] The markings generally recall those of the common orange and grey striped tabbies. The tail is ringed and has a black, untufted tip, important features for the purposes of identifying it in works of art. Leopards (*Panthera pardus*), for example, have spotted tails and lions (*Panthera leo*) have plain tails with a tufted tip.

There are several significant Greek references to the *libyca*. Diodorus Siculus, who wrote a universal history that was published about 49 BC, noted that in a region of what is now central Libya, the wildcats (*ailouroi*) had driven out so many birds from the trees and ravines that none would nest there. This reference is made in the context of a military campaign undertaken by Archagathus, a general of Agathocles of Syracuse in 307 BC, against the Carthaginians. At this time, and indeed throughout the Roman era, North Africa still retained many forested regions.[4]

The natural historian Claudius Aelian, writing in the late second century AD, made many shrewd observations on cats and other animals in his *De Natura Animalium*. One passage on the taming of the Egyptian *libyca* deserves to be repeated in full:

> In Egypt, the cats, the mongeese, the crocodiles, and even the hawks show that animal nature is not entirely intractable, but that when well treated they are good at remembering kindness. They are caught by pandering to their appetites, and when this has rendered them tame, they remain thereafter perfectly gentle. They would never set upon their benefactors once they have been freed from their genetic and natural temper. Man however, a creature endowed with reason, credited with understanding, gifted with a sense of honor, supposedly capable of blushing, can become the bitter enemy of a friend for some trifling and casual reason and blurt out confidences to betray the very man who trusted him.[5]

That this animal was indeed a *libyca* and not a *Felis chaus* or *margarita* is indicated by the animals tamability, a characteristic generally absent from the two other species.

Aelian also notes the predation of wildcats on other animals and birds, and how these animals have evolved defensive measures to avoid it. In these instances, it is not certain whether the wildcats are the *libyca*, or another species; nevertheless, the interest in the stories lies in the preys' methods of escape.

A monkey, pursued by wildcats fled as fast as he could and climbed a tree. The wildcats also climbed the tree,

> very swiftly, for they cling to the bark and can also climb trees. But as he was going to be caught, since he was one against many, he leapt from the trunk with his paws and seized the end of an over-hanging branch high up and clung to it for a long time. [6]

The wildcats gave up the chase, descended the tree and went after other prey. This is also an interesting example of teamwork among wildcats in their hunting.

Aelian notes too that the Egyptian Goose is a fierce fighter and can defend itself from eagles, cats, and all other animals that come against it. Finally, there is the ibis, who also eats dangerous snakes and scorpions without harm to itself.

> It makes its nest on the top of date-palms in order to escape the cats, for this animal cannot easily climb and crawl up a date-palm as it is constantly being impeded and thrown off by the protuberances on the stem.[7]

The *miu*: the domesticated cat

The earliest remains of cats in domestic contexts from Egypt date from about 4000 to 3000 BC, but are probably of tame wildcats rather than domesticated cats. Wildcats of various species were first represented in Egyptian art from about 1900 BC, about the time the *libyca* was domesticated. This is also the time that the first representations appear of what are probably domesticated cats. One bas relief from Coptos of about 1950 BC shows a cat sitting beneath a woman's chair, a common iconographic portrayal in later works of art. By 1450 BC, the cats are a common feature in Egyptian painting of domestic scenes.

For a few hundred years before this era, however, we find the first individuals named after the cat, as other individuals were named after other local animals such as "Monkey," "Wolf," and "Crocodile." The name given to the domestic cat by the Egyptians was the onomatopoeic "miu" or feminine "miit." So we find names such as Pa-miu, "The Tomcat," and Ta-miit, "The Cat."[8]

Among the factors that undermined the serenity and security of Nilotic life, the most significant were deadly snakes, such as cobras and vipers, and rodents, both mice and rats. Since there was little men could do to protect themselves from such dangers, the appearance of an animal that could destroy such vermin would have been a welcome event. Indeed, since snakes can inflict fatal bites on humans, it would have been literally a life-saving event.[9] Since granaries and silos attracted rodents, they represented a reliable source of food for the cats, who would leave the grain alone. Feeding scraps to the cats would assure their presence near their food supplies and homes. As territorial creatures, they would soon strike up associations (if not exactly friendships) with the humans and come to regard the area around their homes as their own. Thus it was just as much a factor of the cats adopting the humans in their territory, as the humans adopting the cats.

Before long, the people began to recognize the benefits of having the cat in the house. Households with cats had more food, less sickness, and fewer deaths. Its personality and behavior compared well to the other pets they had in their homes, such as dogs and monkeys. Its cleanliness no doubt attracted the Egyptians, while its "house training" – the burial of its excrement outdoors in the sand, more preferable to the cat than the fertile earth of the fields – its killing of scorpions, rodents and snakes that may have entered the house, and its general rejection of grain-based food, the staple of the Egyptian diet as for most ancient Mediterranean peoples, must also have recommended it to their service. In exchange for comfort and safety, the cats were willing to give up some of their freedom. Selective breeding would ensure that only the tamest and best-behaved individuals would survive in human company.[10]

It must also be noted that the cat was a new type of domestic animal. Other animals were exploited for their hides, meat, milk, or hair. Some were used for transport, like the horse, donkey, mule, and later the camel. As we saw in the Introduction, the dog was used for hunting, herding, and for guard work but not for killing rats in antiquity. The cat, however, was used solely as a predator of small animals and later as a human companion.

Iconography

Cats occur frequently in the art of the New Kingdom (1570–1070 BC) and the Late Period (1070–332 BC). There are wonderful wall paintings of cats and, of course, some magnificent bronzes. Fortunately, these works have been beautifully illustrated and thoroughly described by Malek. Nevertheless, there are two major categories of images that are of interest to us because of their later use by both Greeks and Romans: the "cat under the chair," and the "cat in the marshes." In addition, there is an important series of bronzes depicting the cat goddess Bastet with her sistrum that will be treated in the sections on religion and folklore below.

Most portrayals of the cat under the chair are in the context of a scene depicting a seated husband and wife accepting gifts and offerings from their servants or children. The cat invariably sits beneath the chair of the wife and sometimes a dog sits beneath the husband. For example, in Figure 1.1, we see the couple Ipuy and his wife Duammeres portrayed on their tomb, which dates to about 1250 BC. A cat sits beneath Duammeres' chair and a small kitten scratches at the garment worn by Ipuy. The cats themselves show the typical color and markings of the *libyca*, which has now been domesticated.

The cat under the woman's chair may symbolize her fertility and the association of both with the goddess Hathor. The dog or the monkey that is frequently found beneath the man's chair, although not on this particular scene, may symbolize his fertility as well.[11] In these tomb paintings, the cat may symbolize the continual force of life even after death. In other scenes, the cats under the chairs play with monkeys, embrace geese, hiss at geese, eat food, or try to break free of their tethers, so they can eat some food that is placed nearby.[12]

Another common theme is the cat hunting birds in the marshes. Often the cat is portrayed with a hunter on his boat or in the marshes attacking water birds. Figure 1.2 shows the family of Nebamun on a small skiff, while the family cat attacks the fowl. The painting is from Nebamun's tomb in the Theban necropolis and dates to about 1450 BC. It is one of the great masterpieces of Egyptian painting. Seldom in any artistic tradition are animals, plants, wildlife, fish, and people portrayed with greater empathy and realism. The cat is a masterpiece in itself and is shown assaulting three different birds at once! Nevertheless the animal is depicted with great naturalism, and is one of the best portrayals in existence. Once again, we see the beautiful golden-tan coat, the darker transverse stripes, and the ringed tail with the black tip (Fig. 1.3).

Figure 1.1 Ipuy, Duammeres, and their cats, tomb fresco, Deir el-Medina, 1250 BC

Figure 1.2   Nebanum and his family, tomb fresco, Theban necropolis, 1450 BC

The cat may indeed have been used to flush out the birds so they could be struck down by the hunter's throwing stick, spear or arrow. Alternatively, during the roosting season, the presence of a cat may force the birds to instinctively protect their nests so that the hunter can have several targets at once. On the other hand, it is more likely that Nebamun merely wanted to show his family together on their eternal journey, and naturally the family cat was included. The cat would do what came naturally when confronted by so many birds and, realistically, it would be quite difficult to train a cat to flush out waterfowl.[13]

The goddess in the house: the sacred cats of Egypt

Throughout history, many have believed that the cat embodies profound spiritual forces. This has been true not only among the ancient Egyptians and the Europeans, but also among the Asian Indians, Chinese, and the Japanese. Part of the reason for this may have been the remarkable sensory acuity of the animal. Its ability to predict the weather, earthquakes, and perhaps even death, has led many throughout the ages to believe in the animal's preternatural power. For the Egyptians, the cat's ability to destroy harmful scorpions, rodents and snakes suggested it was the embodiment of a

Figure 1.3 Detail, showing Nebamun's cat hunting ducks

divine power that both protected the family from evil and misfortune, and also promoted its fertility.

An important religious concept among the ancient Egyptians, as well as other ancient peoples, was animism, the belief that divine spirit pervaded all of nature. Nature was divine and different aspects of nature were embodied in different divinities. Every person, animal, plant, and inanimate object, every tree, glade, brook, and hill was thought to be suffused with a spirit. In this respect, ancient Egyptian concepts were very close to the early beliefs of *polydaimonia* among the Greeks and *numen* among the Romans. Later indeed, when Egyptian religions spread to Europe – especially during the Hellenistic and Roman eras – these concepts proved compatible with comparable Greek, Roman, and Celtic beliefs. This ancient substratum of paganism antedated the later, more sophisticated notions of great gods who controlled various aspects of nature. It also proved to be the most resilient and the most difficult to suppress in later times.

All of nature was a manifestation of divine power and, in pre-agrarian hunting societies, this power would be frequently encountered in the form of animals. In Egypt the lower classes were always in close contact with various domestic and wild animals, hence the religion of animals remained popular with them, even after greater gods were introduced. Indeed, the common folk were frequently excluded from the full worship of the high gods, since only priests were allowed into their sacred precincts.[14]

Associated with the belief of animism was a related magico-sympathetic concept of nature. Many ancient cultures believed that there were no accidents or coincidences in nature, but that everything was related by a divine providence. Therefore it was no coincidence that the cow's horns resembled a crescent moon; this meant that the cow was the sacred animal of the moon goddess. Similarly with the cat: its nocturnal habits and pupils that change from crescent to round meant that it was also sacred to the moon. Indeed, it was thought possible for the moon goddess to be incarnate in a cat.

In spite of its humble origins and lack of a strong cult early in Egyptian history, the cat's religious popularity gradually surpassed that of any other animal, spreading at last far beyond Egypt's boundaries. One of the most misunderstood aspects of Egyptian religion is their attitude towards animals. Animals were not worshipped *per se*, as was frequently claimed by pagan detractors and early Christian authors; rather it was thought that they, as well as all other living beings, were imbued with the same spirit as their creator. The Egyptians did not make a distinction between animals and humans – to them, living beings included gods, people, and animals. Each was made by the creator god, worshipped him in their own way, and were under his protection.

Moreover, some animals were thought to be the visible epiphanies or incarnations of divinities, a function that could also be fulfilled by certain images of the gods. An animal such as the Apis bull could act as the visible incarnation of a divinity during its life, and after death it would be buried with full honors and a successor chosen. This was also true of cats. If a cat had the proper sacred markings, she might have been thought to be the incarnation of the goddess Bastet. At first, the fact that a god could be manifest in a certain animal did not necessarily confer special protection for its species as a whole.

By the Late Period (1070–332 BC), however, most domesticated and many wild animals were regarded as potential epiphanies of divinities, and so a god could well be present in every Egyptian household.[15] This was especially true from the fifth century BC to the end of the pagan era of the country in the fifth century AD, when cats and other animals, especially the ibis, came to be regarded as sacred, imbued with the divine presence.[16]

Indeed, there was an upsurge in popularity of animal cults during that time. This increased popularity may have been caused by the failure of the great gods of the country to protect it during a period of frequent foreign invasion and occupation. Furthermore, Egyptian reverence for animals was also unique to that country, as ancient scholars frequently noted, and Egyptians may have wished to express their national and cultural identity through this form of worship.[17]

Sacred animals were of three types. First and foremost were the Temple Animals, the living incarnations of divinities; the goddess Bastet would have been incarnate in a cat. These animals lived in the Holy of Holies within the temple precinct and had special markings associated with the myths of the divinity. It must be stressed that the Temple Cat and other Temple Animals were not worshipped on their own account, but because it was believed that the divinities were incarnate in their persons. The god manifest in the animal was worshipped, not the animal itself. In the same way, idols were not worshipped by pagans either, but it was thought that the gods would manifest themselves within certain images. These were distinctions lost on most ancient and modern critics. In a similar vein, the divine incarnation of Christ was misunderstood by other pagan critics, like Celsus.

The second type of sacred animals included the members of the same species, kept in the cult center, who received special treatment, care and feeding, but who were not themselves manifestations of the divinity. Thirdly, there were the other members of the species that lived in domestic or wild contexts. These also received special treatment and veneration as members of a sacred species.[18]

The earliest instance of the cat in a religious context comes from a series of ivory "magic knives," dating between 2000 and 1500 BC, that were decorated with animals and mythic beings. Their purpose was apotropaic, that is, to protect individuals from the dangers of everyday existence, illnesses, accidents, and bites from scorpions and snakes. The cat is often engraved on the knives because of its ability to destroy snakes. These knives are usually found in the tombs of women and children. Apotropaic, "good luck," amulets with cats remain common all the way into the Ptolemaic (323–30 BC) and Roman (30 BC – AD 330) periods.[19]

Furthermore, in works concerning the interpretation of dreams, some written as early as 1980 BC, the vision of a cat was a good omen and meant that a large harvest would come. Once again, we are reminded of the cat's role in destroying grain-devouring rodents.[20] Although not a prominent religious role, the manifestation of the cat as an apotropaic animal, giving good luck and warding off evil and misfortune, will continue through the European Middle Ages and into the modern era in European folklore and custom.

From around 1500 BC, it was believed that the sun god Ra, the most powerful divinity in the Egyptian pantheon, could manifest himself in the form of the cat, the "Great Tomcat." Each night Ra, in his incarnation of

Atum-Ra, would journey to the underworld and there, in the form of a cat, would confront his great enemy, the snake-demon Apops (Apophis). At that time he slew the snake with a large knife, thus ensuring his return as the sun the following morning. There are numerous portrayals of this nightly event in Egyptian papyrus texts (Fig. 1.4).

The origins of this connection to the sun, unique to Egypt, are probably related to the cat's eyes. According to Horapollo, writing in the fourth or fifth century AD, the male cat's pupils changed during the passage of the sun through the day (*Hieroglyphica*, 1. 10. 18). We may understand this to mean that during the dim light of the morning, the cat's pupils are nearly round and full. As the sun nears the zenith, they narrow to thin lines, expanding again as the sun sets. The cat's pupils were indeed subject to much learned commentary, as we shall see in later chapters. Furthermore their golden-amber color, unusual in the animal kingdom, and rounded shape may also have suggested this relation.

Horapollo also noted that the sun god of Heliopolis (On), Atum-Ra, was portrayed as cat-shaped (*ailouromorphos*). We may also suggest that the connection with the sun, especially for Atum-Ra, the god of the setting sun who travels beneath the underworld, lies in the cat's reflective eyes that shine on even in darkness. Christopher Smart's poem may help us understand this belief:

Figure 1.4   The sun god Atum-Ra in the form of a cat confronting the snake-demon Apops (Apophis), tomb fresco, Deir El-Medina, 1300 BC

For when his day's work is done his business more properly begins.
For he keeps the Lord's watch in the night against the adversary.
For he counteracts the powers of darkness by his electrical skin and glaring eyes.
For he counteracts the Devil, who is death, by brisking about the life.[21]

There is also the animal's sense of the death of others, appropriate for an underworld divinity.[22] The cat has a well-known propensity for warmth:

For at the first glance of the glory of God in the East he worships in his way ...
For in his morning orisons he loves the sun and the sun loves him ...[23]

Finally, one may note the static electricity of the animal's fur perhaps suggested a connection with a divine light:

For by stroking of him I have found out electricity.
For I perceived God's light about him both wax and fire.
For the Electrical fire is the spiritual substance, which God sends from heaven to sustain the bodies of men and beasts.[24]

These poetic sentiments, expressed in the eighteenth century, reflect the transcendent attitudes of many cultures towards the cat, including the Egyptians.

More often, however, the characteristic changes in the cat's pupils were associated with the movement of the moon as in Yeats' poem:

Does Minnalouche know that his pupils
Will pass from change to change,
And that from round to crescent
From crescent to round they range?[25]

It was this relationship between the cat and the moon that was the most long-lasting, surviving into modern folklore. The earliest connections in this context were with the goddess Hathor and her sistrum. The sistrum was a bronze musical instrument with a handle and a rounded open frame (cf. Fig. 1.5). Within the frame are some bronze rods (from one to four in number) that rattled when shook. Along the curved frame of the instrument, one or more cat figures were usually attached and the figure of Hathor generally appeared in the handle. When the sistrum was shaken quite a noise was produced; it may have resembled that of a tambourine when shaken, only deeper and richer. The noise of the sistrum was symbolically associated with fertility and regeneration symbolized by the cats, because of the animal's reproductive powers. This musical instrument was used commonly in Egypt,

but is also found in archeological excavations all over the European continent and throughout the Roman Empire until the end of antiquity (and
even beyond). A sistrum, perhaps used for the worship of Isis, was even
found in London. It is believed that the site of St Paul's Cathedral in London
was originally dedicated to Diana, another goddess of the cat.[26] Hathor the
goddess was also represented as a cow, and the two appear frequently in
Egyptian works of art through the Roman era.

By the Twenty-second Dynasty (945–715 BC), the cat had become associated with another goddess, Bastet – identified by the Greeks with Artemis –
who became one of the most revered divinities in the Egyptian pantheon in the
first millennium BC. The Twenty-second Dynasty had its capital at Per-Bastet,

Figure 1.5 Sistrum, Hellenistic Egypt, 332–30 BC

the "House of the Goddess Bastet," which the Greeks called Bubastis (Fig. 1.6). Indeed, one of its pharaohs was named Pamiu or "Tomcat" (773–767 BC). The cat was now regarded as the manifestation of Bastet. She was paired with the lion-headed female divinity, Sekhmet, the ferocious protector of Egypt. Just as Sekhmet protected the nation, so Bastet protected the household, especially its women and children. Like Artemis of the Greeks with whom she was later identified, Bastet was a fearsome huntress but also a loving mother. She, or one of her earlier manifestations, also appears on tomb paintings escorting the deceased to the place of judgement.[27]

Her most important role, however, was as the goddess of motherhood, fertility, childbearing, and childrearing. These aspects continued under the

Figure 1.6   Bastet and her sistrum, with kittens, 664–30 BC

Greek goddess Artemis, the Roman goddess Diana, and the Greco-Egyptian goddess Isis, right through the European Middle Ages, and indeed they survive into modern folklore and custom. The cat was an obvious symbol of these important aspects of human life. We have already noted the cats' phenomenal rates of fertility.

High fertility rates were important aspects of ancient and medieval human populations as well, but have unfortunately been neglected by many historians. Before the development of modern medicine and improved diets – brought about in part through the introduction of New World crops into the Old World, and higher living standards brought about through the Industrial Revolution – life expectancies were very low. Census data from Roman Egypt, probably also characteristic of the country during earlier eras as well as of much of the ancient and medieval Mediterranean in general, show a life expectancy at birth of about 22.5 years for females and 25 years for males.[28] The differential in death rates was caused by mortality occurring among women during their childbearing years between the ages of 15 and 44.

Because of the low life expectancies and the high death rates, birth rates also needed to be high. The average woman bore six children during a relatively short life span just to keep the population growth rate stable, neither increasing or decreasing. Married women bore on average nine children. Their rates were higher than average because many women simply did not survive through their marriageable and childbearing years. Many married women bore far more than nine. Marriage was nearly universal for both men and women. If these high birth rates were not maintained, the population would decline at a geometric rate, and would soon be biologically replaced by immigrant groups or become extinct. Surprisingly, these important facts and their impact on the lives of ancient women and on social institutions, including religion, have not been considered by modern historians until the last few years.[29]

Marriage, family, motherhood, childbearing, and childrearing were central to the lives of all women before the industrial age. The cat was thought by Western women to be the living embodiment of this divine force of nature for almost four thousand years. Bearing, nursing, and raising numerous children have been tasks honorably fulfilled by women through the ages, and there was no better symbol of these qualities than the cat. Only aristocratic women could be exempt from nursing, with the use of wet-nurses, who were far beyond the resources of the vast majority. As we have noted, female cats will not only sacrifice their lives on behalf of their kittens but are solely responsible for their upbringing and training. This is especially true for the barn cats and feral cats who must learn to make it on their own from their mothers. This dedication by a small animal to its young has been an inspiration to women for millennia.

The cat has several physical characteristics that may have helped endear it to women. A full-grown cat is nearly the size of a human infant. Its cries can often sound remarkably similar to those of a baby, and its large frontal eyes and rounded face may also have suggested this sympathetic relationship. The animal has a "childlike," playful, and mischievous nature and, when not at play, is usually asleep.

The animal's relationship with motherhood goes far deeper, though. Biologists have long observed that the relationship between cats and their owners closely resembles that between kittens and their mothers.[30] Cats often regard their human owners as a source of food and nurturing. The physical difference in size between a kitten and its mother is proportional to the difference in size between a cat and a human. The padding or kneading motion of the animal's front paws when sitting on their owners is the same motion that kittens use to express milk from their mothers. Cats are also more closely related to humans genetically than any other family of animals except the primates.

Women often cradle the animal in their arms. They frequently carry cats in the same way they carry infants. Cats are often of therapeutic value, especially for the elderly. Blood pressure is lowered and emotional satisfaction is gained simply by petting the animal.[31] Girls and young women may anticipate their own children in the future when they hold them, while elderly women may fondly recall their own infant children in the past. All these factors have endeared the cat to women in many cultures throughout the globe.

Egyptian cats from the fifth century BC through the Roman era, AD 330

Although by the fifth century BC the greatest ages of Egyptian political and military history were but a distant memory, the later period of Egyptian history would have a profound effect on the culture and religion of the West. Among these cultural influences would be the religious associations of the cat with the goddesses Artemis, Diana, Isis, and ultimately the Virgin Mary.

The Greek historian Herodotus, who visited the country during the mid-fifth century BC, provides useful accounts of the great festival of Bastet and of Egyptian cats. Herodotus identifies the Egyptian Bastet with the Greek Artemis.

> The Egyptians do not hold a single solemn assembly, but several in the course of the year. Of these the chief, which is better attended than any other, is held at the city of Bubastis [Per-Bastet] in honor of Artemis.
>
> (*Histories*, 2. 59)

The following are the proceedings on occasion of the assembly at Bubastis. Men and women come sailing altogether, vast numbers in each boat, many of the women with rattles [*krotala*, perhaps the sistrum], which they shake, while some of the men pipe during the whole time of the voyage; the remainder, both male and female, sing and clap their hands. When they sail up to a town, they approach the shore. While some of the women continue to play and sing, others call aloud and jeer at the females of the place. While still others dance, some stand up and lift their dresses. After continuing in this way all along the river, they reach Bubastis, where they celebrate the festival with abundant sacrifices. More wine is consumed at this festival than in all the rest of the year combined. Those who attend, both men and women, not counting the children, number some 700,000 according to native reports.

(*Histories*, 2. 60)

We learn from this important description that the celebration of Bastet was the most popular in the entire country, with a substantial portion of the population, perhaps as many as one half of all the adults of the country, participating.[32] We also hear of "abundant sacrifices," and many of these were no doubt of the cats themselves, who were especially bred for the purpose. We will discuss the role of animal sacrifice in ancient religion below.

Herodotus next records that in his time, all animals in Egypt,

whether domesticated or otherwise, are all regarded as sacred (*hapanta hira nenomistai*). If I were to explain why they are consecrated to the several gods, I should be led to speak of religious matters, which I particularly shrink from mentioning; the points which I have previously touched upon have been introduced from necessity. Their custom in respect to animals is as follows. For every kind there are appointed certain guardians, some male, some female, whose business it is to look after them; and this honor is descended from father to son. The inhabitants of the various cities, when they have made a vow to any god, pay it to his animals in the way which I will now explain. When they make the vow, they shave the head of the child, cutting off all the hair, sometimes half or a third, which they weigh in a balance against a sum of silver. Whatever sum the hair weighs is presented to the guardian of the animals, who thereupon cuts up some fish, and gives it to them as food. When a man has killed one of the sacred animals, if he did it with malice aforethought, he is punished with death; if accidentally, he has to pay a fine as the priests choose to impose. When an ibis or a hawk is killed whether on purpose or by accident, the perpetrator must die.

(*Histories*, 2. 65)

We may wonder what particular sacred animal is being fed the fish! This sacralizing of many animals, although probably not all of them, by the fifth century BC seems to represent the culmination of Egyptian views towards the incarnation of divinities in animals. Herodotus is careful to note that the animals are not worshipped, nor are they gods, but are held sacred to the various gods. Indeed, all cats in the country were sacred, as were many other animals, and this belief continued until the end of paganism in the country.

Herodotus then goes on to discuss the house cats themselves:

> The number of domestic animals in Egypt is very great, and would be still greater were it not for what befalls the cats. As the females, when they have kittened, no longer seek the company of the males, these last, to obtain more of their companionship, practice a curious artifice. They seize the kittens, carry them off, and kill them, but do not eat them afterwards. Upon this the females, being deprived of their young, and longing to supply their place, seek the males once more, since they are particularly fond of their offspring. On every occasion of a fire in Egypt the strangest prodigy occurs with the cats. The inhabitants allow the fire to rage as it pleases, while they stand about at intervals and watch these animals, which slipping by the men or else leaping over them, rush headlong into the flames. When this happens, the Egyptians are in deep affliction. If a cat dies in a private house by a natural death, all the inmates of the house shave their eyebrows.
>
> (*Histories*, 2. 66)

> When the cats die, they are taken to the city of Bubastis [Per-Bastet] where they are embalmed, after which they are buried in certain sacred repositories.
>
> (*Histories*, 2. 67. 1)

In these passages we learn that the mating behavior of male and female cats has not changed much over the last two-and-a-half millennia. As we saw in the Introduction, males of the genus *Felis* will often try to kill offspring of the females in their territories, if they believe these offspring are not their own. This is most likely to happen when a new male is successful in a fight for dominance with the former dominant male. The biological reason for this behavior is related to the establishment of the new, victorious male's genes in the population. Indeed, when the female cat loses her kittens, she will quickly come into heat again. As long as the females are present, they can usually defend their kittens against a new dominant male, but when they leave them to go hunting, their kittens are vulnerable. Natural selection is often harsh and brutal, and nature has her own purposes that are not always understood by humans.

The behavior of the (female) cats when their house catches fire has been frequently observed (see the Introduction). They will indeed re-enter the burning house to rescue their kittens one by one, and will continue until they themselves perish or all their kittens are rescued. Such is the love and self-sacrifice that the animal shows towards its young.

Herodotus next notes that other animals, such as dogs, mongeese, hawks, and ibises also received burial in sacred places. Just as for some pet-owners today, the ancient Egyptians buried their beloved cats and dogs with full honor and ceremony, preparing them to meet their owners once again in the hereafter.

The popularity of Bastet continued through the Ptolemaic (323–30 BC) and Roman (30 BC – AD 330) eras. Thousands of wonderful bronzes of cats and images of Bastet have survived, showing the enormous attraction of her cult for a millennium and a half. Many of these images were religious dedications made in honor of Bastet at her temples throughout the country in return for the benefits she conferred on her worshippers. When the numbers of such dedications became overwhelming to temple personnel, they were buried in pits on the sacred ground, to be found by archeologists of a later age.[33] Indeed the common nickname for the cat, "puss," may have been derived from an alternative name for Bastet, Pasht, but this is unlikely. It seems that the word "puss" is a call-word for the cat found mainly in Germanic languages such as English. It is more probable that the colloquial Arabic word, *bast*, which means "happiness," is related to the Egyptian name of the goddess.[34]

A third goddess, Isis, became associated with Bastet and the cat during the Hellenistic era (323–30 BC). It is through Isis that the cat lore of Egypt was transmitted to Western Europe during the Hellenistic and Roman periods. In the Hellenistic Temple of Horus at Edfu an inscription reads, "Isis is the soul of Bastet," that is, Isis can also become incarnate in a cat. The cult of Isis and her central role in the history of the sacred cat will be fully discussed in Chapter 3.

Another indication of the popularity of the cat is the hundreds of thousands, perhaps millions, of cat mummies that have been found in the country. Many Egyptians fondly hoped that their pets would accompany them into the afterlife. After the death of their cat, it would be taken to a sacred location. There it would be embalmed by a process similar to that used for humans, and mummified. Some cats even had their own elaborate limestone sarcophagi, others, wooden cat-shaped coffins, and a few had beautiful bronze face masks and even bronze cat-shaped coffins. But most were placed in repositories only with their wrappings, often brightly painted with their features and other elaborate designs (Fig. 1.7).[35]

In the Ptolemaic era, individuals that were responsible for caring for sacred cats received exemption from the compulsory labor that had to be performed annually on the irrigation works by most adult males of the

Figure 1.7   Mummified cat, Hellenistic Egypt, 332–30 BC

country. This practice probably continued from earlier times. A document from about 255 BC is addressed to Zenon, an agent for Apollonius, the *dioiketes* of Ptolemy II Philadelphus. In it the *hierodouloi*, or sacred personnel, who feed the cats at the Temple of Bubastis complain that they were wrongly impressed for compulsory labor. "The king rightly granted exemption from compulsory labor to men of this profession throughout the country and Apollonius did the same."[36] A later document from about 242 BC mentions those who are released from compulsory labor on the canals and dykes. Among them are "the dead," "the keepers of the mummies," and "the inhabitants of Somphis who bury the cats." [37]

Many of the mummified cats were unfortunately destroyed in the nineteenth century when hundreds of thousands were ground up and used for fertilizer. Some of the mummies that remain, however, show unmistakable signs of violent death, usually by a broken neck.[38] There is abundant evidence to show that cat sacrifices were frequent.

Nor should this come as a surprise, since many animals, mostly domestic but some wild, were sacrificed in ancient paganism, and indeed, in ancient Judaism. The notion of animal sacrifice ought to be abhorrent to modern civil societies, and its revival by modern "neo-pagans" is nothing more than cruelty to animals and should be suppressed.[39] The ancient world, however, had a different view of the natural and the divine. Sheep, goats, cattle, swine, birds, and other animals, even beetles, were frequently offered as gifts to the gods. The sacrificial cats, often only two to four months old, were offered to Bastet herself for the restoration of her spirit, so she could continue to fulfill her important functions in the world. The sacrificer himself would also be blessed for making the gift to the goddess. Indeed, the word "sacrifice" literally means "to make sacred." However mistaken we may think such views, it was believed that the victim did not die but became part of a spiritual force dedicated to augmenting the goddess's power. Although cats, as well as other animals, were sacred, their sacrifice to the goddess was thought to honor the animal, and in no way detracted from its sacral character. Cat sacrifice is another pagan aspect of the animal that continued through the European Middle Ages and early modern era.

In addition to the evidence from the mummies, ancient literary sources show that Egyptians of the Late Period did indeed sacrifice cats. We have Herodotus' statement that numerous sacrifices were made during the great celebration of Bastet at Bubastis, discussed above, and many of these animals would have been cats, whose remains (with necks broken) have been found in her precinct. Once again, these sacrifices were not taken lightly, and the animal was thought to be honored in becoming a gift to the goddess. A fragment from the lost play, *The Egyptians*, of the fourth-century BC comedian Timocles speaks of an "altar of the cat," and Sextus Empiricus, a philosopher of the second century AD, notes that Alexandrian Egyptians sacrificed cats to the god Horus.[40] This seeming anomaly, that it was good luck to sacrifice a cat but ill fortune to kill one persisted through nineteenth-century Europe.

The temple precinct of Bastet at Bubastis had many personnel in charge of taking care of the Temple Cat and the other sacred cats, and perhaps of sacrificing these latter when necessary. Diodorus Siculus, whose universal history was published in about 49 BC, has important descriptions of the sacred cats in his work. Like Herodotus, Diodorus visited Egypt from about 60 to 56 BC, and gathered materials there for his history. His observations clarify and augment those of his predecessor.

As regards the consecration (*aphieromenon*) of animals in Egypt, the practice naturally appears to many to be extraordinary (*paradoxon*) and worthy of investigation. For the Egyptians venerate (*sebontai*) animals exceedingly, not only during their lifetime but even after death, such as cats, ichneumons [mongeese], and dogs, and even hawks, and the birds called ibis, as well as wolves and crocodiles, and a number of other animals of that kind, and the reasons for this, we shall attempt to set forth, after we have first spoken of the animals themselves.

(1. 83. 1)

Firstly, for each kind of animal that is accorded this veneration, there has been consecrated a portion of land which returns a revenue sufficient for their care and sustenance. Moreover, the Egyptians make vows to certain gods on behalf of their children who have been delivered from an illness, in which case they shave off their hair and weigh it against silver or gold, and then give the money to the attendants of the animals mentioned. These cut up meat for the hawks and calling them with a loud cry toss it up to them, as they swoop by, until they catch it, while for the cats and mongeese they break up bread into milk and calling them with a clucking sound set it before them, or else they cut up fish caught in the Nile and feed the fish to them raw. In such a manner, each of the other kinds of animals is provided with the appropriate food. And as for the various services which these animals require, the Egyptians not only do not try to avoid them or feel ashamed to be seen by the crowds as they perform them, but on the contrary, in the belief that they are engaged in the most serious rites of divine worship (*tas megistas ton theon ginomenoi timas*), they assume airs of importance and wearing special insignia, make the rounds of the cities and the countryside. Since they can be seen from a distance performing services to their animals, all who meet them prostrate themselves and honor them.

(1. 83. 2–5)

These passages show in greater detail than Herodotus the dedication of the Egyptians on behalf of their cats and other sacred animals. Nevertheless, it remains true that the sacred cats and other animals were not worshipped, only that their service was regarded as a serious part of the rites of divine worship. The animals were consecrated (*aphieromenon*), that is, made holy, and venerated (*sebomai, sebontai*), but not worshipped (*sebo, sebizo*).

Despite the time, effort, and resources devoted to the care and feeding of these village cats, the Egyptians received far more in return. In maintaining a force of working cats in their towns and villages, many harmful rodents and snakes were destroyed, thus benefiting the Egyptians not only spiritually but also materially and medically.

Not even the fear of Roman wrath was enough to save the life of a Roman envoy after he had accidentally killed a cat:

> When one of these animals dies they wrap it up in fine linen and then, wailing and beating their breasts, carry it off to be embalmed. After it has been treated with cedar oil and fragrant spices that can help preserve the body for a long time, they lay it away in a consecrated tomb. Whoever intentionally kills one of these animals is put to death unless he kills a cat or an ibis. If he kills one of these either intentionally or unintentionally, he is always put to death. For the common people gather in crowds and cruelly deal with the perpetrator, sometimes doing this without waiting for a trial. And because of their fear of such a punishment, any who have caught sight of one of these animals lying dead withdraw to a great distance and shout with lamentations and protestations that they found the animal already dead.
>
> (1. 83. 5–7)

> Their superstitious regard for these animals (*pros ta zoa auta deisidaimonia*) is deeply implanted among the common people, and the emotions cherished by every man regarding the honor due to them unalterable. Once when Ptolemy their king had not yet been given the title of Friend by the Romans [59 BC], the people were zealously courting the favor of the embassy from Italy, which was visiting Egypt. For they were afraid to give any cause of complaint for war. At this time, one of the Romans killed a cat and the multitude rushed in a mob to his house. Neither the officials sent by the king to plead for the man, nor the fear of Rome which all the people felt, were enough to save the man from punishment, even though his act had been an accident. And we relate this incident, not from hearsay, but we saw it with our own eyes when we made our journey to Egypt.
>
> (1. 83. 8–9)

Diodorus next observes that even during famines, no one dared touch one of the sacred animals. When the family dog was found dead, the whole house went into mourning, and when a sacred animal died in the house, any food in the house was thrown out. If the Egyptians made a military expedition to a foreign country, they ransomed the captive cats and hawks and brought them back to Egypt (1. 84. 1–3).

When asked by Diodorus to explain the reverence felt towards the sacred animals, the priests responded that each one had performed some noble service in the past and many in the present. In the case of the cat, "it is useful against asps with their deadly bite and the other reptiles that sting" (1. 87. 4). They also noted that the ibis, another sacred animal, was known to eat poisonous snakes and even scorpions, without suffering harm to itself.

It is indeed true that the sacredness of animals was frequently overstated and ridiculed by later pagan, Jewish, and Christian authors. Perhaps the most frequent complaint leveled against the Egyptians and their religion was their worship of animals, including the cat. Apart from the Temple Animals themselves, these complaints are not really part of Egyptian religious notions, but the misunderstandings of others.

Nevertheless, the criticism of Clement of Alexandria (c. AD 150–220) is noteworthy for its accuracy and humor, as well as its sarcasm concerning the Temple Animals. Clement describes the grandeur of Egyptian temple worship: the great temples themselves, their sacred processions and ceremonies. This, however, is in contrast with the disappointment that awaits the worshipper once inside the Holy of Holies:

> There is no god within whom we were so anxiously looking for; there is only a cat, or a crocodile, or a snake native to the land, or some other similar animal suited for life in a cave or den or in the mud, but certainly not a temple. The god of the Egyptians then, turns out to be only a beast curled up on a rich purple cushion.[41]

We may indeed wonder what particular beast gets the purple cushion!

A stout defender of Egyptian practices against Christian calumnies was the pagan philosopher Celsus, who wrote *On the True Doctrine* in about 170–180 AD. He notes that the Christians of his time had invented a number of terrifying and offensive doctrines to frighten people into the worship of their faith. Among these were notions of everlasting punishments that even philosophers could never have imagined. Then, in a passage that seems to be a direct response to Clement, he notes:

> In the old religions of Egypt, I recall, a man would be seduced by the magnificence of the shrines – the sacred gardens, the great entrance, the temple surrounded by splendid tents, not to mention the hypnotic effect of the rites themselves, made to be swallowed by

the gullible. But once inside, what did the worshipper find: a cat, or a monkey, a dog, crocodile, or a goat. The design of the old religion was to impress upon the initiate that he had learned a secret knowledge; that the significance of these animals was given to him and to him only. But at least the religion of Egypt transcended the worship of irrational beasts: the animals were symbols of invisible ideas and not objects of worship themselves.[42]

In other words, to Celsus at least, the Temple Animals were symbols of the divine forces of nature, and not objects of worship themselves. Celsus then points out that the Christians do not worship ideas but Jesus, the worship of an individual, not a symbol. It would seem that just as Clement was unable (or unwilling) to understand the concept of divine incarnation, so was Celsus.

Folklore

The cat has nine lives

Although the origins of this famous folk saying must remain obscure, there is a strong possibility that they may lie in ancient Egypt, especially in the worship of the ailouromorphic (cat-form) sun god Atum-Ra. In one tradition, there were nine great gods in Egypt called collectively the Ennead or the Nine.

According to the priesthood of Heliopolis (On), the creator god was Atum-Ra, the cat-god of the setting sun, not Ptah as at Thebes. In the creation story given by this tradition, Atum-Ra, the creator sun, gave birth to Shu (air) and Tefnut (moisture). They begat (earth) and Nut (sky), his wife. This latter pair begat Osiris and Isis, Seth and Nephthys, nine altogether.

A religious text from the Twenty-second Bubastite Dynasty (945–715 BC) reads:

> I am one who becomes two, I am two who becomes four, I am four who becomes eight, and I am one more besides.[43]

The one god thus embodies nine, or has nine lives in one creator being. Another hymn from Heliopolis dating to the fourth century BC sings,

> O Sacred Cat! Your mouth is the mouth of the god Atum, the lord of life who has saved you from all taint.[44]

Indeed, as we have seen, Atum-Ra was represented as a cat at Heliopolis. We recall also that the representation of the sun god in his underworld phase as a cat, one who will strike and kill the evil snake-demon Apophis, can be traced back at least to the thirteenth century BC. Indeed, many of the bronze images of cats found throughout Egypt and dating from the Late Period, may represent not domestic pets or Bastet but Ra. Malek notes that some bronzes have the sun disks and scarab beetles on their heads, both symbols of the sun. [45]

The cat and the fiddle: Bastet and her sistrum

This ancient folk saying seems to have a clear Egyptian origin. As Tabor has observed,[46] this is an obvious reference to the statuettes of the goddess Bastet holding her sistrum, as one glance at Figure 1.6 will show. Bastet is often shown holding the handle of the sistrum in her right hand while the fiddle-shaped frame rests on her right shoulder. Her left hand is usually placed on her breast. For all the world, these statuettes, usually dating from the seventh century BC to the Roman era, look exactly like a cat playing the fiddle!

The association with the cow and the moon can also be derived from the sistrum, which was used not only in the worship of Bastet, but also of Isis, as Plutarch (*c.* AD 46–120) explains in his work *On Isis and Osiris* (376 C–E [63]):

> The upper part of the sistrum is circular and its circumference contains the four things that are shaken; for the part of the world which undergoes reproduction and destruction is contained underneath the orb of the moon, and all things in it are subjected to the motion and change through the four elements: fire, earth, water, and air. At the top of the circumference of the sistrum they construct the figure of a cat with a human face, and below the rattles, the face of Isis on one side and on the other the face of Nephthys. By these faces they symbolize birth and death, for these are the changes and movements of the elements; and by the cat they symbolize the moon because of the varied coloring (*dia ton poikilon ... tou therou*), nocturnal activity, and fecundity of the animal. For the cat is said to bring forth first one, then two and three and four and five, thus increasing the number by one until she reaches seven, so she brings forth in all twenty-eight, the number also of the moon's illuminations. Perhaps, however, this may seem somewhat mythical. But the pupils in the eye of the cat appear to grow large and round at the time of the full moon, and to become thin and narrow at the time of the wanings of that heavenly body.

The sistrum was the most popular instrument associated with the cult of Isis, a goddess who became increasingly influential in Europe during the Hellenistic and Roman periods, as we shall see in Chapter 3. The curved frame of the instrument represented the moon. The face on the handles of the sistra is usually Hathor, the goddess of fertility, later associated with Isis. Hathor is also represented as a cow or as a woman with cow-horns. Hence the reference to the cow and the moon.

Moreover, many of the surviving sistra have a figure of a cat at the top of the curved frame. Some of these cats have a crescent upon their heads,[47] that may have caused the animal to be mistaken for a cow, "jumping over the moon."

It is significant that the changes in cats' pupils is now associated with the moon and not the sun. The enigmatic remarks of Plutarch about the cat's fertility seems to mean that when a female first gives birth, she has one kitten, the second time, two kittens, and so on until the last time she gives birth, she has seven. This gives a total of twenty-eight kittens in all during her fertile years. It must be remembered that cats, as well as humans, did not have the same life expectancy in the past as they do today, for much the same reasons. Aristotle observed that the life expectancy of a cat, presumably one that has survived infancy, was usually about six years.[48]

That this rhyme meant considerably more than a mere child's ditty can be seen in the carvings of cats playing fiddles on the pews and other woodwork in medieval cathedrals. One such carving in Beverly Minster Church, Beverly, England (Fig. 4.2, p. 144) shows a cat playing a fiddle with kittens listening, almost identical to the depiction of Bastet and her kittens in Figure 1.6.[49] There have indeed been many explanations for this symbol but Beadle wisely asks:

> Why a cat with a *fiddle*? Was the idea inspired by the Cat and Fiddle Inn sign, one of great antiquity in England? Among the hostelries that still display the sign is an inn located in a Hampshire town called Hinton Admiral; Frederick Sillar and Ruth Meyler say this inn was listed in the *Domesday Book* (1085) as the home of one Catherine la Fidele. Another possible source, also an inn, was owned by a Frenchman who named it A la Chatte Fidele, after his pet cat Mignonette. Well perhaps ... but inasmuch as cats with fiddles appear frequently in medieval church wood carvings, one suspects that the pairing had some religious symbolism.[50]

Religious symbolism indeed: we shall return to the important passage by Plutarch, and the cat and the fiddle in subsequent chapters.

The cats that saved Egypt

Herodotus (2. 141) preserves a folktale about an attack on Egypt in 701 made by the Assyrian conqueror Sennacherib (704–681 BC). Herodotus calls the Egyptian pharaoh of the time Sethos, the monarch who succeeded

Sabacos (Shabaka 716–702), and so this would be Shebitku (Shabataka 702–690) of the Twenty-fifth Dynasty from Nubia.[51]

It seems that Shebitku neglected the warrior class of the country and took their hereditary allotments of land away from them. So when Sennacherib marched against the country, the warrior class refused to defend it. Shebitku, greatly distressed, entered the Temple of Hephaistos (Ptah) and bewailed his fate. As he wept, he fell asleep and dreamed that the god stood beside him. The god advised him to be of good cheer and meet the enemy with courage, as he himself would send succor.

Thereupon, Shebitku gathered those Egyptians who were willing to follow him in battle, not warriors but tradesmen, artisans, and market people. They marched to Pelusium, which commands the entrance to Egypt from the east, and pitched camp opposite the Assyrian host. When night came, a multitude of field mice (*Mus arouraios*), perhaps the Egyptian field rat (*Arvicanthis niloticus*), devoured the quivers, bow strings, and shield straps of the Assyrian soldiers. The next morning the invaders fled the field, pursued by the Egyptians who slaughtered many of them.

Thus we have the field mice (or rats) devouring the Assyrians' bow strings while the Egyptian army, encamped close by, escaped the same fate. The missing factor in this tale must be the cats who guarded the Egyptian army stores from the mice but were not present in the Assyrian army.

It is not without significance that an almost identical story is told about the Battle of Agincourt in AD 1415. Here it is maintained that the English army carried cats with them to protect their military stores, while the French had none. Sure enough, the night before the battle, rats ate the French bow strings, hence explaining the absence of French archers during the battle, while English bows were protected by the cats. The result was a resounding English victory.[52]

The cats that lost Egypt

Another interesting cat story that belongs more in the realm of folklore than history comes to us from the second-century AD military writer Polyaenus.[53] When the Persian king Cambyses attacked the country in 525 BC, he first advanced to Pelusium. This city was stoutly defended by the Egyptians, in spite of the powerful armaments, siege machinery, and missiles hurled against them. Cambyses, knowing that the Egyptians revered animals such as dogs, cats, the ibis, and other domesticated breeds, placed some of them in front of his own army. Seeing this, the Egyptians halted their own military operations, fearing to harm any of the sacred animals. Thus Cambyses was able to take Pelusium, and conquer Egypt.

Cats in the Near East outside Egypt

Although the cat has also enjoyed a long history in the Near East, especially in Mesopotamia, the history of cats in that region has yet to be written. The Egyptian domesticated cat seems to have been introduced into Mesopotamia by the late second millennium BC (unfortunately, we are not able to be more precise at present). The method of transport to the Near East may have been by ship, as there are New Kingdom representations of cats aboard Egyptian sea-going vessels.[54]

Indeed, the Egyptians may have begun the long and honorable tradition of carrying ship's cats aboard ocean-going vessels. It may also be the case, considering the sacral character of the animal in Egyptian society in general, that the cats came to be regarded as a kind of guardian spirit of their ships just as they were for their homes.

It may also be the case that there was a secondary center of cat domestication in the Fertile Crescent region, as some sixth- and fifth-millennium BC remains have been found from Hacilar in Turkey and Jericho in Israel.[55] It is not unlikely that with the domestication of plants in the Fertile Crescent and the attraction of rodents to grain storage areas, the local *ornata* wildcats would soon follow. Some undoubtedly became tame, if not domesticated. Nevertheless, it remains true that genetically and anatomically all domestic cats are mainly descended from the *libyca*, with some interbreeding with other varieties.

Although the cats mentioned in Near Eastern second-millennium sources are mostly in wild contexts, there are a few references to cats in domestic contexts. By the first millennium BC, references are mainly to the domesticated animal. The word for cat, *su-a*, first appears in the Old Babylonian language (1900–1500 BC), but this seems to refer to the local wildcat, probably the *ornata*. In the later Akkadian (*c.* 900–626 BC) and Neo-Babylonian (*c.* 626–539) languages we find the words *shu-ra-a-nu* and *sa-a* respectively that refer to the domesticated cat. During this era the domesticated cat was often differentiated from the wildcat (*mu-ra-shu-u* or *sa-a-ri*), as well as from the caracal.

Some individuals are described with cat-like characteristics: they lurk like cats, they have cat's feet, or cat's eyes. As in the later Roman era, some have personal names based on the words for the animal.

There were also religious associations in Akkadian and Neo-Babylonian literature. Cats frequently appeared in omen texts. Omens were events that were thought to foretell the will of the gods. If a cat behaved in a certain way or appeared in a certain place, this was thought to have predictive value. Some omen texts contain the formula, "if a cat [*sa-a*] weeps [whines?] in a man's house ... " Others discuss the significance of a cat eating a snake in a temple, appearing in a sick man's house, talking with human speech, or a woman giving birth to a cat. A cat also appears as a divine symbol on an unfinished stele from the Kassite era dating to about 1200 BC.[56]

A wildcat and a fox are mentioned in an Akkadian animal tale; some of these stories served as models for Aesop.[57] It is probable, however, that domesticated cats were introduced into the region by the seventeenth century BC, about the time that they may first have appeared in Greece. An early representation of a cat was found in Lachish, in Israel, also dating to that century.

Some earlier studies of cats maintained that since the *miu* was a protected animal in Egypt, it would never have been given the opportunity to leave the country. This notion was no doubt influenced by the story of Diodorus cited above, that when on military campaigns, the Egyptians would ransom captive cats and hawks and bring them back to the country. However, as is widely known, cats frequently fail to obey orders, rather, they can invariably be expected to do so. This characteristic would make them difficult to constrain; especially futile would have been the task of keeping them from merchant ships with their cargoes of grain and, most likely, rodents and fish. Furthermore, during the seventeenth century much of Egypt was under the foreign domination of the Hyksos, who could not be expected to maintain any Egyptian traditions excluding cats from commerce. The numerous Mesopotamian references to the domesticated cat and the representations of ship's cats on Egyptian sea-going vessels during the New Kingdom make this view untenable.

The only reference to cats specifically in the Near East in the Greek language comes from the apocryphal "Letter of Jeremiah," written sometime in the Hellenistic period (323–30 BC). The letter is a diatribe against idolatry and the author, through his specific knowledge, shows a close understanding of that practice (6: 17–23). Just as broken dishes are useless, so are the images of pagan gods. They are usually covered with dust, the temple doors have to be locked to keep out robbers as the gods cannot defend themselves. Wooden parts of the images are eaten by worms and their faces are blackened by the smoke of numerous lamps (and perhaps sacrifices) that are lit even though the gods cannot see the light. "Bats, swallows, and birds light on their bodies and heads; and so do cats. From this you will know that they are not gods; so do not fear them."

We have now come some 3,000 years: from the Libyan wildcats catching rodents along the Nile valley, the first domesticated cats lurking near Egyptian granaries around 2000 BC, and finally to their revered status in the eyes of ordinary Egyptians from the fifth century BC through the second century AD. The further vicissitudes of the cat in Egypt, how the animal fared under the Christians and later the Muslims, will be discussed in Chapter 4.

In subsequent chapters several themes that have first been observed in Egypt will be repeated in later cultures. The first and most obvious are the artistic representations of "the cat under (or beside) the chair," and "the cat in the marshes." More profound, however, are the sacred beliefs towards the animal found among the Greeks, Romans, and many medieval Europeans. Finally, there are the folklore and folk customs that still survive today in modern Europe. Many of these themes can be traced back to ancient Egypt, as we shall see.

We may conclude this section on ancient Egyptian cats by citing some more lines from the eighteenth-century English poet Christopher Smart. In his poetry he seems to have captured better than anyone the feelings of many humans towards the animal over the millennia, including the ancient Egyptians:

> For he purrs in thankfulness, when God tells him he's a good cat ...
> For every house is incompleat without him and a blessing is lacking in the spirit ...
> For the divine spirit comes about his body to sustain it in compleat cat ...
> For he made a great figure in Egypt for his signal services.[58]

2

GREECE

Aye, an' I'm bringin' hares, geese, an' foxes,
Easels an' weasels, moles, hedgehogs an' cats,
An' otters too, an' eels from Lake Copais.
(Boeotian merchant in the agora [or market-place]
of Athens: Aristophanes, *Acharnians*,
878–80, 425 BC)

After Egypt, the original home of the domestic cat, Greece became the most important location for the distribution and spread of the animal. Beginning in the eighth century BC, the Greeks sent out colonies to southern Italy, France, Spain, the Balkans, and the Black Sea. Available evidence shows that the cats accompanied the colonists on their ships, as we might expect of opportunists who enjoyed dining on fish, shipboard rats, and mice.

Europe would offer numerous opportunities for the new immigrant. It would occupy a unique ecological niche, that of a small predator, performing valuable services, who is comfortable in human association. Aside from the ferret with its limitations discussed below, the cat will occupy this position virtually alone. New opportunities abound, but also new dangers. Cats must adapt to a new climate, not entirely different in southern Greece than in northern Egypt, but growing much colder further north. The terrain will often be hilly or mountainous, not the flat alluvial plain of the Nile valley. New predators, as well as some older ones, will also be encountered. There are lions, foxes, lynxes and wolves, but these usually shun human contact because they present a danger to the farmer's domesticated animals. Here the dog becomes a useful ally of the cat, by keeping these large predators at bay and warning the village of their presence.

The earliest Greek cats: *c.* 6000–500 BC

Cyprus: 6000 BC

Pride of place for the earliest cat in the region later occupied by Greeks

48

comes from the island of Cyprus at the Neolithic site of Khirokitia.[1] The remains consist of a lower mandible and teeth from a domestic context. Measurements have determined that they belong to a large member of the species *F. sylvestris* and date to about 6000 BC. The lack of other skeletal remains makes it impossible to determine to which variety of *F. sylvestris* the mandible belongs. Nevertheless, as we have already seen, the *libyca* is the most amenable to human companionship of all the species of wildcats, and this makes it probable that the individual was a tame (not domesticated) *libyca*.

This wildcat, or its immediate ancestors, must have been transported to the island, since there is no fossil record of wildcats on Cyprus. This is because the Mediterranean basin has remained full of water since the beginning of the Pliocene, 5.2 mya (million years ago), after several earlier interludes when it was a dry desert basin. Since, as we saw in the Introduction, the species *F. sylvestris* evolved some 5 mya, it is unlikely that the species traveled across the water to the Mediterranean islands on its own. A desert basin like the Sahara would also have been inhospitable for *F. sylvestris*, as well as for its prey animals, the birds and rodents.[2]

These facts make it likely that the cat remains found on Mediterranean islands were descended from individuals that were transported there by man. It also means that all cat remains on the islands are probably those of the *libyca* or *catus*, since only a fool would attempt to transport the fierce *sylvestris*. Indeed, it is probable that the latter animal would not allow itself to be transported by sea, and would jump ship at the earliest opportunity.

It is of course also possible that the Cyprus cat was killed for its meat, but this is unlikely. It is doubtful whether humans would have transported the cat all the way to Cyprus, merely to slaughter it and eat its meat. It is more likely that the animal was transported deliberately by sea by humans who valued its companionship and its ability to kill rodents. It is not without significance that the first cat appears on the island at about the same time as agriculture begins there, since this activity has always attracted mice. We have already noted this relationship in Egypt. The specimen is the earliest example of the special relationship between the *libyca* and humans, earlier indeed than the first recorded examples from Egypt itself. It is also obviously the first example of a ship's cat, since it had to be transported by sea to the island.

The Bronze Age and Dark Age of Greece: 1600–800 BC

Remarkably, there are several depictions of the cat on frescoes and other objects of art that survive from the Late Bronze Age of the Aegean and Greece, 1700–1200 BC.[3] Most notable is a probable Minoan representation of a cat from a fresco found at Akrotiri on the island of Thera (Santorini) dating to before 1628 BC (Fig. 2.1). The animal is shown in a Nilotic environment, once again chasing ducks. Although the animal is blue in color and has elongated spots on its coat, it has a flatter feline face with jaws agape, and a feline body. The characteristic ringed tail of small Egyptian wildcats is portrayed in a typical curved, upright position.

The animal in question has sometimes been identified with the serval cat and not a *libyca* or *catus*, but this is unlikely. In second-millennium BC Egypt, the serval was an exotic import from sub-Saharan Africa. When it was depicted in Egyptian art, it was frequently as a gift or trade object from Nubia.[4]

One of the earliest representations of a cat from Crete occurs on a seal stone dated stylistically to about 1800–1700 BC. Another early depiction of the cat is from the palace of Mallia in Crete: a remarkable set of a jug and two cups decorated with molded reliefs of cats, trees, and marine elements. There is also a stunning fresco from the palace at Ayia Triada of a cat hunting birds amidst Cretan flora, and another from Knossos with a similar scene. Three Cretan seal stones depict cats chasing ducks (Fig. 2.2). A final representation of a Bronze Age cat comes from the Minoan site of Palaikastro in eastern Crete.[5] This is a terracotta head dating to about 1400 BC. One of the symbols in the Linear A syllabic script used on Minoan Crete is a cat.[6]

There are also several portrayals of cats from mainland Greece during the Late Mycenaean era (1700–1200 BC). Most striking is a bronze dagger inlaid with silver and niello from Grave Circle V at Mycenae. This object dates to approximately 1600 BC and depicts four cats hunting ducks in a papyrus marsh (Figs 2.3, 2.4), two on one side of the dagger and two on the other side.[7] The felines have sometimes been described as leopards (*Panthera*

Figure 2.1 Cat chasing ducks in Nilotic setting, fresco from Akrotiri, Thera (Santorini), before 1628 BC

Figure 2.2 Cat hunting ducks, from Minoan seal stone, Akharnes, Crete, *c.* 1600 BC

pardus), but it is obvious that the animals in question are small cats (*libyca* or perhaps *catus*). This can be seen in the flatter profile of the cat in side one of Figure 2.4 compared to the longer snouts on the lions from the same set of daggers, which are characteristic of larger pantherines such as leopards. Although one feline on side two of Figure 2.4 is seen face-on, it is clear he is a small cat as well. The small size of the two felines compared to the ducks shows that they are cats and not larger animals. The bodies of both cats are only slightly larger than the ducks they pursue. Surely, the artist is skilled enough to depict a leopard at the correct scale if that were his intention.

Finally, the markings on the animal's body also resemble those on the *libyca* and its immediate domesticated descendant in Egypt as portrayed in wall paintings (Fig. 1.3). The markings are not spots, but broken lines comparable to the broken stripes on the coats of the *libyca* and the *miu*, the domesticated Egyptian cat. They are also portrayed with the typical ringed tail of the *libyca* and not the spotted tail of the leopard. The *F. chaus* does not

Figure 2.3   Two cats hunting ducks, from inlaid Mycenaean dagger, *c.* 1600 BC

have pronounced markings. Coincidentally, the warm, golden color of the bronze also is a close match for the coat of the *libyca*.

The cats depicted on the daggers closely resemble the famous "cat in the marshes" scenes in Egypt, discussed in Chapter 1, especially the tomb fresco of Nebamun from the Theban necropolis dating to about 1450 BC (Fig. 1.3). Indeed, the pose of the cat on the upper part of the blade in Figure 2.3 and side one of Figure 2.4 closely resembles that of the cat in the Nebamun fresco, when allowance is made for the narrow field of the dagger. Both cats

Figure 2.4 Drawing of side one and side two of Mycenaean dagger

are shown with duck wings in their mouths, and their hind feet rest on other ducks.

Another Mycenaean inlaid dagger from Pylos shows three small cats with spotted bodies and ringed tails stalking through a rocky landscape with reeds. Moreover, four identical gold images of two cats come from Shaft Grave III at Mycenae. These objects consist of two heraldic cats standing on top of a palm tree (Fig. 2.5). So far as we know there is no word for cat among the surviving documents in the Mycenaean Greek Linear B tablets.

Nevertheless, several remains of cats have been found throughout the Bronze Age Aegean islands, including Thera, Kea, and others from Cyprus. There are also numerous remains from Bronze Age Troy (see Appendix 2). Here, as we have seen, many of the animals were probably domesticated. All cats found on the islands were probably brought over from mainland regions or are descended from such animals. The only suitable animals for such transport would have been the *libyca* or the *catus*. Moreover, the fine representations of the animal by Minoan and Mycenaean artists show an intimate knowledge of the animal. As in Egypt, the cats – long after their domestication – are frequently portrayed as hunting, an activity much admired in antiquity. We can thus be sure that the domesticated cat was present in Minoan and Mycenaean Greece from at least 1600 BC.

There is nothing to suggest that there were any religious beliefs associated with the cat during the Bronze Age. Although some cats are portrayed in heraldic positions, none are of a specifically religious nature. Still, the lack of artistic representations of cats in religious contexts does not prove the lack of such associations. There are no specific representations of cats in religious contexts in classical Greek or Roman art either, but we know from literary texts that such powerful connections existed. It is possible that Egyptian religious beliefs concerning the cat, especially those associated with Hathor and Bastet, were brought over with the *miu* itself. Certainly the

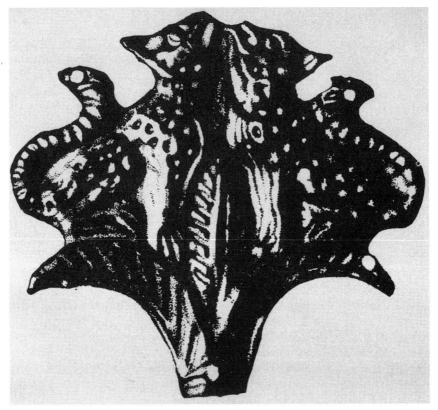

Figure 2.5   Cats in heraldic pose, gold Mycenaean ornament, *c.* 1600 BC

goddess Artemis is represented on the Linear B tables as well as many other female divinities such as Potnia, "The Mistress," later called Potnia Theron, "Mistress of the Animals." By the fifth century at least, the cat had strong associations with Artemis.

There were close connections between Egypt and the Aegean world, especially during the time when Egypt was under Hyksos control, from about 1782 to 1570 BC. Although the Hyksos were not Minoan Cretans, there was certainly a close economic and cultural association between the two cultures. Massive quantities of Minoan pottery have been found at the Hyksos capital of Avaris (Tell el-Daba) as well as Minoan-style frescos.[8] Hyksos artifacts have also been found from the palace of Knossos.

This is a likely time for the cat to have spread into the Aegean and southern Greece. Central control over Egypt was lost, and the cats would lose little opportunity to accompany Cretan traders around the eastern Mediterranean on their fish- and mouse-laden vessels. Moreover, as was noted, cats accompanied Egyptian ocean-going vessels during the New Kingdom (1570–1070 BC).

Between 1300 and 1200 BC, the Minoan and Mycenaean culture of Greece came to a destructive end at the hands of sea-raiders. The following era, that of the Greek Dark Ages, from about 1200 to 800 BC, marked a nadir for Greek culture. There are no certain representations and few remains of cats from this time. Still, the cats of the Bronze Age probably survived the massive destruction of sites on the mainland, Crete, and the islands. Considering the cat's ability to adapt and take advantage of changed environments and circumstances, it is certain that if it was present during the Bronze Age, it could survive on its own during the Dark Age as a feral cat, barn cat, or perhaps village cat, as it has throughout the ages.

Cats, unlike warlike and destructive humans, are survivors. As was seen in the Introduction, cat colonies have managed to survive for over a century on hostile, remote, sub-Antarctic islands with a complete lack of human intervention. They could surely have survived on the hospitable Aegean islands and the Greek mainland through the Dark Ages of Greece. Certainly by the Archaic era, 800–500 BC, the cat was a well-established element of the Greek natural environment and has remained so ever since.

Archaic Greece: 800–500 BC

It is at the beginning of this era that domesticated cats from Greece probably made their way throughout the Mediterranean on ships sent out by colonists. Important representations of cats occur in the coinage of the Greek colonies of Rhegion (Rhegium, Reggio di Calabria) and Taras (Tarentum, Taranto) in southern Italy, dating to the mid-fifth century BC (Figs 2.6, 2.7). The coinage of Rhegion, founded around 720 BC depicts a seated male figure, identified with the city-founder, Iokastos. On the floor beside the man, an obviously domesticated cat characteristically stands on its hind legs and plays with something (piece of wood, meat, cloth) in the man's hand. In the coinage of Taras, founded about 710 BC, the founder Phalanthos sits on a chair with a cat beside him. The fifth-century historians Herodotus (especially 4. 151–9, regarding the foundation of Cyrene) and Thucydides (especially 6. 3–5, concerning Sicilian colonies) have preserved a great deal of factual information about colonies that were founded in the eighth and seventh centuries BC. This shows that, in general, such information was widely available to later eras.[9]

This marvelous series of coins indicates that the Greeks may well have taken their domesticated cats with them on their journeys to found colonies. Obviously they were also ship's cats, and pets as well. The cats were clearly domesticated rather than Italian wildcats or feral cats, or else they would not be depicted in a domestic context. The most likely place for the cat to have come from is mainland Greece. In other coins from Rhegion, a duck or a dog sits under Iokastos' chair, indicating that these may have been brought over as well.

Figure 2.6   Coin depicting the founder of Rhegion, Iokastos, and a pet cat, *c.* 720 BC, on a coin from Rhegion dating to *c.* 435 BC

More importantly, we have depictions of the earliest unmistakable Greek domestic cats. Although the coins date from the mid-fifth century, the city-founders Iokastos and Phalanthos are from the eighth. Thus these are also the first representations of domestic cats in Italy and seem to indicate an early introduction to the peninsula. There must have been an interesting story to go along with the figures, but it has long since perished. It is as if American coinage depicted a seated George Washington playing with a cat beside his chair! The cats could have been descended from Mycenaean Greek cats or more recent imports from Egypt or the Levant.

There is also a series of small bronze cats from the island of Samos that dates to the eighth century BC.[10] It is not possible to tell whether these represent domestic cats, but once again, their presence on an island indicates that they did. The cats are frequently attributed to an Egyptian workshop, but they are frankly too crude to have had an Egyptian origin and may have been made in Greece or the Levant.

The next earliest representation from Greece is on the famous Arkesilas Vase from Laconia and dates to *c.* 550 BC (Fig. 2.8). Here the cat is crouching down into a sphinx position and flourishes its tail in a character-istic manner beneath the seat of Arkesilas, the king of Cyrene. The king is

Figure 2.7 Coin depicting the founder of Taras, Phalanthos, with a pet cat, *c.* 710 BC, on a Tarentine coin dating to *c.* 450 BC

supervising the measurement of the herb silphion for export, and various birds and a monkey grace the scene. The artist is closely familiar with the animal, which by this time was common in Greece.[11]

Cats of the classical and Hellenistic eras: 500–30 BC

It is during this period that we first find a large body of Greek literary and artistic sources concerning the cat. We also encounter the unusual classical Greek word for the cat, *aielouros*, in the fifth century, subsequently *ailouros* in the fourth century and later. It comes from two words: *aiolos*, moving, and *ouros*, tail. As we would say, "moving tail" or, more colloquially, "waggy tail." "Ailouros, the animal (so-called) from moving and holding forth its tail," is the definition in several ancient Greek etymological works.[12] One might expect this word to be used more appropriately for the dog, but a perfectly good term, *kuon*, was already long in use for this animal. Moreover, the description is more apt for cats than for dogs. Cats' tails are often in motion when they are not asleep, and this is especially true in the presence of humans. Indeed, an entire "tail language" may be postulated for the animal by the position and movement of its tail in different circumstances: hunting, stalking, jumping, balancing, pursuit, aggression, anger, fear,

Figure 2.8   Arkesilas, the king of the Greek colony of Cyrene in Libya, with a
cat under his seat. Laconian kylix, *c.* 550 BC

contentment, and happiness. Cats' tails are more expressive than dogs', they
have a wider range of movement and are more indicative of different moods.

Nor are cats the only animal that the Greeks named from the characteristics of their tails. The word "squirrel" comes from the Greek word *skiouros* or
"shadow tail." This probably derived from the typical sitting pose of the
animal, with its tail upraised along its back. In a hot, Mediterranean climate,
this may have suggested that the animal was shading himself from the sun.

It is somewhat surprising to learn that another member of the cat family,
the cheetah (*Acinonyx jubatus*) or hunting leopard was also domesticated by
the Greeks. In a lost play, the playwright Sophocles asked, "Is it likely the
cat grows up into a leopard?"[13] This passage probably referred to the cheetah,
as it was something of a common animal in fifth-century BC Athens, as we
learn from numerous vase paintings,[14] a number of which depict adult cheetahs and cheetah cubs in domestic contexts. The vase paintings invariably
show men walking the animals on leashes, or playing with younger ones

inside the house and sometimes on their lap. They were used for hunting large prey, a tradition that continued in the Near East and North Africa until recently. It is interesting, too, that cheetah cubs with their spotted coats, rounded ears, and large paws are also depicted on small perfume jars that would normally be found in women's quarters, indicating that the Greeks were probably able to breed the animals in captivity.

Aesop's fables

The collection of Aesop's fables provides a wonderful portrayal of barnyard society in classical and Hellenistic Greece. In these stories, the cat first emerges from our sources as an individual, distinctive personality. Although Aesop was an actual author who lived in the sixth century BC, many of the fables ascribed to him were written centuries later. Furthermore, the exact date of an individual fable is virtually impossible to determine. Thus it seems best to treat the corpus in a single place, rather than scattered over two or three chapters. The only exception will be those fables with Christian themes, which will be discussed in Chapter 3. It is quite possible that a few cat fables do in fact belong to the classical or Hellenistic periods. There may even be one written by Aesop himself.

Aesop was a slave on the island of Samos, but came originally from Thrace. He lived in the early sixth century BC and was a contemporary of Sappho. His fables were collected together in one book by Demetrius of Phaleron in the late fourth century BC, and this collection survived until the tenth century AD.[15] This was the principal source used by Phaedrus and Babrius.

Phaedrus wrote in Latin and lived approximately from 18 BC to AD 55–60. Book 1 of his animal tales was derived primarily from an Aesopic collection, probably that of Demetrius, while books 2–5 contain material from other sources and those invented by Phaedrus himself. There is only one cat fable in the manuscripts of Phaedrus (book 2, number 4), but some of his fables that feature weasels or ferrets (*galai*) have cats substituted for them in later recensions and appendices.

Babrius was a hellenized Italian who lived in Syria from about AD 50 to 100. His book is dedicated to Alexander, king of Cilicia under Vespasian. His real name was probably Barbius, but the letters of his name were transposed by error over the years. Again, only one cat fable survives in his text (no. 17). However, as in Phaedrus, several others which feature weasels, have cats substituted for them in some later recensions.

In addition to these basic texts, there are seven other collections of fables that were attributed to Aesop and contain stories about cats. Some of these stories merely repeat those in the earlier texts, but some are different.

Perotti's Appendix of Phaedrus contains thirty fables not found in surviving manuscripts of Phaedrus. Nicolo Perotti (AD 1430–80) was a humanist scholar who transcribed the fables from an earlier manuscript which is now lost. The appendix contains one cat fable.

The Augustana Recension has some 231 fables unknown to Phaedrus and uninfluenced by Babrius. The Augustana manuscript (from Augsburg, Germany) contains three cat fables. In one (no. 165), cats have been substituted for weasels in a story recorded by Babrius (no. 31) and Phaedrus (4.6). The manuscript dates to the tenth century AD and is based on an archetype of the fourth or fifth century. The original compilation may have been made in the late first or early second century.[16]

One cat fable is to be found in Pseudo-Dositheus, *Hermeneumata*. The supplementary Latin fables of Phaedrus contain one original cat fable, and two others repeated from Phaedrus. The fables collected by Odo of Cheriton contain six cat fables, two of them with a Christian context. The Codex Bruxellensis 536 contains two, both with Christian themes. Finally, there is a possible Byzantine cat fable with a Christian theme written by Nicephoras Gregoras in the thirteenth century. Altogether, the ancient, Byzantine and early medieval animal fable tradition contains some sixteen different cat fables and a possible seventeenth written by Gregoras. There are twelve with non-Christian themes and four or five with Christian themes. In several of the later collections, cats have been substituted for weasels.

The fables are notoriously difficult to date and it is unfortunately impossible to attribute a specific fable to Aesop himself. All we can say is that Phaedrus' fables antedate the Augustan era and Babrius' the era of Claudius. The later, supplementary editions and collections may also contain some early fables, but this cannot be known with certainty.[17]

In the fables, domestic cats are represented in three different contexts — the house cat, the barn cat, and the feral or wildcat. Once again this latter context may well include the *sylvestris*, as there is no way of distinguishing the two in the wild. The Greek word used for "cat" is always *ailouros* in the collection. The Latin word in Phaedrus is *feles*. *Catus* is used in the later Latin collections and *gatus* in the latest one. *Murilegus* was also a late term for the cat, although its literal meaning is "mouse catcher." This indicates that other animals, including the ferret, could also be called *murilegus*.

The following fables are from the Aesopic corpus; they concern cats and do not have Christian themes. Where different animals (especially ferrets or weasels) are substituted for cats in other appendices or collections, this will be pointed out in the notes. As mentioned earlier, the five fables from the corpus with Christian themes will be discussed in Chapter 3.

The barn cat

The most frequent portrayal of the cat in the ancient traditions occurs in the context of the barnyard. It interacts with barnyard animals, usually chickens, but sometimes mice.

THE CAT AND THE ROOSTER

A cat, setting a trap for some chickens, suspended himself like a bag from pegs. But a rooster (*alektor*) with hooked spurs, a shrewd fellow, saw him and jeered at him in shrill tones: "I have seen many a bag before now, and know what they look like; none of them had the teeth of a living cat." [18]

THE CAT AND THE HEN

A hen once fell sick. A cat leaned over her and said: "How are you getting along? What do you need? I'll get you anything you want. Only take care of yourself and don't die." The hen replied, " If you get out of here, I won't die."[19]

FELINE SOPHISTRY

A cat wanted to find a plausible reason for killing and eating a cock which he had caught. He alleged that he made himself a nuisance to men by crowing at night and preventing them from sleeping. The cock's defense was that he did men a good turn by waking them to start their day's work. Then the cat charged him with committing the unnatural sin of incest with his mother and sisters. The cock replied that this also was a useful service to his owners, because it made the hens lay as well. "You are full of specious pleas," said the cat, "But that is no reason why I should go hungry." So she made a meal of him – showing how an evil nature is bent on wrongdoing, with or without the cloak of a fair-sounding pretext.[20]

THE ROOSTER CARRIED ON A LITTER BY CATS

A rooster had some cats as his litter-bearers. A fox saw him proudly borne along in style and said: "I advise you to watch out for treachery; if you were to take a good look into the faces of those fellows, you would conclude that they are not porters with a load, but hunters bringing home their booty." When the team of cats began to feel hungry, they tore their master to pieces and divided the kill.[21]

Domestic cats

The following fables contain stories about cats in domestic contexts. Readers expecting to find the famous "Aphrodite and the Cat" or "Metamorphosis" in Handford's translation will be disappointed. This is because in all the manuscripts and recensions the animal protagonist is a ferret (*gale*) and not a cat. Nor do we find a cat substituted for the ferret in a later recension of the tale. Lamentably, the same is true for the "Parrot and the Cat," which also has a ferret as a protagonist rather than a cat. Once again, it is the reluctance of some modern translators to believe that the ferret or domesticated weasel was a house pet among the Greeks and Romans that has led the cat to be substituted for the ferret. Nevertheless, the two fables will be recorded in the section on ferrets.

The first fable considered here from the Aesopic tradition with a reference to a cat is a fable of LaFontaine (1621–95) called "The Battle of the Rats and the Weasels," originally derived from Odo of Cheriton. It will not be repeated here in full since the cat only appears briefly in the second line. It begins,

> The weasel race abhors,
> As much as that of the cats,
> The entire nation of the rats.

The ensuing lines portray a battle between rats and weasels. The weasels are victorious and the rat generals, who have various insignia on their helmets and uniforms, are too encumbered to escape into their holes and cracks. The rank and file, unencumbered by such regalia, are able to escape.[22]

THE CAT, THE RAT, AND CHEESE

A householder, on finding that a rat (*ratus*) was eating the cheese in his cupboard, took counsel with himself and placed a cat (*murilegus*) in the room, but the cat devoured both the rat and the cheese.[23]

THE MICE TAKE COUNSEL ABOUT THE CAT

The mice held a meeting to consider how they might defend themselves against the cat. One wise mouse spoke up and said, "Let a bell be tied to the cat's neck, then we will be able to hear him wherever he goes and be on guard against his sly assaults." All the mice thought this a very good plan, but one of them asked, "Who is going to tie the bell on the cat's neck?" "Not I, certainly," said one of the mice. "Nor I," said another. "I wouldn't go near him for all the world."[24]

THE MOUSE IN THE WINE JAR AND THE CAT

Once a mouse fell into the foam of some wine when it was fermenting. A cat passing by heard him squeaking and asked him why he did so. "Because I can't get out," answered the mouse.

"What will you give me," asked the cat, "if I pull you out?" "Anything you want," said the mouse. "If I free you this time," said the cat, "will you come to me hereafter when I call to you?" The mouse promised under oath that he would do so, and the cat pulled him out of the wine jar and let him go. Afterwards, when the cat was hungry, he went to the mouse's hole and told him to come out, but the mouse refused. "Didn't you swear to come to me when I called?" said the cat. "Yes brother," replied the mouse, "but I was drunk when I swore."[25]

THE CAT'S BIRTHDAY DINNER

A cat on the pretense that he was celebrating his birthday, invited some birds to dinner. He waited until all his guests were inside the house, then shut the door and proceeded to eat them one after the other.[26]

Feral or wild cats

Here one may encounter the feral cat among his wild brethren. Some of the most famous cat fables belong in this series.

THE EAGLE, THE CAT, AND THE WILD SOW

An eagle had made her nest high up in a lofty oak; a cat (*feles*) having appropriated a hollow in the middle of the tree, had borne her kittens there; and a sow, that denizen of the woods, had deposited her litter at the bottom. Then by deceit and wicked malice the cat wreaks havoc on the community formed by chance. She climbs up the bird's nest and says: "Destruction is in store for you, and perhaps also for poor me. For the rooting up of the earth that you see every day means that crafty sow intends to overturn the oak so as to attack our offspring on the ground." After this terrifying blast, which confused the wits of the eagle, she crept down into the lair of the bristly sow. "Your little ones," she says, "are in great danger; for once you go out to feed with your tender litter, the eagle is ready to carry off your little pigs." Soon, this home too was beset with alarm, the wily cat retired to safety in her hole. From there she wanders forth at night on tiptoes, and once she and the kittens (*prolem*) have their fill of food, she pretends to be terrified and keeps watch all day long. The eagle, fearing the downfall of the tree, continues to sit still in the branches. The sow, in order to prevent the capture of her young ones, never issues forth from her lair. Why say more? Both of them starved to death together with their offspring, thus providing the cat family with an ample feast.

In this fable we see how much evil a double-tongued person often creates.[27]

THE OWL, THE CAT, AND THE MOUSE

An owl hunted up a cat and proposed that he ride the cat and they go out traveling together. The cat carried him to the home of a mouse. The owl asked the cat to announce himself. He did. When the mouse heard his voice, he came to the door and said, "What do you want, or what do you have to say?" They replied, "We want to talk to you." The mouse realized that they had evil intentions against him. He said, "To hell with you, Mister Cat, and that fellow who's riding you, and with your houses and your sons and daughters, and to hell with your whole family. You came here with no good in mind, and I hope you meet with the same when you go away."[28]

THE FOX WITH MANY TRICKS AND THE CAT WITH ONLY ONE

Renard the fox met Tibert the cat and asked him, "How many tricks or deceptions do you know?" "I know only one," said the cat. "What's that?" asked Renard. "When the dogs chase me," replied the cat, "I know how to scramble up a tree and get away from them. And you, how many tricks do you know?" "I know seventeen," said Renard, "and besides that I have a bag full of others. Come with me and I will teach you my tricks, so that the dogs will never catch you." To this the cat agreed and the two went forth together. Soon the hunters with their dogs began to chase them, and the cat said, "I hear dogs, I'm afraid." "Don't be afraid," said Renard, "I'll show you how to escape alright." "This is enough for me," said the cat, "I'm not going any further with you, I'm going to make use of my own trick." And thereupon he jumped into a tree. The dogs let the cat go and pursued Renard, whom they presently overtook. They bit him all over, some in the shins, some in the belly, some on the back, and others on the head. Then the cat, sitting on a high place in the tree called out, "Renard, Renard, open up your bag of tricks! Now, surely, all your clever shifts are no good at all."[29]

The portrayal of the cat in the Aesopic corpus

Aesop's fables are metaphors for common human problems and concerns. They depict everyday encounters among barnyard animals, familiar to readers throughout history. The animals are portrayed realistically with a refreshing lack of sentimentality. Some people indeed would impart a further, symbolic interpretation to the animals. For example, the cat may represent the night and the rooster, the day. Be that as it may, the fables have appealed to readers over the millennia because of their simple, direct style, and the universality of the stories that have transcended the bounds of time and place.

The cat is "typecast" in the fables. Whatever the age or tradition of a particular fable, the cat emerges from the corpus with a realistic and distinctive personality. It is a crafty predator, an especial terror to mice, an opportunist who is willing and capable of taking advantage of another animal's mistakes or distress to obtain a meal.

Barns were a familiar sight in the ancient Greek rural landscape. They were used to store straw and hay, wild herbs for winter feeding, dried fruits, olive oil, olives, wine, grain, beans, and nuts. Xenophon recommended that grain be stored in dry, airy, and unplastered chambers within the house or in a separate granary. Some farms had large stone towers for the storage of grain, attached to the farmhouse. Some of the foundations and lower courses of these structures still survive. These would make excellent rodent-proof granaries.[30]

The Aesopic portrayal of the barn cat is especially notable and bears many similarities to present-day barn cats. My informants with such cats tell me that they are almost never made into pets, as their nature is too wild, although they tolerate humans, who on occasion give them supplementary food. While this food would reduce the effectiveness of the cats as mousers, the supplementary diet would tide them over in case of a dearth of prey animals and would perhaps lessen or eliminate any predation on the chickens.

In earlier years in this country, before modern silos, grain was stored in bins in the barn. Naturally this situation attracted numerous mice and rats, and it was the task of the cats to rid the barn of as many rodents as possible.

The semi-wild condition of the barn cat would explain why none of the fables show them directly interacting with humans – this simply was not a common occurrence. It is quite the opposite with dogs, oxen, and horses which are frequently portrayed in human company. It is likely that there was little interaction between the two species in the home either. Like the barn cats, the house cats were left on their own to kill the rodents for food, with little or no human intervention.

The portrayal of wildcats also shows them as pitiless hunters, sneaky and devious, who make their dens in trees, where they would be protected from many predators. Their "one trick," to escape immediate danger by climbing a tree, has protected the animal from predation, both human and animal, over the millennia.

Other animals in Aesop, related to the cat either as prey animals or competitors

Perhaps the most remarkable animal in this context is the domesticated weasel or ferret (*Mustela furo*), a deadly and effective predator of mice, and a valiant fighter. From the evidence of the fables, the ferret was the principal and worthy competitor to the cat as a mouser and later a ratter.

The ferret hunts mice, rats, and rabbits which can also be a major threat to farmer's crops.[31] The method used by the ferret is to burrow directly into the rodent's den and destroy everything in it. When employed to hunt rabbits, the ferret is muzzled, as it was in Roman times. When the rabbits were chased out of their dens, they were captured by humans above ground and used for food. The weasel family has a streamlined body and powerful forepaws, making them excellent burrowers. Their teeth are marvels of killing effectiveness. However, the animal does have major limitations as a human companion. It must be caged and kept in a warm location.

> The ferret is an animal that although exhibiting considerable tameness, seems incapable of attachment and when not properly fed or when otherwise irritated is apt to give painful evidence of its native ferocity. In a word, it is not a trustworthy pet but is a useful partner in the hunting of rabbits and rats.[32]

For these reasons, the animal is banned as a pet in some states in the USA, mainly because of its attacks on children.[33]

Although wild weasels or polecats are hardy animals that can withstand the coldest northern winters, ferrets are quickly killed by cold and have to be kept in warm, sheltered cages. This suggests that the animal was first domesticated in a warm climate and not in Europe.

In the standard text of Phaedrus, our earliest surviving animal fabulist, there is only one fable devoted to the cat ("The Eagle, the Cat, and the Wild Sow"), and this could well be a *sylvestris* rather than a *catus*. There are three fables concerning ferrets. In the standard text of Babrius there is also one cat fable, and three with ferrets. In the Augustana Recension, there are three cat fables and four ferret fables.

In the later recensions, however (Pseudo-Dositheus, Byzantine authors, supplementary Latin fables from Phaedrus and his paraphrasers, Perotti's Appendix, Odo of Cheriton, and the Codex Bruxellensis), there are thirteen cat fables (some with Christian themes discussed below) and only one with ferrets. Furthermore, as we have seen, some early fables with ferret protagonists have them replaced with cats in later recensions. Finally, some modern translators have translated the word for ferret or weasel (*gale* or *galee*) with "cat," thus expressing a modern distaste for the former animal. This would seem to represent a gradual favoritism for the cat over the ferret as a domestic pet over several centuries. The ferret was never entirely replaced by the cat, since its descendants are still pets and efficient rodent-killers today.

Although this is not a book about ferrets, a few observations are in order concerning this adversarial relationship, as well as some suggestions as to why the cats not only held their own but gradually gained the upper hand. The Old World weasel family or genus includes the ferret, and the European and steppe polecats. The ferret (*Mustela furo*) is a domesticated weasel descended either from the European polecat (*Mustela putoris*) or the steppe polecat (*Mustela eversmanii*). Recent research suggests that a descent from the Eurasian *eversmanii* is more likely. The exact location and process of the animal's domestication are still not understood, but it is possible that it was analogous to the domestication of the cat. Human grain-production attracted rats and mice, and this in turn attracted the polecat. A symbiotic relationship developed between the two species, setting up the basis for domestication. [34]

The same problem occurs with ancient terminology concerning the ferret as with the cat. In Liddell, Scott, Jones, *gale* refers to both the wild and domesticated weasel (*gale katoikidios*, or *enoikidios*), just as the Greek term *ailouros* refers to the wild *sylvestris* and the domesticated *catus*. This also is true for the Latin term *mustela*. The word *gale* never means cat, despite the translation of many modern authors. Finally, although there is a superficial resemblance between the two species, they are significantly different animals, with different behaviors both in the wild and in the house, and different vocalizations. No Greek or Roman author would consciously confuse the two.[35]

In the Aesopic corpus, cats are never mentioned in direct conflict with ferrets, but this undoubtedly was a common occurrence. Most references are to domestic weasels or ferrets, but two refer to wild weasels or polecats. A few tales will indicate the nature of this dangerous predator of mice and rats, and its relation to humans. The following two tales refer to a wild weasel or polecat.

THE UNAPPRECIATED WEASEL

> A man trapped a weasel (*gale*), tied it up, and proceeded to drown it where the waters came together in a hollow. The weasel said: "What a miserable recompense you make me in return for the help I give you in hunting down mice and lizards!" "I admit your claim," the man answered, "but there's more to it than that; you were strangling all the chickens and stripping the whole house bare; you did more to harm me than to help me."[36]

The following tale probably refers to a wild weasel that frequents a household and not a ferret.

THE WEASEL AND THE MAN

A weasel (*mustela*), caught by a man and eager to escape impending death, said to him: "Spare me, I pray you, for I keep your house clear of troublesome mice." His captor replied: "If you were doing this for my sake, it would be something to thank you for, and I should have granted you the pardon for which you ask. But as it is, since you do the job to profit by the scraps that the mice would have nibbled, as well as to feed on the mice themselves, don't set me down as your debtor for imaginary services." And so saying, he put the culprit to death.

This applies to those busybodies – let them recognize it – who work for their own private advantage while vaunting their useless services as benefactors to an unwary public.[37]

The following fable shows an interesting relationship between a snake and a ferret in a domestic context.

THE SNAKE, THE FERRET, AND THE MICE

A snake and a ferret were fighting each other in a certain house. When the mice in the house, who were forever being devoured by these enemies, saw them fighting, they began to walk out leisurely; but when the snake and the ferret saw the mice going out, they left off fighting with each other and went after the mice.[38]

Cats will hunt, kill, and eat snakes, which at one time were also used to hunt and kill rodents in Greece.

One of the most famous of all Aesop's fables is the "Ferret and the Man," or "Metamorphosis." As we have noted, the animal protagonist has almost always been translated as a cat, but in all the manuscripts it is a domesticated weasel or ferret.

THE FERRET AND THE MAN

Once a ferret (*gale*) fell in love with a handsome young man, and Aphrodite, the mother of desire, revered goddess, gave her the privilege of changing her form and becoming a woman, one so beautiful that any man would yearn to possess her. When the young man of her choice saw her, he too was overcome by desire and planned to marry her. When the main part of the dinner was over a mouse ran by. Up sprang the bride from her richly strewn couch and began to chase it. That was the end of the wedding banquet. Eros, having played the game well, departed. He was defeated by nature.[39]

THE PARROT AND THE FERRET

A man bought a parrot to which he gave the run of the house. It was tame and one day it jumped onto the hearth and kept up a chatter. The ferret watched it and asked who it was and where did it come from. It answered that the master just bought it. "O most audacious of animals," said the ferret, "how can a newcomer like you make such noise while I who was born in the house am not allowed to? If I do they are angry and shoo me away." "O mistress of the house," answered the parrot, "why not take a hike. The family does not dislike my voice as it does yours."

This fable is for philologists who are always criticizing others.[40]

From the corpus we see that the wild polecat or weasel, like the wild *libyca*, was an opportunist who did not shun human settlements, especially when mice and also chickens might be present. It seems that they may have even invaded houses in search of food. In "The Snake, the Weasel, and the Mice," we learn of house snakes that also hunted down mice, the only reference to this practice in the corpus.

A formidable competitor, the ferret nevertheless had several selective disadvantages in relation to the cat. First of all, its method of hunting mice and rats by burrowing into their underground dens, although effective and well suited to rural environments, was not well adapted to urban areas. Here, streets were often paved and houses built of brick or stone, and so the ferret would have little opportunity to hunt its prey. Cats that often hunt by ambush and wait for their prey to pass close at ground level would be much more effective in these environments. Even in rural contexts, where more homes may have used wattle and daub construction with beaten earthen floors, the homeowner would no doubt have some reservations about having his walls and floors torn up by ferrets. This was especially true when another effective hunter was easily available.

A further problem with the ferret, expressed in the fables "The Unappreciated Weasel," and "The Weasel and the Man," is that its diet is more varied than that of the cat. We have already noted that the family of Vulpavines, of which the weasel is a member, is omnivorous. It is recommended that ferrets be fed bread, milk, and meat scraps, while feral cats do not need to be fed at all. The ferret might therefore represent competition for the farmer's other provisions, whereas the cat would not, since it will only eat freshly killed meat, unless desperate. For many poor farm families, this could have been the difference between having a cat or a ferret. Finally, the ferret's inability to withstand cold weather would place it at a distinct disadvantage in Europe compared to the feral cat, particularly those that had interbred with the cold-acclimated *sylvestris*. Polecats in rural areas undoubtedly helped control rodent populations but their depredations of chickens would not make them welcome to the farmer.

In "The Parrot and the Ferret," we see that cats were not the only whiners in ancient households! There was another territorial animal that refused to brook a rival as well. Although a cat is almost always substituted for a weasel in translations of this fable, it is obvious that the weasel is the correct one. A cat with its climbing ability and ambush tactics would soon have made short work of the parrot!

Dogs were the most beloved of all pets among both the Greeks and the Romans. Yet dogs and cats do not interact in any fables of the Aesopic corpus, nor in other ancient literary sources. Nor are dogs ever mentioned as predators of mice and rats. This is an important point. If dogs were predators of mice this fact would surely have been recorded somewhere in the corpus. Every other conceivable predator of mice was noted, cats, owls, snakes, and weasels, but dogs were absent. As we saw in the Introduction, the primary functions of the dog in Greco-Roman society were as guard dog, sheep dog, and hunting dog, as well as the lap dog, the common household pet.[41] Although dogs were able to hunt and kill mice and rats, this was primarily the function of the cat.

Since in general the cat did not overlap the functions of the dog, there would be little competition for a place in farmyard society. Since both animals were valuable to the farmer, it is reasonable to assume that the dogs would be trained to give the cats a modicum of tolerance, and that the cats and dogs could coexist. If it came to physical confrontation, the cat could usually hold its own, if only by beating a hasty retreat and resorting to its "one trick."[42] Our ancient literary sources do not depict the cat and dog in conflict or as competitors for human toleration and respect.

Nevertheless, such conflicts were inevitable and, on occasion, even encouraged. This can be seen in the famous Popopoulos relief of about 510 BC found near Athens, one of the finest pieces of Greek bas relief from that time (Fig. 2.9). Here we see two seated men, one on the left faces right, with a small dog on a leash, while the other faces left and has a cat on a leash. Two other men each stand behind the seated ones. Both the dog and cat are poised to strike, the snarling dog has its forepaws extended in front, its back arched upwards, and its tail curled (a pose the Greeks referred to as *proskynesis* or "fore-dogging"). The cat is also ready to spring, with its arched back tightly coiled, tail low to the ground, and ears back. The cat is not intimidated by the larger size of the dog, and appears as if to strike. This is a graphic scene, whose tension and excitement one can still feel over two-and-a-half millennia.

Another depiction of a cat and a dog occurs on the celebrated fifth-century BC kylix painted by the Cat and Dog Painter (Fig. 2.10). Here we see peaceful coexistence between the two species. The handsome cat stands on a small table or stool in the center of the scene and faces right. He has a

Figure 2.9   Bas relief showing cat and dog about to fight. Popopoulos Relief found
near Athens, *c.* 510 BC

collar and is on a leash held by a boy who stands at the center. The cat is
well represented in profile with his upright triangular ears and flattened
face. Traces of his original coat markings survive, but they are indistinct.
There is no trace of fear or anxiety in its pose. The dog stands facing the cat
and shows interest in it, with his ears perked up and tail curled upwards.
Nevertheless he remains calm and controlled. The cat is in the center of the
scene.

Figure 2.10   Cat and dog, by the Cat and Dog Painter, Athens, *c.* 450 BC

Today as we have seen, though, street-wise Greek village cats have an intimate knowledge of their neighborhood territory including its dogs:

> Within the district ... they also know every inhabitant, human or animal. They see a dog at a distance, and know at once how to behave towards that particular creature ... Dogs usually know better than to risk confrontation, and instead lurk in hiding places from which they can see without being seen. Female cats will attack only if their kittens are in danger: their actions are swift, sudden, and fearless, and the astonished foe turns its tail in terror.[43]

The stand-off between the barn cat and the chickens (*Gallus gallus*) is especially notable and accurate according to my informants. Generally speaking, the barn cats leave the hens and the roosters alone, but there is an uneasy truce between the two species and, under certain circumstances, cats are not above taking a weak or sickly individual. However, one of my informants tells me that after twenty years of association with barn cats, she never knew a cat to take a chicken, or more remarkably, a chick, which were also raised in the barn. This is not to say that it never happened, but happened so rarely (if at all) that the cats would not be suspected. She felt that the dogs were the more likely culprits. The presence of the cat in the barn for these many millennia implies a reasonable expectation by the farmer that the cat will do no real harm to the other animals, or at least do more good than harm.

Furthermore, the rooster itself is a formidable animal, not to be trifled with, even by a hungry cat. One of my informants told me that she even used roosters on occasion to guard her young children and to prevent them from straying outside their play area. Doubtless the goose would also be a match for a cat and it has certainly been known to frighten away some human trespassers.[44]

Finally, there are the mice (*Mus musculus*) that are mentioned frequently throughout the fables. Mice are portrayed as cunning and conniving, devouring the food of the homeowner and farmer, but not as carriers of disease. Usually they are no match for the cat or the ferret in intelligence or strength.

One animal missing from the early fables is the black rat (*Rattus rattus*). So far as is known, there is no word that represents rat in either classical or koine Greek, but the word *ratus* occurs in late Latin and is used in the one late Latin fable recorded by Odo of Cheriton. In Chapter 3, the arrival of the black rat in the Mediterranean will be discussed. Although an occasional visitor to the Mediterranean region from at least the eleventh century BC, it became a permanent resident there in the first century AD. The larger brown rat (*Rattus norvegicus*) does not appear in Europe until the seventeenth century AD.

The natural history, or study, of the cat

Many ancient Greek scholars made shrewd and mostly accurate observations about the behavior and biology of the cat. Furthermore, the cat was also used in medicine for its healing properties. In general, studies concerning different aspects of nature were called natural histories, literally, "inquiries into nature." Hence our term, museum of natural history, used to describe an institution devoted to the study of nature, not necessarily the "history" of nature in the modern sense. While no ancient natural history devoted specifically to the cat survives, scattered references to the animal can be found in authors from the fourth century BC to the first century AD and even later, some from the greatest intellects of their eras.

Although some authors, such as Claudius Aelian, Aetius of Amida, and Alexander of Tralles, wrote at the time of Roman rule over Greece, many of these medical writers and naturalists based their own works on those of the Hellenistic period. Once again, as in the case of the Aesopic tradition, it seems best to treat the whole topic in one place, rather than separately in two chapters. One important philosophical debate concerning animals in general was whether they possessed reason as did humans, or whether the capacity of reason was denied to them.[45] The Pythagoreans, Platonists, and Neo-Platonists maintained the former view while the Aristotelians, Stoics, and later the Christians maintained the latter. The view that animals shared reason with humans may indeed have ameliorated their treatment in some instances, preventing their abuse, sacrifice, and consumption as food. As the Neo-Platonist Iamblichus observed:

> In this way too, we classify all humans as related both to each other and to all animals. For their bodily origins are by nature all the same ... And much more are they related through their souls being no different in nature, I mean in their appetites, anger, and again in their reasonings (*logismoi*), and above all in their senses. But, as with their bodies, some animals have souls more finely tuned, others less so, but they still all by nature have the same origins. And this is shown by their passions being the same.[46]

Nevertheless, it remains true that the actual treatment of animals may have more to do with religious beliefs and the practical uses of the animals than to philosophical notions. For example, although the early Christians opposed the idea that animals shared reason with men, they succeeded in abolishing the practice of animal sacrifice, thus benefiting animals such as the cat who were sacrificed but not eaten in the pagan tradition. The opposition to animal sacrifice would, of course, not benefit those animals who were killed anyway and eaten for their meat. The medieval Christians on the other hand, although outlawing animal sacrifice, massacred cats by the millions as agents of Satan. Finally, although the sacral position of the cat in Egypt and among many in Roman Europe benefited the species as a whole, it was of little use to the individual cats who were sacrificed.

Three specific characteristics of the cat receive the most frequent notice by our ancient naturalists: reproduction; predation, including night vision; and the suitability of the animal for taming as a human companion. Also of interest is the cat in medicine, both as a cause of illness and as a healing force.

One notion that many of these accounts share, especially the later ones, is the magico-sympathetic concept of nature, discussed in Chapter 1 and called *sympatheia* by the Greeks. To many naturalists and laymen of the Hellenistic and Roman eras, all of nature was harmoniously unified in both necessary and symbolic ways by divine spirit. This was also true of the cat. For example, in this way of thinking, the resemblance of the cat's pupils to the phases of the moon was not accidental, but was caused by a sympathetic association. There were no accidents or coincidences in nature since it was thought that everything was linked together by divine providence.

Aristotle has accurately observed many behavioral characteristics of the cat in his *Historia Animalium*. In reproduction,

> They do not copulate hindways, but the male stands erect and the female places herself under him. Female cats are naturally lecherous (*aphrodisiastikai*) and lure the males on to sexual intercourse, during which time they caterwaul.
>
> (*HA* 540 a; cf. Pliny *NH* 10. 174)

Claudius Aelian (6. 27) provides another description of the animal's love life:

> The male cat is extremely lustful, but the female is devoted to her kittens (*philoteknos*), and tries to avoid sexual intercourse with the male, because the semen he ejaculates is extremely hot and fiery, and burns the female organ. Now the male cat, knowing this, makes away with their kittens, and the female in her yearning for other offspring yields to his lust.

As for other solitary cats, the female must be stimulated to ovulate during intercourse. This is accomplished by barbs on the male's penis, and is a painful experience for the female. Hence the caterwauling by the female. We have already discussed the fact that a dominant male will kill kittens in his territory if he believes they are not his own.

Aristotle also notes that cats and mongeese share many similar characteristics; indeed, both are members of the Viverrine family as noted in the Introduction. "Cats and mongeese (*ichneumones*) bear the same number of young, as dogs, live on the same diet, and live for about six years" (*HA* 580 a; cf. Pliny *NH* 10. 179). Once again, we are reminded that animals and humans in the past did not live as long as those at present. Presumably, the cats that survived infancy would live to six years, the life expectancy at birth was probably about five, similar to feral cats at present.

Cats are clean and, "abhor all foul-smelling objects, and that is why they dig a hole before they discharge their excrement, so they may get it out of sight by throwing earth upon it" (Aelian, *HA* 6. 27). Pliny the Elder (d. AD 79) adds that this is done to hide the animal's presence from its prey (*NH* 10. 202). Finally, Aelian notes that cats, like polecats, prey on birds as well (*HA* 612 b). Pliny (*NH* 11. 172) accurately notes that cats' tongues are so rough they can scrape away skin – this is indeed one of the tongue's functions in helping to devour prey.

Once again, the cat's eyes and nocturnal habits attracted much attention from naturalists. Pliny noted that the eyes of many night hunters, including the cat, shine and flash at night. He implies that this may startle or spook prey animals (*NH* 11. 151). In other words, although flashing eyes may give away their presence, it may also frighten the prey, and cause them to remain still. Of interest to the serious ailourologist is the explanation for the cat's night vision given by the sixth-century AD medical writer Alexander of Tralles:

> Why are some able to see during the day but not at night? This is because they have a heavier optical vital spirit (*optikon pneuma*) that does not allow the air to be seen. For at night the air becomes heavy because of the cold and the absence of the sun, while during the day, the air becomes lighter and warmer. Therefore, cats, hyenas, and bats can see more clearly at night than in the day, because they have a lighter and brighter optical vital spirit.[47]

Some naturalists believed (wrongly), that the cat's pupils changed with the phases of the moon, contracting as the moon wanes and increasing when it grows full.[48] This error was caused in part by the notion of *sympatheia* between the cat and the moon. Others maintained that the total number of offspring borne by the cat was twenty-eight during their life span, the number of days in a lunar cycle.[49]

In an important passage, the sixth-century AD medical writer Aetius of Amida notes that cats can be the cause of illness:

> The excrement of sick cats provides plenty of causes for illnesses of the following types, depending on the cats' coat varieties (*tes choas tou pantos dermatos*). A whitish (*leukotera*) coat produces a phlegmatic disorder, a blackish one (*melantera*) a melancholic state, and a pale coat (*ochrotera*), a choleric one. [50]

Indeed some individuals are allergic to cats, and this has been discussed in many modern veterinary and medical works, although the allergies are caused by the cat's dander and not its excrement. We note again the concept of *sympatheia* in this passage, with the blacker cats (*melantera*) producing melancholic dispositions (*melagcholikoteran*).

What is of special interest here, however, is the coat colors themselves. The "pale" color may indeed refer to the natural color of the *libyca*-type cat seen in works of art from ancient Egypt through the Roman Empire. Of greater significance, though, are the black and white coats, mentioned here for the first time. These late medical writers often repeat earlier medical authorities. Aetius, for example, bases most of his work on the second-century AD medical authority Galen and the fifth-century Oribasius. According to Aetius, Galen gives antidotes for the cat-caused maladies, and it is therefore possible that Galen was also the source of the information about the cats. This view is supported by the humoral theory in the passage, a theory that was revived by Galen from the Hippocratic school. It is not certain, however, that the cat passage was based on Galen and no surviving work of Galen gives such information.

Although, as we shall see below, the existence of the black cat in the Mediterranean from about 500 BC has been postulated by Todd, based on genetic research, the date of the introduction of the white cat into that region has not been known. Once again, the passage from Aetius is the earliest to give a physical description of these two color types, which date therefore to at least the sixth century AD, and probably earlier.

One reason for the concern with cat excrement and disease is the frequent use of this substance in ancient medical pharmacopoeias. Cat parts and excrement have been used in medical cures since the pharaonic era in Egypt. In Greek pharmacopoeias, the parts and excrement of virtually every animal were used for some medical purpose. It is doubtful whether these particular animal remedies were very effective. Nevertheless, ancient pharmacopoeias consisting mainly of folk remedies from herbs do contain many medicinally useful substances, such as digitalis, atropine, ephedrine, and salicin, derived from willow bark. The latter was used as a pain suppressant and is chemically related to salicylic acid, the main ingredient in asprin. Not surprisingly, cats were used for medicinal purposes as well – indeed their dung, mixed with vinegar was highly regarded by pharmacologists as an external medicament![51]

Finally, we learn from Plutarch that cats and ferrets are only eaten in times of famine.[52] It is also possible that the skins of cats were used for garments or other purposes, but the source of this particular information is the satirist Anaxandrides, who once again was mocking Egyptian ritual practices concerning animals.[53] In Chapter 1, we discussed the taming of the *libyca* as seen in our Greek sources. From Plutarch (482C) we learn that some naturalists were interested in taming the European *sylvestris*:

Some breed and grow fond of savage dogs and horses and may also do so with lynxes, cats, monkeys, and lions, but cannot endure a brother's faults.

Aristotle (*HA* 580 b) also has an interesting description of the reproductive capacity of mice and mice plagues. "The reproduction of mice is a most astonishing thing when compared with other animals both for the number of young produced and the speed of it." Aristotle noted that one pregnant female mouse was caught in a jar of millet seed and when the jar was opened a short time later, there were 120 mice inside. When a plague of mice has overrun a field, very little of the crop remains. Indeed, on small farms the reaping equipment is made ready to reap the crop the next day, and when the farmer goes to his fields the following morning, he finds that the entire crop is gone, having been devoured overnight. Farm hands try to dig them up, and turn pigs on them that will dig up their holes. Foxes and polecats (*galai agrai*) can also hunt them but are no match for the speed and volume of the mice's reproduction. Strong rainstorms are the only way their predations can be halted.

Like the cat, the mouse had religious associations, this time with Apollo. One of Apollo's epithets was Smintheus, the Mouse God. Mice were associated with causing disease, making depredations on crops, but also with curing disease. White mice were even kept as apotropaic pets in Apollo's temples to protect against disease and depredations. As was discussed earlier, the keeping of pet mice will cause no great harm to society, provided they are fed, kept clean, and their reproductive capacity limited.

Religion: Artemis and her cat

There is very little direct evidence concerning the cat in Greek religion during the classical era (500–300 BC), the Hellenistic era of the East (300–30 BC), or the pre-Roman era of western Europe. Nevertheless, critical associations of the animal with the goddess Artemis in Greece and Diana in Italy were made in this period. Furthermore, this was probably also the time that various Celtic rituals first arose concerning the cat, rituals that survived as folk traditions and customs in modern France and England. These developments will be discussed in Chapter 3.

The relationship between Artemis, Diana, and the cat was a momentous one for the history of the animal. Though providing religious protection for it during pagan times, the association doomed the cat to suffering, cruelty and virtual annihilation in many towns of continental Europe during the Middle Ages, when Diana became identified as the demonic leader of witches.

We have already seen that the Greeks had identified the Egyptian goddess Bastet with their own Artemis.[54] Along with this identification came the association of Artemis with the cat.[55] Furthermore, some Greek sources note that the animal was also sacred to Athena Glaukopis, Athena of the Shining Eyes, sometimes called "Athena the Cat," an apt description of the cat's eyes, especially at night.[56]

Artemis was the most popular goddess in ancient Greece, especially among women. She was a virgin hunter, also known as *Potnia Theron*, Mistress of the Animals. With her companions the nymphs, she roamed the hills and forests. Furthermore, although she was merciless to her prey, she was the protector of the young of all species. She and the hunters that followed her example never hunted immature or small prey animals such as wildcats, squirrels, or dormice.[57]

Hunting was always regarded as a noble practice in antiquity, and indeed even in many regions of my own country today. In ancient Egypt, hunting scenes were commonly painted on the walls of the tombs of the nobility. Prowess in hunting was a characteristic of royalty in Egypt, Mesopotamia, Macedonia, and in the Roman Empire, and was frequently associated with success in war.

Artemis was also the goddess of fertility, who protected women in childbirth. As we noted in Chapter 1, his was a very important factor in ancient populations. Because of high death rates and low life expectancies of only about 25 years, birth rates were also high. If they were not maintained, the population would decline at a geometric rate. Birth rates among married women were some nine children during a relatively short life span.[58] Artemis was also the protector of the young and watched over little children. Girls brought offerings to her before their marriages. Indeed, all women throughout Greece had an intimate and sacred relationship with the goddess, since marriage, motherhood, childbearing, and childrearing were central to their lives. This was also later true of the goddess Diana among the Romans.

Artemis probably had more shrines, temples, and sacred precincts than any other divinity. The city of Sparta was sacred to Artemis Orthia and her great temple at Ephesus was one of the Seven Wonders of the ancient world, an honor given to her temple only among all those of other divinities.[59] Artemis was the goddess of the moon, too, a celestial body frequently associated with the cat, as we have seen.

Lastly, Artemis was associated with diseases that afflicted women, as her brother Apollo was with diseases that afflicted men. In Homer, Artemis can actually cause diseases by shooting arrows of disease (*toxa*) into the women, but she could also cure diseases, as could her brother. Thus she was also a goddess of healing and one recalls the role of the cat in reducing rodent populations and their associated diseases.

The personality of Artemis is not as contradictory as some have supposed, and there is no need to invoke two different divinities merging into one through the conquest of an earlier matriarchal or matrilineal society with a goddess of fertility and childbirth by a later "patriarchal" society with a hunting goddess.[60] Nevertheless, there is also no doubt that the goddess was something of a composite, taking the attributes of many of the local female divinities found throughout the northern Near East, Aegean, and Greece, as well as Egypt. Religious syncretism was a common characteristic of the Greeks from earliest times, and usually involved he identification of a small, local divinity with a greater and more powerful one who had similar attributes. A comparable process can be seen in the development of the Egyptian solar god Ra, who gradually subsumed the local gods Ammun of Thebes and Atum of Heliopolis under his own name as Amun-Ra and Atum-Ra.

It seems clear that Artemis embodies many of the characteristics of the cat. Both are pitiless hunters who are nevertheless also associated with motherhood, fertility and childbirth. Both protect the young and, as we have seen, there is no animal of any species that is more protective of its offspring than the mother cat, who will literally give up her life for the sake of her kittens. The warding off of diseases and harm, especially for women and children, was a characteristic of the animal that we have already observed in ancient Egypt. Finally, there is the connection with the moon which has endured all the way from ancient Egypt, through the Roman Empire and the Middle Ages to modern-day folktales.

Another of Artemis' talents was her ability to enter into the body of a cat, or to assume the shape of a cat, as we learn from Ovid in the *Metamorphoses*, Lucian, and the mythographer Antoninus Liberalis.[61] Ovid (43 BC – *c*. AD 18), who regularly uses earlier Greek versions of myths for his work, wrote that when the gods were at war with the giants, they fled to Egypt to escape. There, they hid in lying shapes (*et se mentitis superos celasse figuris*). Jupiter became a ram, while Diana (the Roman Artemis) became a cat. The notion that gods can assume the shape of animals seems to be derived from Egyptian ideas, as we have seen. Now this idea has been transmitted to the Greek and the Roman world as well; it was to play a significant role in the future history of the animal, as we shall see.

The goddess has been one of the most enduring features of Greek country life, still surviving today in folklore, as her Roman counterpart, Diana, has survived in the West. Today she is called the "Great Mistress," the "Lady of the Mountains," or the "Queen of the Mountains," and is still seen by the peasants hunting and roaming the hills with her consort of maiden nymphs, now often called Neriads.[62]

Finally, in this context, we will discuss the cat portrayed on a great funeral monument from fifth-century BC Athens (Fig 2.11). Although the religious content of these grave stelae may not be readily apparent, or may indeed be absent, it seems best to discuss it at this point, since it relates to views of death if not of an afterlife. This grave stele dates to about 440 BC and is one of the great works of Greek art. Created by one of the masters of the Parthenon Frieze and now in the National Museum, its subject is the death of a young man who perhaps died during the military conflicts of that decade. A cat is portrayed on the stele. It is unfortunate that the head of the animal has broken off, but enough survives to show that it was indeed a domesticated cat. In these monuments, the most prominent emotion is the beloved's loss of everything of meaning in this life. As in Homer's *Iliad*, the dying soldier's entire life passes before his eyes, his home, family, and loved ones, before the final darkness of death overcomes him forever. In general, the ancient Greeks did not believe in much of an afterlife, and very little of their prodigious intellectual effort was expended in considering such issues. This remains true in Greece today, especially among the peasantry, who tell of a dark and gloomy afterlife to which all departed spirits go, regardless of the religious or ethical qualities of their lives.

On the monument we see the departed young man's left hand holding a small bird, probably a pet, while his right hand is raised to the bird's cage. A young relative, perhaps the man's son or younger brother, stands facing the viewer with a sad expression and downcast eyes. On a ledge beneath the cage a small cat sits in a characteristic sphinx position; it is probably another pet. We imagine that this must have been a favorite place for the cat to sit.

As is often the case on such monuments, the loss of dearest relations and favorite possessions is beautifully expressed. The young deceased may not have been married, and his most cherished relative expresses grief and loss, while his bird and cat will be gone forever.

The funerary stele of Salamine, who died in about 420 BC, shows a young girl and a cat.[63] It is one of the earliest monuments to show the connection between the animal and young girls.

The distribution of the cat by the end of the first century BC

According to many conventional accounts of the animal's distribution in western Europe, domesticated cats did not make an appearance in Italy, let alone the rest of the continent, until the beginning of the Imperial era (30 BC – AD 500).[64] However, literary, artistic, genetic, and archeological evidence demonstrates conclusively that the animal was widely distributed throughout the continent by the third century BC. Thus it was not the Romans that brought the cat with them during their conquests, but merchants and travelers from the Greek colonies in Italy and southern Gaul (France) at a much earlier date. Perhaps Phoenician traders from North Africa also brought them to the same regions, as well as to their colonies in Spain at the same time.

In Greece, as we have seen, there is no doubt that cats were a common feature of farm and village life by at least the seventeenth century BC. They

Figure 2.11 Funeral monument showing the departed with a young relative, bird, and cat. Sculpted by one of the Parthenon sculptors, Athens, *c.* 440 BC

may have survived the Greek Dark Age and were well established by the sixth century BC, when we find many artistic representations.

Of course, the domesticated animals were well established in Egypt and the Near East from an early era. It is probable that ship's cats found their way on the vessels of Phoenician colonists to North Africa and southern Spain, and settled there in the ninth and eighth centuries BC.

The coins of Rhegion and Taras show that cats were very probably taken by Greek colonists to their new homes during the eighth century. If they were taken to Rhegion and Taras, there is no reason why they should not have been taken elsewhere, for example, southern Europe and probably the Black Sea region. In any event, it would be difficult to stop a cat, who wanted to leap aboard a ship to dine on fish and mice. It would be equally difficult to stop the cat from "jumping ship." Furthermore, as we shall see in the next chapter, cats were well established in Italy by at least the fifth century BC, when they were represented in domestic scenes in Etruscan tomb paintings from Tarquinia. The first osteological evidence for Italian cats also dates from that century. Evidence from feline population genetics collected by Todd (discussed immediately below) has shown that the Greek colony of Massilia (Marseilles), founded by Phocaeans in about 600 BC, was a major point of distribution of the animal up the Rhone and Seine rivers to the rest of Gaul (France) and Britain.

The most remarkable evidence for the early distribution of the cat in Europe comes from Gussage All Saints, an Iron Age hill fort in Dorset, England. The site was occupied from the Iron Age through the early Roman era. Here we find the bones of no fewer than seven individuals, including five kittens, that date to the mid-third century BC.[65] According to Harcourt, the analyst of the bones, the individuals are domesticated cats and not European wildcats, which are native to Britain as well. There is no doubt that this view is correct. As we have seen, wildcats will avoid human settlement if at all possible, and so if their remains are present, it is because they have been hunted, killed, and butchered for eating. In this instance, the bones should be disarticulated and show signs of butchering marks. The remains from Gussage All Saints, however, are articulated, and the cats are breeding within the community, all factors demonstrating domestication. That such an overwhelming presence of cats is found in a small settlement in southern England already by the third century BC indicates a wide distribution of the animal, not only in Britain, but also in Gaul at an early date. This fact is also supported by the research on cat population genetics undertaken by Todd.

The types of coat colors and patterns on cats (phenotypes) are determined genetically.[66] Through the study of the variable genotypes (mutant alleles), that are associated with coat types or phenotypes, Todd was able to establish some general dates and patterns of distribution of different feline mutant alleles throughout the Near East and Europe. Figures 2.12 and 2.13 are cline maps showing the frequency of certain mutant alleles that appear in different geographical areas. Because of genetic complexities, some cats with the mutant allele do not display the corresponding phenotype. That is why the maps show the alleles and not the coat types.

Coat types, however, are only outward manifestations of the animal's complex, internal endocrine chemistry. Behavior patterns such as fear and aggression can be manipulated in many animals merely by cross-breeding

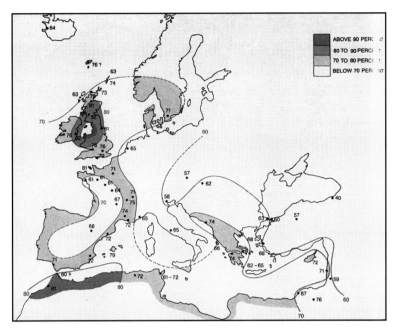

Figure 2.12   Allele distribution of nonagouti cats

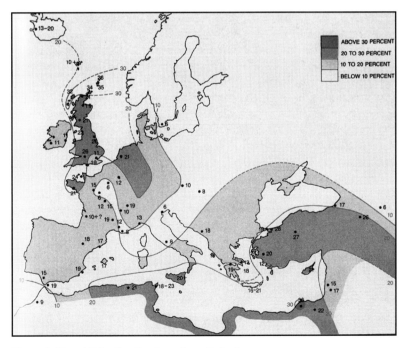

Figure 2.13   Allele distribution of sex-linked orange cats

one coat type with another, and the same is true for cats. Urban cats in different countries share many of the same mutant alleles with each other, but not with cats in neighboring suburban areas. This is because different selective forces required by urban life exert powerful influences on feline genetics. The maps represent, therefore, the complex adaptations of cats moving from one ecological niche to another, or from a feral, predatory life style to a more settled domesticated one.

In general, humans have in the past exerted little control over the breeding of cats. Two exceptions are the selection of a novel coat color or pattern, an all-white or all-black cat for example, and through selective migration. In the first instance, however, when the mutant allele reaches 10 per cent in a population, it is no longer considered a novelty and loses its appeal.

Selective migrations have played an important role in the distribution of cats and their wild-type, and mutant genotypes. Water barriers that have prevented the distribution of most animals are veritable highways for cats, since they adapt well to ship-board conditions. Human preferences for a specific phenotype that would be overwhelmed in a settled cat population, can become dominant in a migratory population with fewer local cats. The new migrant mutant types, preserved and secured by human selection, now come under the forces of natural selection in their new homes. Perhaps the new mutant forms impart some intrinsic superiority, such as resistance to disease, broader nutritional requirements, better hunting ability, or better adaptability to the presence of humans or other species.

There were three basic cat genotypes in the ancient world. The first was the "wild," non-mutant type represented by the grey tabby in Europe and the Egyptian domesticated cat (the *miu*, represented by the modern Mau breed), first bred in North Africa, and discussed in Chapter 1. Originally, the "wild" type grey-tabby coat belonged to the *sylvestris*, but through centuries of interbreeding with the *miu* its fearsome personality was modified to levels acceptable for a human companion.[67]

Some ancient artistic representations from Italy dating from the mid-fifth century BC until the first century AD represent colors and coat types (Fig. 3.4). They show that the *miu* or *libyca*-type was a common coat phenotype during that period. We may well conclude that this was the first type to be introduced into Greece and western Europe, and long remained dominant in many regions. Interbreeding with the local *sylvestris* gradually produced the domesticated grey tabby. We may also suppose that this genotype, the one most closely related to its wild ancestors, shared some selective advantages over more recently introduced ones, especially skill in hunting.[68]

The first mutant allele to be introduced into the Mediterranean region was the nonagouti type. Agouti refers to a characteristic of many wild mammalian coat types: each hair has a band of reduced pigmentation below the tip, giving it a salt-and-pepper or brindle pattern. It is named agouti after a South American rodent whose coat exemplifies the pattern. Nonagouti cats lack this pattern, and have solid colors, usually black. This mutation began about 500 BC in the eastern Mediterranean, perhaps in Greece or Phoenicia (Fig. 2.12).

One finds this genotype most pronounced in northwestern Africa and central Britain. The reasons for this pattern of distribution seem to be that when the cats were first introduced, perhaps through Carthaginian traders, they were the only domesticated cats in the region. With few or no competitors, they were able to genetically dominate the area and hold out against more recent types. Furthermore, there is evidence that the nonagouti mutant is favored by the urban environment and fosters a closer cat–human affiliation. This would also explain its formidable presence in urbanized areas of modern Britain and France.

One will also notice the corridor of distribution along the Rhone and Seine rivers in Gaul, with its southern terminus at the Greek colony of Massilia (Marseilles). This colony, founded in about 600 BC by Phocaeans, was a critical point of distribution for the animal up the Rhone valley to the rest of Gaul and into southern Britain, as can be seen not only in the distribution of the nonagouti type but also the sex-linked orange mutation.

This second form of ancient mutation seems to have been introduced after the nonagouti, perhaps during the Roman Empire. The sex-linked orange mutation is responsible for a wide variety of coat phenotypes. The most common are called marmalade (or orange tabby), tortoiseshell, and calico. The latter two are almost always females, since the coat phenotypes depend on heterozygosity.[69]

The cline map (Fig. 2.13) for the distribution of this mutant allele shows an unusual pattern, with heavy representation in the eastern Mediterranean, especially in Egypt and Anatolia, but a relative absence in Italy, the Rhone–Seine corridor, and southern Britain. Todd believes that Asia Minor may have been the original home of this genotype, and from there it spread by sea to the central and western Mediterranean. Its strong presence in central and north Britain may indicate once again that the new migrant did not face overwhelming competition from the wild and nonagouti genotypes already present.

Alternatively, the strong presence of the sex-linked orange allele in Scotland, Iceland, and the Faeroe Islands may indicate their transport there by Vikings in about AD 1000 from their trade connections in the eastern Mediterranean and Black Sea regions. This may also explain the high frequencies of dominant white in the same northern areas of Europe. The highest frequencies of this genotype are found in western Turkey, probably their original home, and they may have been transported from the region by Vikings who favored their color.

The reason for the relative lack of this mutant allele in Italy, the Rhone corridor, and southern Britain (compared to the central and northern parts of the country, and Scotland) is probably the long, stable, and continuous presence of large populations of cats in those regions during the Roman Empire. When the sex-linked orange cats reached those areas, they represented but a small fraction of the genotypes already there. They must also have enjoyed some selective advantage in North Africa, perhaps a human predilection for their coat color, or ability to tolerate the climate and terrain.

At present, a third mutant allele, the blotched tabby is becoming increasingly dominant. "The type is clearly spreading like an epidemic that will apparently engulf all cat populations."[70] The type emerged in England about three hundred years ago and has spread through France, using the same Rhone–Seine corridor, though this time the cats are emigrating from north to south. It has also spread to the English colonies in North America, Australia, New Zealand, and Oceania, and outdoes many of the earlier types in those regions.

By the second century BC, the domestic cat had also reached India.[71] A beautiful Hindu poem reads,

> The cat laps up moonbeams in the bowl of water thinking them to be milk.[72]

This was probably accomplished through the overseas trade that the Hellenistic world had established with India and the East. Direct contacts between the Mediterranean and India were opened up for the first time by the conquests of Alexander the Great. He believed correctly that through trade with India, Arabia and southern Persia could become as prosperous as Phoenicia. To open up trade routes from the Persian Gulf to India was one of the reasons for his making the disastrous crossing of the Gedrosian Desert in southern Pakistan and Iran in 325 BC.

In any event, the Hellenistic era witnessed a great expansion of trade with the East, both with India overseas and China overland. The termini for much of this overseas trade were the Red Sea trading ports of Egypt, especially Berenice and Myos Hormos, controlled by the Ptolemies of Egypt and later by the Romans. We have seen that the Egyptians used ship's cats in their ocean-going vessels from the New Kingdom era (1570–1070 BC). It is likely that the Indian cats were transported there by this method.

By the end of the Hellenistic era in the East and the Roman Republic in the West (about 30 BC), therefore, we find a general distribution of the animal throughout the Mediterranean and Europe, as well as east to India. Many of the phenotypes – the "wild" nonagouti (or *miu*-type), sex-linked orange, black, and perhaps the white – that are still common today were already widely known. By the time of the Roman Empire, the cat enjoyed a distribution throughout the Old World. During this period, it continued its role as the protector of the household from evil and misfortune – especially in the form of disease and starvation. Its religious role, however, assumed a new prominence with the introduction of Greco-Egyptian cults such as that of Isis into Europe. Indeed, many of the folk traditions concerning the cat that persist in modern Europe have their origins in Gallo-Roman Gaul and Romano-Celtic Britain.

3

ROME

How silently and with what light a tread do cats creep up to
birds, how stealthily they watch their chance to pounce on
tiny mice.

(Pliny the Elder, *Natural History*, 10. 202 (94), *c.* AD 70)

In this chapter we shall consider the history of the cat in the Italian peninsula from the time of the first Greek colonies in the eighth century BC and
the Roman Empire as a whole through the end of the fifth century AD. This
is the next critical stage of the animal's development as a permanent feature
of European life. As was discussed in Chapter 2, recent research has shown
that the cat was already broadly distributed in the Mediterranean and western
Europe well before the time of the Roman conquests. Nevertheless, during
the Roman era, in addition to its traditional place as defender of the household from disease and rodent depredations, the cat now assumed new roles
in religion, folklore, and folk customs that have continued until the present
day.

The earliest Italian cats: 800–500 BC

In modern literature concerning cats, one often reads that they were not
introduced into Italy until the beginning of the Imperial era, about 30 BC,
after the defeat of Ptolemaic Egypt by Octavian. Thereafter, Egypt became a
Roman province, and so at last the cats would have made their way to Italy.[1]
However, it is improbable that the Greek cats, well established there since at
least the eighth century BC, could be kept out of neighboring Italy for very
long. Indeed, as we have seen, there are strong indications that cats were
introduced into Italy at least by the eighth century BC. It is also possible that
the first cats arrived even earlier on Mycenaean Greek vessels (1600–1200
BC), since they had numerous trading posts along the western and southern
coasts of Italy, but this cannot be proven until more Italian osteological
material from that time is recorded and analyzed.

As was noted in Chapter 2, the earliest signs of the domestic cat in Italy come from an unlikely source, a marvelous series of coins from the Greek colonies of Rhegion (Rhegium, modern Reggio di Calabria) which was founded about 710 BC and Taras (Tarentum, Taranto), founded about the same time in southern Italy (Figs 2.6, 2.7). The coins from Rhegion, minted in the mid-fifth century, depict the founder of the city, Iokastos, with a cat under his chair or playing with a cat beside his chair. This shows that the Greek colonists very probably brought cats with them as well as the cultivation of vine and olive crops.[2] The coins from nearby Taras also depict the founder, Phalanthos, with a cat by his chair.

The first Greek colony in mainland Italy was Cyme (Cumae), founded in about 750 BC. Thereafter, numerous colonies were founded throughout the southern part of Italy. In addition to Rhegion and Taras, the most prominent of these were Neapolis (Napoli) founded in 735, Poseidonia (Paestum), Thurioi (Thurii), and Croton (Crotone). Furthermore, the Greeks also founded colonies in Sicily, the most famous being Syrakosai (Syracuse, Siracusa), founded in about 735 BC from Corinth. Indeed there were so many Greek colonies that the Romans called the entire region Magna Graecia, "Great Greece."

It is reasonable to assume that the transport of cats to Rhegion and Taras would not have been isolated incidents, but that the colonists brought many with them to their new homeland. Indeed, it would be quite impossible to keep ship's cats on board if they wanted to escape onto land. The first Italian cats would have occupied a specialized ecological niche unique to themselves: a small predator of rodents who would not eat the farmer's grain-based food and, if given the chance, would make a clean, civil companion, especially to women and children but also, as the coins show, to men as well. It is likely that their population increased upon their introduction into the peninsula.

Fortunately, thanks to recent archeological research, a clearer picture of their spread throughout the peninsula is emerging. The important recent work of Michael Mackinnon and others has shown that the earliest recorded osteological evidence for domesticated cats in Italy dates from the fifth to the third centuries BC (see Appendix 2).[3] These early individuals were found in Ostia and Selle in Campania. As will be seen below, Ostia was a major Italian center for the worship of Isis and her companion, the sacred cat goddess Bubastis (Bastet). Once again the archeological evidence can only show the presence of individuals and not their absence. Future research will give us a better understanding of the introduction and spread of the animal throughout the Italian peninsula.

The coins are depictions of the earliest known domestic cats in Italy. Although they date to the fifth century, they portray scenes from the late eighth. The earliest representation of a cat from an Italian context may be seen in the Etruscan Bucchero Ware raised bowl or compote, perhaps from Chiusi, dating from the sixth century BC and now in the Museum of Fine Arts in Boston (Fig. 3.1). The bowl stands on a base with a stem. Along the lip of the bowl are the heads of four cats. They have upright, triangular ears, distinctive cat's eyes and rounded faces.

That cats were well established in peninsular Italy by the fifth century BC can also be seen in the superb fresco from the Etruscan Tomb of the Triclinium at Tarquinia, dating to about 470 BC (Fig. 3.2). This scene portrays a symposium or dinner party in which the guests recline on couches. A large, obviously domesticated cat, with the *libyca*-type coat coloration and markings, strides deliberately to the right among the couches.[4] His interest is drawn to two domestic fowl under the right-hand couch.

Three Apulian and Campanian vases dating to the late-fifth to the mid-fourth century also depict the cat. These are in the Greek colonial artistic tradition of southern Italy. The earliest, a *kotyle* dating to about 400 BC, shows a nude youth standing towards the right and holding a small bird in his raised right hand. A cat clings to the youth's shoulder with his paw raised to strike the bird. The second cat scene is on the lower register of a *pelike* from Apulia (southern Italy) and dates to about 350 BC. Here a white goose and a cat confront each other.

The third vase is the famous Campanian *lekane* dating to about 330 BC (Fig. 3.3). It shows two women, one of whom is nude and sits at the right,

Figure 3.1   Etruscan Bucchero Ware bowl with cat's heads along the rim, from Chiusi, sixth century BC

Figure 3.2   *Miu*-type cat at an Etruscan banquet, fresco from the Tomb of the
Triclinium, Tarquinia, *c.* 470 BC

while another draped companion stands at the left. The seated woman has
just released a dove from her raised right hand, while a cat, standing on his
hind paws, watches the bird intently as if to leap at it. The seated woman
also has a ball on her lap and her companion has two balls in each of her
hands, doubtless more toys for the cat. The cat coat is once again of the
libyca type; the orange color of the painted figures on the vase probably
closely mimicked the true coat color of the cat.

The women may represent goddesses – the seated one is perhaps
Aphrodite and her companion Peitho. If so, this would be an important
connection between the cat and the goddess of love and fertility. The true
importance of the vase, however, is its portrayal of the important relationship between cats and women, a relationship that will transcend all
geographical barriers and even time itself.

Cats of the Roman Republic: 500–30 BC

There are few literary passages in Latin referring to the cat compared to the
large numbers in the corpus of Greek literature. Furthermore, there were
numerous Latin literary references to the dog as well. There were probably

91

Figure 3.3 Two women playing with a cat, Campanian *lekane, c.* 330 BC

several reasons for these differences. Firstly, the dog was always the most popular pet in the Roman world, especially among the elite men who were generally responsible for the literary tradition. Its characteristics of loyalty and faithfulness accorded well with Roman values of *pietas* and *fides*. The cat does not represent either of these virtues particularly well. Nevertheless, the lack of literary sources is more than compensated for by the large number of inscriptional references during the Imperial era discussed below.

Again, the values associated with the cat, freedom, independence, and autonomy, were not particularly suited to Roman tastes. The Romans had a strong sense of duty and obligation to others, expressed in their adherence to Stoic philosophical concepts. According to the Stoic ideals that many Romans shared, all humans, animals, and indeed all of nature is interlinked in a harmonious whole, governed by a divine providence. All people were thought to share the inheritance of divine reason from the creator. This reason (Logos) pervaded nature and operated through natural laws. Living in harmony with the laws of nature assured a happy and honorable life for the individual and the community. "Homo sum, nihil humani alienus a me puto," observed a famous Stoic saying. "I am a human being and I think nothing human is alien to me."

Doubtless the Romans found it difficult to appreciate the cat's more "Greek" values. To the Greeks, freedom (*eleutheria*), independence, and autonomy (*autonomia*) were the most important human concerns. Indeed, as far as is known, the Greeks invented the concept of freedom, and the word first appears in 479 BC in Pindar's *Isthmian Odes* 8.1.[5]

To the Romans, *libertas* did not mean complete freedom and autonomy in the Greek sense. For example, when the Greeks were given their *libertas* from Macedonian control by the Romans in 196 BC, they thought they were being given freedom and autonomy. Instead, according to Roman concepts, the Greeks had been given the great *beneficium* of *libertas*, and therefore ought to show the same duties and obligations towards the Romans that a client would show to his patron and benefactor.

Furthermore, where dogs were natural Stoics, cats tended to be Epicureans in many respects. According to this latter school of thought, which most Romans despised, the chance combination of atoms in a void explained everything in the universe. There was no divine providence or purpose to the cosmos. Ethics were thought to be determined by the autonomous decisions of individuals, not by reference to a greater spiritual power. Humans were autonomous, independent, and ought to live like atoms, as unconnected as possible to the city's institutions or religions. "Live obscurely" was a favorite Epicurean motto: they believed one ought not get involved with the chaos and turmoil of the city's politics or religion, nor compete for prestige or political ambition.

As one will observe, Epicurean values accord well with the cat, but obviously do not duplicate the animal's independent nature. Mother cats will fight to the death on behalf of their kittens and a group of tough tom cats can cooperate to annihilate a pack of large fearsome brown rats. Still, in the end, cats resemble Epicureans and dogs, Stoics.

Many tombstones were erected by bereaved Romans to their pet dogs, but none are known for cats. The Romans wrote poems and elaborate epitaphs in honor of their dogs. There was also a religious association with the dog and the afterlife that the cat could not share: the hope that the loyal and beloved pet would remain the owner's constant companion in the afterlife just as he had been in this life.[6] Who knew where the cats would be?

Roman greatness was expressed in many fields – military professionalism, law, government, architecture, public works, and public health, for instance. Scientific investigation, however, was not among their greatest achievements, as the Romans well knew. Works on science and natural history were mainly written by Greeks. It is only the naturalist Pliny the Elder who deigns to discuss the cat in scientific terms, based on the knowledge of his time. Finally, the animal was especially important to women in the Roman world, whose voices are not often heard in the elite literature produced by men.

Despite the bias in our literary sources, we learn from archeology and Latin inscriptions that the cat was an immensely popular animal among ordinary Roman subjects during the Imperial era, especially women. Like animal fables, inscriptions can often represent groups lower down the social scale than those who wrote the great works of poetry and prose. Although they wrote the inscriptions in Latin in the West and Greek in the East, the authors were seldom either Roman or Greek in ethnicity. The inscriptions come from all over the Empire, from small towns and villages, as well as larger cities.

The first literary source concerning the cat in Italy appears in the comic playwright Plautus (c. 251–184 BC), at the beginning of the Latin literary tradition. In two of his plays, the *Persa* and *Rudens*, we encounter the unfortunate terms *feles virginaria* and *feles virginalis*.[7] These phrases may seem innocent enough, literally "the cat of the virgin," but in fact, the context makes clear that they refer to despoilers of virgins. The terms have been translated as "virgin mousers;" perhaps "virgin predators" would be more apt.

In both passages, unsuspecting young girls have been taken advantage of by young men. In the *Persa*, a girl has been kidnapped while her father was away, and sold to a pimp. When the father returns and finds out what has been done, he calls the seller of his daughter a *feles virginaria*, and hauls him before the magistrate. In the *Rudens*, a girl has been shipwrecked and used as a slave by a pimp. He is finally caught and called a *feles virginalis*. The meaning of the terms is clear from the contexts of the plays: they pounce on innocent, unsuspecting, and often helpless young women, the same way that cats catch mice.

Another sexual sense of a related term occurs in the fourth-century AD Gallic author and poet, Ausonius: *"feles pullaria,"* a seducer or predator of young females.[8] The man in question, Marcus, is described as a *pullaria* or kidnapper, and Ausonius believes that if the concept of reincarnation is true, he should be born again as a dung beetle.

The great statesman Cicero (106–43 BC), also spoke of the cat in a few passages in the context of Egyptian religious attitudes to the animal.[9] In a significant passage in *Tusculan Disputations*, written about 45 BC, Cicero extends his remarks to the behavior of animals in general and the role of pain and suffering in life.[10] He notes that the Egyptians would submit to any punishment before they harmed an asp, a cat, a dog, or a crocodile. In this we recognize the Egyptians' views of their sacred animals, especially the ibis and the cat. But Cicero's main point was that the Egyptians were quite willing to suffer pain and even death on behalf of a principle, however misguided in Cicero's eyes.

He then went on to state that for the animals,

> Do they not go through cold, through hunger, ranging the mountains and traversing the forests in their wanderings? Do they not fight for their young so fiercely that they sustain wounds, and shrink from no assaults, no blows?

Cicero then states that humans, when acting in accordance with the great principles of nature, ought to be willing to risk no less. Indeed, he noted that this was in full accordance with the Stoic beliefs that he shared. So in the end, even the cats are Stoics. To his everlasting credit, he gave his own life in defense of his beloved Republic.

From the Roman scholar and agronomist, Marcus Terentius Varro (c. 116–27 BC), comes the sage advice to construct chicken houses and rabbit houses, so that cats will not be able to enter them. The same sentiment is voiced by Columella in the first century AD. It is probably the European wildcats, *sylvestris*, that are the culprits here, because no farmer would put up with a domesticated cat who went after the chickens for very long.[11]

As was seen in the last chapter, by the end of the Roman Republic, cats were already widespread throughout western Europe. During the Empire, the evidence for the cat and its role in human affairs becomes much more plentiful.

Cats of the Imperial era: 30 BC – AD 500

To the cats, as well as to the humans of the era, the Roman Empire represented something of a golden age of peace, prosperity, and civil society. There was a general lack of religious fanaticism:

> The various modes of worship, which prevailed in the Roman world, were all considered by the people, as equally true; by the philosopher, as equally false; and by the magistrate as equally useful. And thus toleration produced not only mutual indulgence, but even religious concord.[12]

The archeological evidence shows that the earlier colonies of cats that had occupied western Europe since the third century BC were now spread through peaceful commerce to all corners of the continent. As we shall see at the end of this chapter, it is probable that the domesticated cat spread as far as China during this era via the trade established by the Romans with that region.

The Roman Empire was far from a cultural unity. It was, in fact, a "multicultural" society in the best sense of that abused term. The Romans did not care about the culture of their subjects nor did they make any coercive attempts to change it. As far as the Romans were concerned, their subjects could speak any language, worship any gods, wear any clothes, dance to any music they chose with no interference from the central government.

Indeed, the central authority during the early Empire was relatively weak. There were only some 170 imperial officials for an Empire of some 70 million people. Most important local administrative decisions were made by the hundreds of city states throughout the Empire. They elected their magistrates, made their laws, policed their streets, and supervised public and private buildings in their cities, with little or no interference from the capital. Many even coined their own money as a symbol of political autonomy. The armies were generally stationed on the frontiers, far removed from most civilian populations. Most Roman subjects passed their entire lives without ever seeing a Roman imperial official or soldier.

There were only three rules the Roman government insisted upon for their subjects. The first was to be civilized. The inhabitants of the Empire went unarmed in their city's streets, the cardinal principle of a civil society. This was because criminals who committed capital crimes such as murder, rape, theft, and arson were severely punished. Living in a civil society also meant not belonging to a religious group that practiced human sacrifice or cannibalism, such as the Druids of Gaul or Britain. Such religions were suppressed. It was unfortunate that false charges of human sacrifice and cannibalism were leveled against the Christians, both by the pagans and by some Christian groups against each other.[13]

The second rule was to pay taxes, which averaged a modest 10 per cent of the crop. Thirdly, Roman subjects were discouraged from revolting against Roman rule. Within these rather broad parameters many millions throughout Europe, North Africa, and the Near East lived in relative peace and harmony with each other for about 250 years, the only period of time in history where this was the case.

There was a great deal of cultural sharing during the *Pax Romana*, especially in religion. For example, we find Egyptian gods worshipped in Britain as well as those from Persia. Attitudes towards cats probably also varied considerably from region to region, and indeed, from individual to individual. For some, the cats not only demanded but received religious adoration from their owners. To others they were probably a nuisance, especially their caterwauling at night and occasional piddles on the rug. But to most subjects of the Empire, as shown by inscriptions and archeology, they were useful animals, treated with some consideration because of their predatory capability, and were especially popular with women. There was probably little uniformity in attitudes or beliefs.

There are many works of art that portray the cat during the Roman Empire. Those without obvious religious associations will be discussed here. Perhaps the most famous is the mosaic from Pompeii, now preserved in the Naples Museum, that must date from before AD 79 when the city was destroyed by Vesuvius (Fig. 3.4). Here we find the portrayal of a cat hunting birds in the marshes, a theme we first encountered in Egypt during the second millennium BC. In the top register the cat stands towards the right with his paw planted on a bird. In the lower zone we find two ducks, four smaller birds, several fish and shells in the marsh. The cat, with his paw on one bird, looks at the other birds and fish in the marsh with wide-open, greedy eyes. The dark blue background of the mosaic indicates that this is a nocturnal hunt. The coat of the cat is of the Egyptian *libyca* type, showing that even at this late date the type remained common. There are other mosaics with the same theme from the vicinity of Rome, but they are not as well composed. The subject was clearly popular with the Romans.

Figure 3.4   Cat hunting ducks, Pompeian mosaic, before AD 79

Another mosaic from Pompeii depicts a large two-handled bowl on a pedestal (Fig. 3.5). On the rim are two parrots and a dove. Beside the pedestal lurks a cat, again with *libyca*-type coat. He has one paw raised, probably to climb the pedestal.

A fine marble relief of Hadrianic date, now in the Museo Capitolino (Fig. 3.6), depicts a cat being taught to dance! On the left a girl is seated facing right and playing her lyre. In the center a cat stands on its hind legs, its head and forepaws raised towards a brace of ducks that is hung above it from a tree branch. One wonders if this attempt was successful!

Figure 3.5 Cat watching birds in a bird bath, Pompeian mosaic, before AD 79

Figure 3.6　Cat being taught to dance, Italian frieze of Hadrianic date (*c.* AD
117–38)

Another performing cat can be seen in the discus of a lamp from the
Imperial period in the British Museum. Here the trainer squats down with a
monkey on the left. On the right is a cat ascending a ladder. Above the
ladder are two hoops, perhaps for the cat to jump through.

A second-century Latin tombstone from Rome is of especial significance.
It was erected by Calpurnia Felicla "Little Cat," or "Kitten," for her husband
Germullus and for herself (Fig. 3.7). Below the inscription a small cat stands
towards the right, clearly an allusion to the woman's name.[14] As we shall see
below, the names Felicla and Felicula, "Kitten," were among the most
common cognomens for women in the western Empire.

Portrayals of the cat come from the provinces, too, especially Gaul and
North Africa. From Auxerre (southern France) there is a fragmentary sculpture of a cat wearing a heavy collar. There are some five funeral stelae from
Roman Gaul with cats. Three of these show a young girl seated in a niche
holding a cat in her arms while another shows a standing boy holding a cat
in the crook of his left elbow. The most famous is from Bordeaux and depicts
a young girl. It dates to the second century AD (Fig. 3.8). She stands facing
the viewer and holds her pet cat in front of her chest. The cat also faces the
viewer while his tail dangles down. A rooster pecks at the cat's tail.

One may see religious symbolism in the stele, but such sentiments were
seldom made in such memorials. Like the great funeral stele from Athens of

Figure 3.7   Tombstone of Calpurnia Felicla ("Kitten") and her husband, with bas relief of a kitten or small cat. Rome, early Empire

the fifth century BC, this simply portrays the loss of the girl while her cherished cat and favorite rooster remain behind.[15] It has been said that rituals of death are more for the living than for the dead, and this is certainly true of these humble memorials. Upon visiting the departed during festivals of the dead and at other occasions, the family would be reminded of their loved ones with their favorite pets, just as they were seen together in life.

From Arausio (Orange, southern France) there was another mosaic, now lost, that depicted a black cat crouching to the right with his head turned towards the viewer, a dead mouse in his mouth.[16] The mosaic, dated to the early Empire on stylistic grounds, is the earliest depiction of the black cat. The image may have had an apotropaic significance, helping to ward off rodents as well as evil and misfortune from the household. If so, this would be the earliest known use of the black cat as a symbol of "good luck."

In Roman Alesia (east–central France), there is the enigmatic figure of a boy sculpted in high relief who holds a cat in his upraised tunic (Fig. 3.9). The cat faces forward and wears a collar with a bell. This relief, dating to the second or third century, is part of the pedestal of an offertory table in the

Figure 3.8 Tombstone of Laetus's duaghter with her pet rooster and cat. Found in Bordeaux, *c.* AD 75–125

cellar of a private dwelling that was used for domestic cults. The religious significance of the sculpture will be discussed below.

A mosaic from Volubilis, Morocco, depicts a cat named Vincentius ("Conqueror") who wears a red collar and a bell. He is pouncing on a mouse or rat named Luxurius. On an ornament (*corniola*) from Cherchel, Morocco, we find an inscription, "catta" and "felix," with a figure of a cat between the

Figure 3.9   Base of offertory table showing a boy with a cat in his raised tunic. From Roman Alesia

words.[17] The word *felix* means lucky or happy; it may indeed be the name of the cat, or it may simply denote that the cat is lucky or fortunate, an attribute that can be traced back to ancient Egypt.

Finally, from Wales comes a bowl found on the slope of Mt Snowdon, dating to the first century AD. On the handle of the bowl is a wonderful cat's head portrayed in the Celtic curvilinear style. The bowl is now in the National Museum of Wales.

One of the most surprising aspects of the cat in the Roman Empire is the large number of individuals that have cognomens or nicknames derived from the animal, such as Felicula, Felicla, Catta, or Cattula, and numerous variants. This information is found on inscriptions throughout the Empire. However, some names such as Catus, used as a cognomen (the third name of the traditional Roman three names), meant sharp-witted and had nothing to do with a cat. Similarly, the cognomen Catulus actually meant "puppy" or any young animal. The common nomen or family name, Cattius also probably had little or nothing to do with the animal in most cases.

Most male Romans had three names. The first name is the praenomen, given by the family at birth; the second name is the nomen or family name; and the third name is the cognomen. The cognomen may denote a particular branch of a family, or it may be a "nickname" given to the individual by the family. So in the name, Gaius Julius Caesar, Gaius is the praenomen, Julius is the family (or *gens*) name, and Caesar denotes the branch of the family. In Roman inscriptions, the three names are often but not always given. Some individuals only had one or two names. In Latin an -ius or -us ending is masculine and an -ia or -a ending is feminine.

Most women in the Roman tradition had two names. They took their first name from the nomen or family name of their fathers, and kept it after marriage. Many of these nomens have subsequently become common women's names used in many societies for centuries; for example Julia, Aemelia (Emily), Caelia, Caecilia (Cicely), Cornelia, and Lucia. Sometimes, women would take both the nomen and the cognomen of their father, such as Sergia Paullina. In most cases women would have a cognomen given by the family, such as Julia Felicia ("Fortunate"), or Julia Felicla ("Little Cat").

There are hundreds of inscriptions throughout the Latin-speaking western Empire in which the cognomen or nickname for women is either Felicula or Felicla, "Little Cat" or "Kitten."[18] In fact, these cognomens are among the most common for women during the Imperial era. For the city of Rome alone, there are over 250 of these cognomens from surviving inscriptions.[19] The names are also common in North Africa, Spain, Gaul, Germania (western Germany and parts of eastern France), Italy, and even Britain. The only province in which the names do not occur, based on present evidence, is Noricum (western Austria), but here the later, related name with the same meaning, Cattula, is used. It seems that Noricum only became Romanized, with a sufficient number of Latin-speaking people, relatively late in Imperial history, when the use of the later word for cat, *cattus*, had replaced the earlier word, *felis*. These cognomens were also used for men, especially Feliculus, but the proportion seems to be about 50 to 1 in favor of females.

The inscriptions with the names are usually tombstones, erected by a close family member, often a spouse, but frequently a son or daughter, or a father or mother. Other inscriptions are dedicatory in nature. Sometimes an individual has made a dedication in honor of a divinity to fulfill a vow, and the inscription has survived. It is unfortunate that the tombstones and dedicatory inscriptions cannot be dated with much accuracy based on their appearance in the corpus of inscriptions. But from internal evidence and the fact that the writing of inscriptions seems to have died out during the mid-third century, we may date most of them to the first two centuries AD.[20]

It is also difficult to assess the social origins of the commemorators. Some were perhaps wealthy, but most of the tombstones and dedications were small and simple indicating individuals of no great means, probably of middle-class status.

Inscriptions containing the cognomens Cattus and Catta "The Cat", are also common from the western Empire. This word for the animal will eventually replace the earlier term *felis*. For example, from Pannonia (eastern Austria and western Hungary) we find Aelia Catta and Sempronia Catta; from Dalmatia (Croatia), Ulpia Catta. From Milan, Italy, we find Sextillia Catta. For men, we find the word Cattus probably used as a cognomen in Belgica (Belgium), by Quintus Cattus Libo Nepos, a centurion. From Pannonia (Croatia) there is Priscus Cattus, a cavalryman from a Pannonian squadron.[21]

The cognomens Cattulus and Cattula, "Little Cat," (not to be confused with Catulus, "Little Pet" or "Puppy") are common in Roman North Africa, as we might expect from the origins of the animal. But this nickname, like Felicula, is found in every province of the Latin-speaking western Empire. The numbers of inscriptions with these cognomens are fewer than those with Feliculus and Felicula, probably because Cattulus was a name introduced relatively late when fewer inscriptions were being made.

From Roman Vienne (southeastern France), we also find that Catia Bubate (probably her nomen and cognomen) set up a tombstone to her daughter Titia Catia.[22] The cognomen Bubate associated with Catia is surely a variant of the name of the cat goddess Bubastis (Bastet). This indicates that the name Catia could be associated with a cognomen relating to the cat.

We also find the name Cattius or Cattia used for both nomens and cognomens. From the example of Catia Bubate, we may infer that, at least in some instances, this nomen may also be associated with the later Latin name for the cat. The close resemblance of the words cattus and Cattius may have suggested a relationship between the animal and the name amongst some who bore it. Furthermore, the nicknames or cognomens given to some with the nomen Cattius often refer to the common attributes of the animal, such as good fortune. Although many of these nicknames are widespread, in some cases this does not seem to be a coincidence, considering the ancient associations with these attributes.

Many individuals with nomens or family names related to Cattius have cognomens that are associated with good fortune, such as *Felix* or *Fortunata*. From Rome we find S. Cattius Felix, a policeman (*vigilis*), Cattia Fortunata, and a dedication made by Quintius Cattius Felix to Cattia Faustina ("Auspicious"). From Misenum comes Cattius Sossius Felix and from Apulia (the region near Rhegium), Cattia Fortunata.[23] In an inscription from ancient Bovianus, Italy, we find a list of names apparently from the same family, Cattius: Publius Cattius Optatus ("the Best"), (...) Cattius Ferox ("the Ferocious"), Gaius Cattius Celer ("the Swift"), and Marcus Cattius Dexter ("the Propitious", or "the Favorable"). From Noricum (Croatia) we find the lovely name Cattia Serena.[24]

Some soldiers also had the name Cattius as a nomen or cognomen. From Rome we find the soldier (*miles*) Gaius Cattius Aniensus Lucilianus and from Etruria (Tuscany), we find the cognomen for the Praetorian Guardsman Gaius Julius Cattius Hasta.[25] Another soldier, the centurion C. Julius Aelurio helped to set up an honorific inscription in the early third century in Roman Numidia.[26] His cognomen refers to the Greek name for the animal Latinized to Aelurio.

The most significant inscriptional reference to the cat also comes from a military context. This is from the Praetorian Camp in Rome dating to AD 144. On the inscription, honorably discharged veterans from the Praetorian Guard are listed by cohort and century. We learn that the sixth century of the third cohort of the guards was named Catti, or "The Cats."[27] As interesting as this is for the use of the animal as a symbol in military contexts, far more important is the fact that this is the earliest datable use of the word *cattus* for cat.

The earliest examples of the name *cattus* used for cat from our literary sources do not occur until the time of Palladius in the fifth century. This has led many to believe that the name was not used before that time. However, as we have seen, there are numerous examples of the word *cattus* from the early Empire, many coming from North Africa.

Indeed, it is probable that some of our inscriptions from North Africa with the word *cattus* antedate this inscription. Some such tombstones contained the abbreviation H. S. E. "hic situs est," or "he lies here." About AD 100, this abbreviation was replaced by D. M. "Dis Manibus," "to the spirits below." So some of our tombstones could antedate the inscription from Rome but this cannot be proven.[28]

The ancient, north African Berber word for the cat was *kaddiska*, probably related to the Nubian word for the animal, *qadis*.[29] This word was likely transmitted to the Latin-speaking immigrants in North Africa, especially during the early Imperial era. The word was transcribed into Latin as *cattus*, two "t"s probably used to differentiate it from the Latin word *catus*, meaning sharp-witted. It seems that the Berber language has in general not accepted any loan words from other languages, not even from Arabic, but has retained its original Hamitic vocabulary.[30] Thus it is unlikely that the word originated in the Latin-speaking world and spread to North Africa.

From North Africa, the word probably spread to Rome and western Europe, and finally to the eastern Empire. Thus the words *cattus* and *catta* probably spread to the East, where they became *kattos* and *katta* in the Greek language. The earliest reference to the Greek word *kattos* is from the fifth-century church historian Evagrius.[31] This would be one of the few loan words from the Latin West that was transmitted to the Greek East.[32]

From the western Empire the word spread further to the German tribes along the Danube and Rhine frontiers. Hence the near universality of the word "cat" and its variants was probably related to the universality of the Roman Empire and its role in cultural transmission.

Thanks to the inscriptions, we learn a great deal about the popularity and spread of the animal throughout the Empire. They fill in the gaps of our rather meager literary tradition and show that the animal was popular, especially among women. The use of the word in military contexts will be discussed below. The inscriptional evidence concerning the cat goddess Bubastis and the related goddess Isis will also be discussed below.

The archeology from the western provinces of the Empire also shows that the cat was ubiquitous throughout the region by the fourth century AD. As is discussed in Appendix 2, the survival of cat remains depends to a large extent on chance finding and preservation, the vicissitudes of the body after death, soil and climatic conditions, the date at which a site was excavated (those excavated before the 1960s seldom recorded animal bones), the resources of the archeological expeditions and their skill at identifying and recording the bones. The absence of cat bones does not prove the absence of the cat from that site. Furthermore, a single bone from a site does not mean that only one cat was present, only that one bone was found. One seldom finds just one cat in a community; where there is one, there are bound to be others. Thanks to their high fertility rates, where there are a few, there will soon be a lot more. Roman cats are found in three different archeological contexts: forts and other military installations, towns and other civil settlements, and villas and native farmsteads.

One remarkable aspect of the archeological survival of cat remains is the large number that come from military sites. They are found along the Rhine and Danube frontiers, as well as from the military fort of Pevensey in Sussex, England on the south coast. It seems that the Roman army was well aware of the value of the animal in protecting its military and food stores from rodents. Since Pevensey was a fourth-century naval fortress that protected the country from Angle and Saxon sea-raiders, perhaps the cat found there was a naval ship's cat, one in a long line of dedicated service.

It is worth considering here the relationship between cats and the Roman army. We have already noted several military inscriptions referring to the animal. Another comes from Arabia Nabatea (Jordan). It reads, "Leg[io] III Cyr[enaica] Feliciter Invicta." A crude but distinctive cat stands to the left with upraised tail, rounded face, and triangular ears.[33] The Third Legion Cyrenaica was stationed in Arabia Nabatea from about AD 123, giving a terminus post quem for the inscription. *Invicta* means undefeated; the adverb *feliciter* is related to the word *felix* and has many meanings in Latin – those with a military connotation include "auspiciously", "luckily", and "successfully", terms associated with the cat for millennia.

There are several reasons for the relationship of cats with the military. First and most obvious was the protection the animal provided for military stores. These would include not only food but, as we have seen, leather straps, other leather materials, and bow strings. Cats are predators and the symbolism of the cat destroying rodents just as the soldiers crush their enemies was probably compelling. Moreover, as we have seen, cats were regarded as lucky, another characteristic that would recommend the animal to the Roman legions. It has been suggested that the possible use of emblems of the cat on military regalia were as apotropaic words and devices, warding off evil from the soldiers.[34] The Third Cyrenaica was stationed in Egypt before its redeployment in Arabia which would only reinforce these notions.

Cat remains found in towns and civil settlements tend to be clustered in Austria, Switzerland, Germany, Belgium, and the Netherlands, most likely because soil and climatic conditions are favorable to their preservation. Furthermore, the excellent archeological services of those nations strive to preserve animal remains. The important center of Marseilles is also represented, one of the prime locations for the distribution of the cat in the pre-Roman era.

For Italy, we have already discussed the early remains found at Ostia and Campagna. From the house gardens of Pompeii we find the remains of domesticated house cats that were buried there before the eruption of AD 79. Cats of the Roman era are found throughout the peninsula.

As was discussed in Chapter 2, the location of some of the earliest domesticated cat remains in western Europe outside Italy come from Gussage All Saints in Dorset, England, accurately dated to about 250 BC.[35] More cat remains were found from the same site during the early Roman period, 60 BC – AD 130. The same site is also the location of the earliest remains of the house mouse (*Mus musculus*) in Britain, also dating to about 250 BC. Not surprisingly, cat remains have been found from the earliest levels of Roman London, from AD 50 to 125.[36] Numerous remains have been found from Roman villas as well, Lullingstone in Kent for example.[37]

Naturally, there are quantities of osteological material from the Roman East as well, Egypt, Greece, and elsewhere. One such individual, from the

Roman Red Sea port of Quseir el-Quadim, will be discussed fully at the end of this chapter.

The cat and the rat: religion and public health

The introduction of the black rat into the Mediterranean as an endemic species occurred in the first century AD. The rat was not a natural migrant, but was probably brought in from south and southeast Asia through the trade that the Romans maintained in those regions. This animal represented the greatest natural opponent of the cat, when it fought in packs, as well as a new opportunity as a prey animal. Furthermore, the black rat has probably been responsible for more human deaths than any other single cause. In the Introduction, the role of the animal in spreading disease and destroying food supplies has already been discussed. The worst disease it carried was the bubonic plague.

The role of the cat in controlling rat populations during the classical era has not always been appreciated.[38] Some of the most important aspects of both Greek and Roman public health policies were those that suppressed rats and mice. One of the consequences of these policies was the absence of the bubonic plague. For a millennium, the classical world was virtually immune from this disease, even though all the factors for its spread were present. Needless to say, the cat played an important role in this respect, but it has not been given the credit it deserves. This section will help address this neglect.

The role of religion in public health

Religious beliefs played an important role in the formation of public health policies. Many of these policies helped to suppress rodent populations as did the cat itself. Naturally, Greek and Roman policies of 2,000 years ago were not as advanced as those of today, at least in modern, industrialized societies, but such trite comparisons do little to advance our knowledge of antiquity. However, Greco-Roman policies do compare favorably to those in most other pre- and non-industrial societies.

Classical public health policies were ultimately based on Greek and Roman social and religious beliefs. The study of the relationship between religious values and social, economic, and political institutions is something of a taboo subject among US academics at present.[39] This is unfortunate, since most characteristics of classical civilization, as for many others, cannot be adequately explained in simple materialistic terms. If religion were merely "the opiate of the people," there would be no reason to study its influences on society, but this view is false. "Consciousness precedes Being," noted Vaclav Havel, "and not the other way around, as the Marxists claim."[40] The late twentieth century shows the limitations of ignoring the effect of religion on society; the influence was even stronger in the past. As in other ancient traditions, the Greek and Roman gods were gods of nature: for example, Zeus was not only the god of the sky, he was the sky, and Poseidon was not only the god of the sea, he was the sea. Reason and wisdom were also regarded as part of the natural world and were embodied by the goddess Athena. Since the time of Homer, cooperation with the gods meant cooperating with nature, and living in harmony with them was one of the highest of human virtues.

In the *Iliad* (ll. 207–18), for example, Athena comes down to stop the anger of Achilles towards Agamemnon, and asks him, "I have come from the heavens to restrain your anger – if you will comply." Achilles responds, "Goddess, it is necessary that I honor the word of you two, angry though I am in heart. So it will be better. If a man obeys the gods, they listen to him also." Although Achilles has the free will to disobey, obedience will be rewarded by divine favor, and since he is no fool, Achilles does as Athena asks. The Greeks and Romans saw no contradiction between philosophy or reason, and nature.

Greeks and Romans believed that nature was holy and divine and many believed that the gods of nature worked through natural laws. Since the time of Pythagoras, it was thought that a knowledge of natural laws led to a knowledge of the divine.[41] This principle was also maintained by both the Stoics and Epicureans, although they disagreed about the role of the gods in nature. The same principle motivated many scientists during the Scientific Revolution, including Isaac Newton.

The Pythagoreans were also the first to call the universe a cosmos, because of the orderliness they saw in nature. The cosmic order was based on the principles of justice and harmony among disparate elements.[42] Heracleitus added that the laws of justice and harmony upon which the cosmos is based are the product of a universal divine reason or logos.[43] Living in harmony with natural laws assisted by reason was a fundamental religious belief; it was also the operating principle of classical cities, regardless of whether they had democratic or aristocratic governments.

The Greco-Roman medical tradition was firmly based on concepts of God, humanity, and nature. It rejected divine causation and the fatalism associated with that concept. Individuals had free will and were primarily responsible for their own health. Diseases were usually attributed to ignorance or negligence, and they developed in accordance with natural laws. They were not a consequence of the wrath of the gods, and were therefore often the result of human free will. Disease could be prevented by the individual through living in harmony with nature: following proper regimen, observing the principles of personal hygiene, and by living a balanced and moderate life. The community as a whole was also responsible for the collective health of society and provided facilities that were beyond the resources of individuals.

Fundamental truths were discovered by the Greeks in many fields of medicine and science. Francis Bacon could state in 1620 that "the school of Democritus [also Epicurus and Lucretius] went further into nature than the rest," including those of his own time.[44] The achievements in pharmacology, hygiene, public health, anatomy, physiology, and surgery, itself a Greek word coming from *cheirourgia,* were especially notable. Hemostasis, the tying off of blood vessels during surgery, antiseptics, some thirty times more powerful than the first modern antiseptic, phenol, developed by Lister in the 1870s, and anesthetics, based on opium and atropine compounds, were all known and used in operations, some of them major, by the Greeks and Romans. Hemostasis was not reinvented until about 1550 by Ambrose Paré and effective antiseptics were not redeveloped until the 1870s by Lister.[45]

Urban public health policies and facilities were numerous: paved streets; covered drains; public baths; public gymnasia; public physicians; latrines; sewage disposal; subsidized food; and clean water supplies often brought in from great distances. Harsh legal penalties were imposed for failing to clean the streets in front of residences, for polluting public water supplies, for constructing open drains, and even for failing to clean private cisterns.[46]

Greeks and Romans believed the laws of the gods were the laws of nature. Herbal remedies, many of them effective, were called "hands of the gods." Since natural laws showed that rats and mice carry dangerous diseases, they did not make pets of them and massacre the cats. They favored the cats, who were sacred to Isis or Diana, and let them keep the rodent population under control. All water was in some sense "holy water," whether from rivers, springs, or the ocean, and bathing was a holy and a purifying act. Greek and Roman cities went to great lengths to avoid contaminating the water supply before it was made available for human use. Their methods compare favorably to those of industrialized cities through the 1840s and non-industrialized cities today. Originally, these provisions were of religious inspiration. Finally, it was held that the city ought to be located in a healthy environment, not near a swamp, and to provide basic public health policies and facilities for its people.[47]

The bubonic plague

The virtual absence of the bubonic plague among Greek and Roman populations, even though all the vectors for its spread were present, is of considerable interest. Of the numerous rodent-borne diseases that have afflicted the human race because of poor public health and personal hygiene, perhaps the most disastrous has been the bubonic plague. This disease is caused by the bacterium *Yersinia pestis* (formerly called *Pasturella pestis* until 1970) which in turn infects the *Xenopsylla cheopis* flea. The favorite home of the flea is the black rat or house rat, *Rattus rattus*, although the flea is perfectly happy to live on filthy humans and their squalid clothing, especially furs.

The bacterium and infected rodent hosts are still endemic to Central and South Asia, as well as the Mediterranean. The plague is normally spread when infected fleas bite the rats and spread the disease to them. When large numbers of rats and fleas live in close proximity to unwashed humans, the plague can spread rapidly, especially in urban areas.[48] Other rodents and other fleas including the human flea (*Pulex irritans*) can also spread the plague, but the black rat and *X. cheopis* are the major culprits.

The main vector in the transmission of the disease is the black rat, endemic to Europe since at least the first century AD and still widespread throughout the Mediterranean.[49] Unlike its larger cousin, the brown rat (*Rattus norvegicus*, which normally does not carry the plague), the black rat is not a natural migrant, but must be carried from place to place by man, usually in trade goods transported by land or sea. It is the transportation of infected rats and their flea passengers that causes the plague to spread. As we have seen, rats and mice carry about thirty-five dangerous diseases, including the plague and typhus. Throughout most eras of Western history, they were regarded as a threat to humanity, and every effort was made to eliminate them.

The original home of the black rat was southern India and Southeast Asia. The first certain evidence for the rat in the Near East comes from Iraq in about 1500 BC. From there, it spread to Egypt and the Levant. By the first century AD, the rat was well established throughout all of Europe including England. The close commercial relationships between the Hellenistic and Roman worlds with China and India, over both land and sea,[50] ensured the infusion of new blood into the Mediterranean and European populations which kept them viable.

The first probable reference to the plague in the West occurs in I Samuel: 5–6, concerning an epidemic at Ashdod about 1080 BC.[51] It is generally believed that the expansion of trade with the East that occurred after Alexander's conquests reintroduced the disease into the Mediterranean region. The only definite reference to the plague in classical antiquity, however, occurs in a passage of Rufus of Ephesus. At the time he wrote, about AD 50, he knew of only two outbreaks, one in the Near East in about 300 BC and another that occurred in Libya about AD 50.[52] Apart from these two episodes, there is no evidence for an epidemic, let alone a pandemic (or continent-wide epidemic) of the plague in the Hellenistic or Roman eras.

Three factors in particular are responsible for the spread of the black rat: the provision of a safe, comfortable home; making nourishing, wholesome food available to him in abundant quantities; and the elimination of his natural predators, especially cats.[53] Fortunately, the Greeks and Romans denied the rat all three of these basic necessities.

The non-occurrence of an epidemic or pandemic of the bubonic plague during the classical, Hellenistic, and Roman eras is of great importance. All the factors necessary for the introduction and spread of the disease were present in the classical world, especially the Roman Empire, but no epidemic occurred. The rat, the flea, the bacillum, large cities linked together through commerce and administration were all present, as were close commercial relations with South Asia. This made it just as likely that an epidemic would have occurred in the Roman Empire as in other times when all the same factors were present. Although the classical world was helpless in the face of other epidemics of communicable infectious diseases such as smallpox, so was the rest of the world before the nineteenth and twentieth centuries.[54]

The first line of defense against rodent-borne fleas was personal hygiene. "It was the great contribution of the Greeks that they created a system of personal hygiene which set an example for all time," noted Henry Sigerist, perhaps the greatest historian of medicine in our century.[55] Indeed, as Sigerist notes, the level of hygiene in a society has often been linked to its collective intelligence, both in the past and at present. Both the Greeks and the Romans tried to bathe daily. If no facilities were available in the home, most cities and towns provided public ones. Frequent bathing in clean water and the wearing of clean linen and wool clothing will deter the growth of fleas.

Another policy that would reduce the numbers of rats in cities was paving the streets, a practice that epidemiologists believe is the most important factor in the reduction of disease in developing countries. Furthermore, in urban areas, public buildings, houses and storage facilities were usually built of stone, brick, or concrete, with tile roofs, which would prevent the intrusion of rodents and other pests.[56]

The disposal of human and animal wastes from the cities was also important, since mice and rats will eat the wastes. Many Greek and Roman cities had magistrates that oversaw the collection of solid wastes from individual homes and their transport to the countryside.[57] There the wastes were deposited in dung heaps which would compost the material and remove harmful bacteria. Finally it would be spread on local fields as manure. The cesspits were not connected to the city sewer systems. This would not only lessen the amount of sewage entering nearby rivers but also prevent sewer rats from entering private homes. Their contents would not leach into the rainwater cisterns since these were required to be waterproof and cleaned regularly. Furthermore, the cisterns were usually placed at a higher level than the pits.[58] The harshest penalties were levied against anyone dumping waste of any kind into the street or public water supply.[59]

The large city of Rome had exceptional waste removal problems. In addition to the above procedures, some solid and liquid waste flowed from the public latrines through the sewer system and into the Tiber. Nevertheless, the Romans never drank from the river, unlike many of the inhabitants of the world today who still obtain their drinking water from polluted sources.

If drinking water contaminated with sewage causes diseases such as cholera, typhoid, intestinal parasites, and dysentery, then drinking water uncontaminated with sewage will not cause these diseases.[60] If the aqueducts of late nineteenth-century London reduced the levels of cholera and other diseases for that city, then the aqueducts of Rome probably had the same effect. It is reasonable to assume that many of the same public health measures which reduced mortality in nineteenth-century Europe and America would have had the same consequence for the Roman population.

In Roman cities the garbage was cleaned up from the streets by the perpetrators. If they could not be found, the owners of the property facing the street had to clean the mess, or as a last resort it would be cleared up by the city, that would then charge the property owner for the service. It was the responsibility of each urban resident to keep the street in front of his home clean. Excrement was disposed of properly wherever possible. These policies deprived rodents of a basic source of food.

Housing and storage facilities built of stone, brick, and concrete with tile roofs discouraged the rat. As the eminent bacteriologist Shrewsbury notes:

> The brick-built house with its slated or tiled roof was also inimical to it, and the national [English] development of this type of dwelling was probably the most important single factor in the eventual disappearance of the house-rat from the bulk of England.[61]

Indeed, Greek and Roman urban housing was built largely of brick, stone, and in Italy, even brick-faced concrete. This was especially true of the Mediterranean region. Further north, wood and half-timber construction was used, but this older-style construction was gradually replaced during the Empire by brick and concrete. Even Roman London had some concrete streets.[62] The roofs were generally tiled. Urban streets were often paved, thus denying entrance to the black rat through burrowing into dwellings from the ground or street. Storage facilities for grain both in the cities and in the countryside were usually constructed of solid masonry or concrete.[63]

It has not been generally appreciated that Roman cities with their paved streets, sewers, brick and concrete dwellings and storage buildings were largely rodent-proof. They must have presented formidable, if not insurmountable, obstacles to the health and well-being of mice and rats. Rodent-proof dwellings were common among the elite, but also for the masses, especially in large cities, who often lived in brick-faced concrete apartments, especially during the Empire.

Compared to later eras, the Roman Empire was something of a golden age for urban public health: their public health policies and personal hygiene compare favorably with most of the rest of the world until relatively recent times. Indeed, when public water supplies are taken into consideration, Roman cities were probably safer to live in from the perspective of public health than cities in western Europe and the United States through the 1870s. These medical practices and public health policies alleviated the suffering and prevented the deaths of millions during the centuries of the Hellenistic era and Roman Empire.

Furthermore, cats have played an important albeit unappreciated role in rodent predation. What the stone, brick, tile, and concrete failed to stop, the cats took care of, as they awaited their prey in silence and shadow. Indeed, it seems that the cats were especially useful in the cities. Here, the main competitor of the cat, the ferret, would be of little use, since that animal is a burrower and destroys rodents in their underground dens. This would often not be possible in the brick, concrete and stone cities of the Greeks and Romans. Ambush is a far more effective predatory strategy under these conditions. "The best hunters are those who wait," especially in the cities.

Finally, in village settings, cats would also be formidable adversaries of the black rat. In wattle and daub construction with thatched roofs, the black rat would frequently make its nest in the thatch. This is why the black rat is often called the roof rat or tree rat. The cat's excellent climbing ability would be put to good use under such circumstances. Here again the ferret's burrowing ability, while effective against mice, would be of little value.[64]

In later eras dogs have made excellent ratters, but as we have seen, our sources indicate that dogs were used for hunting large game, for herding sheep, and as household pets. They were apparently not trained to be mousers and ratters until the seventeenth century.[65]

There is abundant evidence that the Romans, like their Greek predecessors, understood the value of the cat, as well as of the ferret in destroying rodents. This understanding will also be seen in the animal fables from the early Christian tradition given below. The fourth-century agronomist Palladius also recommended cats for destroying moles that dug up fields and gardens.[66]

Cats, therefore, along with the hygiene and public health policies of Roman cities, must be given their due credit for the absence of the bubonic plague from the Roman Empire. Doubtless they also helped to check other rodent-borne diseases and protected food supplies as well.

The Romans tried too to limit mankind's other great natural enemy, the mosquito. They were well aware that mosquitoes caused dangerous diseases, perhaps including malaria, long before the cause was discovered by Ronald Ross and Patrick Manson at the turn of the century.[67] The draining of swamps, the covering of drains and cisterns, and the frequent cleaning of water facilities, indicate the knowledge that standing open water was a public health threat, and all helped to reduce the scourge of this insect.

These public health policies helped reduce water- and rat-borne diseases and prevented many deaths. As Andrew Jones notes, it was Rome's sanitary engineers, rather than its legions, that were the true secret to the Empire's success, "Without clean water, Roman colonists would have been wiped out by epidemics."[68]

The sacred cat in Europe

One of the characteristics of Roman paganism was a broad toleration for other religious traditions, so long as they did not practice human sacrifice, cannibalism, or commit treasonable actions. Within these parameters, the religious traditions of the entire Roman world were permitted to flourish unhindered by the government. This was even true of the Celtic traditions of western Europe, once the barbarous practice of human sacrifice was suppressed by Roman authorities in Gaul and Britain.

Indeed, the *concordia* among the many pagan religious traditions during the Roman era, the ability of worshippers of numerous pagan gods to live in peace and harmony with each other, annoyed many Christian critics. St Augustine (d. 430) complained that although the pagans worshipped many false gods, there was no religious divisiveness among them.[69] The Christians, however, who ostensibly worshipped a single God, were continuously at war with one another concerning various heretical beliefs.[70]

A great many pre-Christian, pagan, and Celtic folk traditions and customs have survived into modern Europe. Among the more notable of these are the festivals of Halloween, New Year's Eve, and Carnival. Although these traditions have undergone many changes over the centuries, their essential pagan characteristics can still be discerned. Many folk customs and traditions from France and Britain relating to the cat can plausibly be dated to the time of the Roman Empire, when the cat becomes well established in western Europe.

Isis and Bubastis (Bastet)

The cult of Isis and her sacred cat companion Bubastis was widespread and influential throughout the Roman Empire, both in the East and the West. Isis was originally an Egyptian divinity, whose cult was transformed when the Macedonians under Alexander conquered the region in 332 BC. At that time the native cult was suffused with Greek theological notions and artistic representations. The great temple of Isis and Sarapis at Alexandria, the Sarapeum, and its cult statues were some of the greatest religious monuments of the classical world.

It is mainly through the worship of Isis and Bubastis that Egyptian beliefs of the sacred cat spread throughout Europe and survived until the present day. A knowledge of their religion is therefore critical for the understanding of the history of the animal in Europe. As we shall see in the Epilogue in the section "The afterlife of the sacred cat" (pp. 162–70) the religious attributes of Isis are also the attributes of the cat and often of the "witch" in modern European folklore and custom.

At first it may seem improbable to some that Egypt once played an important role in the religious history of the West. This may be because today, Egypt seems remote, peripheral, isolated, and exotic, if not alien, to western culture and religion. It may seem unlikely that the country once made important contributions in these areas. Furthermore, recent attempts to exaggerate Egypt's role in the cultural formation of the West, especially for classical Greece, have helped to discredit the notion of Egyptian cultural transmission in general.[71]

There is, nevertheless, abundant evidence for the enormous popularity of Isis in the western Empire and indeed, throughout the Empire in general, especially among women. Virtually every town in every province had a temple to her and Sarapis.[72]

According to the ancient Egyptian religious tradition of the pharaonic era, the gods Isis and Osiris were husband and wife as well as brother and sister. In addition, the two had an evil brother named Seth. One day Seth and Osiris fought and Osiris was killed. Seth tore his dead brother in pieces, which were then scattered abroad. Isis gathered the pieces together on her sacred island of Philae near Syene (Aswan) in Upper Egypt and restored Osiris to life.

During the reign of Ptolemy I, the ancient Egyptian cult of Isis and Osiris was transformed into a new, syncretic, universal religion. The god Osiris became Sarapis. A splendid temple to the divine pair, the Sarapeum, was constructed in Alexandria which became a beacon of religious devotion to the entire Mediterranean. The images of Sarapis, Horus, and Isis were sculpted in the medium of Hellenistic art by the great sculptor Bryaxis. The ancient Egyptian theology of the religion was given by the hellenized Egyptian priest Manetho. This was recast into a Greek model by Timotheus, one of the priests of the Eleusinian mysteries at Eleusis near Athens. Finally, hymns were composed by one of the founders of the great Museum and Library of Alexandria, Demetrius of Phaleron, also near Athens, who believed that his eyesight was restored through the intervention of Isis.

One of the most important sources of information about the goddess comes from Lucius Apuleius, who wrote a novel entitled *The Golden Ass* in about AD 150. In this work, the hero, also called Lucius, wishes to become an owl and goes to a witch for a magic potion. He is turned into a donkey by mistake and, in the form of that animal, has numerous adventures in second-century AD Greece. In the end he escaped from the theater in Corinth and fled to Cenchreae, Corinth's eastern port. There in a precinct sacred to the goddess, he prays for deliverance and then goes to sleep on the beach. His prayers are answered by Isis herself, who promises to redeem him back into humanity. Apuleius gives a vivid description of the goddess rising from the sea, in answer to his prayer:

> She had an abundance of hair that fell gently in dispersed ringlets upon the divine neck. A crown of interlaced wreaths and varying flowers rested upon her head; and in its midst, just over the brow,

there hung a plain circlet resembling a mirror or rather a miniature moon – for it emitted a soft clear light. This ornament was supported on either side by vipers that rose from the furrows of the earth; and above it blades of wheat were disposed. Her garment, dyed many colors, was woven of fine flax. One part was gleaming white; another was yellow as the crocus; another was flamboyant with the red of roses. But what obsessed my gazing eyes the most was her pitch-black cloak that shone with a dark glow. It was wrapped around her, passing from under the right arm over the left shoulder and fastened with a knot like the boss of a shield. Part of it fell down in pleated folds and swayed gracefully with a knotted fringe along the hem. Upon the embroidered edges and over the whole surface sprinkled stars were burning; and in the center a mid-month moon breathed forth her floating beams. Lastly, a garland wholly composed of every kind of fruit and flower clung of its own accord to the fluttering border of that splendid robe.[73]

In this description we see the symbols of Isis and Isaic religion. She is the goddess of the moon, the night, and the starry sky. She is also the goddess of the earth's fertility and of all living things. The color of her sacred robe was black, which represents the night sky. We can see Isis, "The Queen of the Black Robe," in ancient frescos from Pompeii and in several surviving statues (cf. Fig. 3.10).

When she has risen from the sea, she addresses Lucius:

Behold Lucius, moved by your prayer I come to you – I, the natural mother of all life, the mistress of the elements, the first child of time, the supreme divinity, the queen of those in hell, the first among those in heaven, the uniform manifestation of all the gods and goddesses – I, who govern by my nod the crests of light in the sky, the purifying wafts of the ocean, and the lamentable silences of hell, – I, whose single godhead is venerated all over the earth under manifold forms, varying rites, and changing names. Thus the Phrygians that are the oldest human stock call me Pessinuntia, Mother of the Gods. The aboriginal races of Attica call me Cercropian Minerva. The Cyprians in their island-home call me Paphian Venus. The archer Cretans call me Diana Dictynna. The three-tongued Sicilians call me Stygian Proserpine. The Eleusinians call me the ancient goddess Ceres. Some call me Juno. Some call me Bellona. Some call me Hecate. Some call me Rhamnusia. But those who are enlightened by the earliest rays of the sun, the Arii, and the Egyptians who excel in antique lore, all worship me by my true name, Queen Isis.[74]

Figure 3.10   The goddess Isis represented as Euploia, the guardian of sailors and
ships, with her steering oar, dark red robe, and *hydreion* filled with
Nile water. Fresco from Pompeii, before AD 79

Initiates into the cult of Isis were also promised a blessed afterlife, as was
Lucius, the protagonist of the Golden Ass:

> Only remember, and keep the remembrance fast in your heart's deep
> core, that all the remaining days of your life must be dedicated to
> me, and that nothing can release you from this service but death.
> Neither is it aught but just that you should devote your life to her

who redeems you back into humanity. You shall live blessed. You shall live glorious under my guidance: and when you have traveled your full length of time and you go down into death, there also on that hidden side of earth, you shall dwell in the Elysian Fields and frequently adore me for my favors. For you shall see me shining on amid the darkness of Acheron and reigning in the Stygian depths.[75]

In Greek theology, the Elysian fields are the garden-like destination of those related by blood or other religious union with the gods. In Homer's *Odyssey* 4. 561–70, Menelaos is told he will not die (he is an *athanatos*, a deathless one) because of his relationship to the gods through his marriage to Helen, a daughter of Zeus:

> … it is not the gods' will
> that you shall die and go to your end in horse-pasturing Argos,
> but the immortals will convey you to the Elysian
> Fields, and the limits of the earth, where fair-haired Rhadamanthys
> is, and where there is made the easiest life for mortals,
> for there is no snow, nor much winter there, nor is there ever
> rain, but always the stream of the ocean sends up breezes
> of the West Wind blowing for the refreshment of mortals.

Apuleius describes the initiation rite of Isis, as much as he is able considering the religious prohibitions of revealing the details of the experience. The initiate became mystically united to the divinity:

> I approached the confines of death. I trod the threshold of Proserpine; and borne through the elements I returned. At midnight I saw the sun shining in all his glory. I approached the gods below and the gods above, and I stood beside them, and I worshipped them. Behold, I have told you my experience, and yet what you hear can mean nothing to you.[76]

In the vision of Lucius at Cenchreae Isis claimed to be the embodiment of all gods and goddesses of the world. In other words, all peoples worshiped some aspect of her divinity in a tolerant, inclusive monotheism. Hence Isis was frequently described as *myrionymos* "Isis of the numberless names," in inscriptions. The view that all religions had some validity and indeed, all were in effect worshipping one divinity under different aspects, was also a major principle of contemporary Stoicism.

Isis herself was easily assimilated with native female divinities of Europe, especially Artemis and Diana. There was no rigid orthodoxy or dogma associated with paganism, no "true doctrine" that had to be defended at all costs, in blood if necessary. Thus religious syncretism was the norm, a vast borrowing of divinities and religious traditions, usually from the eastern Empire, and a transmission of them to the West.

There is no better symbol of her syncretic power than the image of Artemis of Ephesus that resides at the Villa Albani at Rome (Fig. 3.11). Here we see Artemis with her many breasts, the nurturer of all life. She wears a crescent moon on her chaplet, and is crowned with a lighthouse. We also see many of her sacred animals, the cat, the goat, the lion, and various birds. The animals also have human-like breasts. The cat images on her garment are almost identical to those of the goddess Bubastis (Bastet) that we have seen from the later eras of Egyptian history. The upper row of cats have the horns of Isis surmounted by her sacred rosette symbol. Her compassionate, loving demeanor and her outstretched arms beckon all her children to her embrace. The image of the lighthouse belongs to Isis as we shall see immediately below. It remains a symbol of religious faith to the present day.[77]

Another important image of the goddess is on the tondo of a silver patera found at Boscoreale, Italy and dating to the first century BC. Here we see the goddess with attributes associated with Isis and Artemis: the bow and crescent moon of Artemis, the sistrum and uraeus of Isis, a lyre, a lion sacred to Cybele, a female dog, perhaps a representation of Anubis, a stalk of wheat and fruits of various kinds and a cornucopia. She wears an elephant headdress, symbolic of her African origins.

A final work of art from Roman Alesia (central France) may also show the religious connection of Isis and the cat (Fig. 3.9, p. 102). This is the boy or young man sculpted in high relief and found on the pedestal of an offertory table from an underground shrine. He holds a cat in his upraised tunic. The exact identity of this figure may never be known but the cat links him to Isis or Diana, since no other divinity from the region is known to be associated with the animal, who indeed was a relatively recent immigrant into Gaul. Through a process of elimination, the figure could well represent Harpocrates, young Horus, who was frequently linked to his mother Isis. Another similar pedestal comes from Ostia and depicts Isis herself with the Egyptian god Bes.

With the introduction of Isis into the western Empire came a renewed association with the female goddess of fertility and motherhood and her sacred cat. That the cat was sacred to Isis during the Roman Empire can be seen in the passage in Plutarch's *On Isis and Osiris*, discussed in Chapter 1 in the context of the folk image of "The cat and the fiddle" (pp. 42–3). Isis's sacred instrument was the sistrum (also discussed in that chapter). Examples of this rattle and sculptural reliefs depicting priestesses of Isis holding the instrument are found throughout the Empire. It had a loop that contained three or four bars that rattled when shook. The loop represented the moon and small cats were attached to it, usually at the top, but sometimes at the base. On the handle was a representation of the goddess Hathor,

Figure 3.11 Statue of Diana or Artemis of Ephesus, the nurturer of all life, showing images of Bubastis on her garment, together with other attributes of Isis. Rome, Villa Albani, early Empire

sometimes represented as a cow, or of Isis. An inscription of Cleopatra VII (d. 30 BC) from Aswan reads, "I play the sistrum before thy fair countenance, leader of the goddesses in Bigeh, that thy countenance may lighten and thine heart be glad, thy spirit be in peace …"[78]

Indeed, as was discussed in Chapter 1, Isis became identified with Bastet and assimilated the cat goddess into her worship during the Hellenistic and Roman eras. The Greek name of Bastet was *Boubastis*, while the Latin version was Bubastis, and we will use this latter name for her during the Roman and medieval eras. As was noted, an important Hellenistic hieroglyphic inscription from the temple of Horus at Edfu states that "the soul of Isis is present in Bastet," that is, that the goddess Isis can be incarnate in the cat goddess Bastet. In a Greek hymn to Isis, she was described as the "goddess of Bubastis, bearer of the sistrum."[79] The introduction of the cat goddess Bubastis into Europe and her association with Isis is of fundamental importance for the history of the animal in western Europe. Indeed, as will be seen in the Epilogue, her worship seems to have continued through at least the early Middle Ages. Most of the Latin dedications to her date to the first two centuries AD and associate the cat goddess with Isis.

Ostia, the port city of Rome, seems to have been especially important for the introduction of Isis and Bubastis into western Europe. Numerous inscriptions, dedications, and the Sarapeum survive from this bustling port with direct trade connections with Alexandria, Egypt, as well as the rest of the world. Rome's grain supply was heavily dependent on grain imported from Egypt and delivered by huge freighters. The description of one of these vessels, the "Isis," will be given below.[80]

Several Roman inscriptions refer to Bubastis, many of them from Ostia. In that city, Caltilia Diodora Bubastiaca, a priestess of Bubastis, dedicated a silver statue of Venus weighing one pound, and two gold wreaths to Isis-Bubastis. In Rome, a tombstone was erected by T. Flavius Ampliatus, a freedman of the imperial family, to his wife Ostoria Successa, a priestess of Bubastis's temple (Bubastium). In the Roman province of Pannonia Superior (Croatia), the freedman Gaius Philinus made a dedication to "Isis Augusta and Bubastis." [81]

Also from Ostia, fortune has preserved a significant inscription from the early Empire concerning its temple of Isis and Bubastis (Fig. 3.12). The inscription is an inventory of sacred objects that belonged to both divinities, and from it we gain an insight into the great wealth of the temple. Among the items belonging to Isis were seventeen sacred standards of the goddess, one bust of Sol, the sun god, four silver statues, two bronze altars, a bronze image of a dolphin, a silver patera, a royal ornament (*basileum*) befitting the Queen of Heaven, decorated with gems, a silver sistrum inlaid with gold, an inlaid gold couch frame, a necklace of beryl gems, two bracelets (*spatalia*) with gems, seven necklaces with gems, ten gems set in gold, one *analempsiaca* crown and a crown with twenty-one topazes and eighty-four garnets, linen vestments, and a belt with silver segments. To Bubastis, whose name appears on line 17, belonged silk garments of purple and green, a marble wash basin on a pedestal, a *hydreion* (water vessel), a golden belt and key, and numerous linen garments of white and purple. Clearly, the temple of these goddesses was wealthy and powerful and the religion was a force to be reckoned with in Ostia.[82] The inventory of temple objects also lends support to Apuleius' description of the wealth and splendor displayed in the procession of Isis at Corinth.

Some Roman names contain the theophoric element Bubastis, as in the example of Caltilia Bubastiaca. In Rome, Cornelia Mo(desta?) Bubastica set up a tombstone to her husband, a freedman of the imperial family, Marcus Ulpius A(…); a mother named Bubastûs set up a tombstone to her son Sulpicius Sardonychus; and a Greek inscription gives the name of Aurelius Boubastous.[83]

The most significant evidence for the widespread popularity of Bubastis in Europe is the bitter invective leveled against her worship by Christian authors from the second through the sixth centuries. The magnitude of their opposition to her cult indicates that they saw it as a serious threat, as we shall see below.

The Roman essayist Lucian of Samosata satirized the Egyptian notion of divine incarnation into an animal, "If you seek the god within, it is either a monkey, an ibis, a goat, or a cat!"[84] In this statement, we recognize the religion of Isis and Bubastis. As we noted in Chapter 1, the Egyptian Bastet was also assimilated with Artemis (the Roman Diana) by the Greeks. This association will contribute to the important connection of Isis with Artemis or Diana. Along with the worship of Bubastis in Europe came the goddess's cult image as discussed in Chapter 1, the female cat with her kittens with a sistrum on her shoulder, "the cat and the fiddle." As we shall see in Chapter 4, traditions concerning the worship of a cat goddess, portrayed as a bronze cat with her kittens, the typical depiction of Bubastis, continued in the Belgian city of Ieper (Ypres) until AD 962, when it was finally suppressed.

In the context of Isis, it is not difficult to see the religious significance of the color black for the cat. At this time black was not the color of evil or misfortune, but simply the color of the night. The night itself was not filled with evil demonic spirits, but with the moon and the stars and the gentle love of Isis for her creation. It is probable that at this time the black cat assumed its sacral character, which has survived all the way into modern European folklore, as we shall see in the Epilogue.

The black robe was Isis' sacred color, and she was called "Queen of the Black Robe." One order of her priests were the Wearers of the Black (*melanephoroi*), although most wore white linen. Isis is frequently portrayed in her dark robe in frescos and in sculpture (Fig. 3.10). It is not difficult to see how a black cat would have been especially sacred to her and regarded as her symbol. According to the magico-sympathetic principles discussed in

RES · TRADITAE · FANIS · VTRISQVE
SIGNA N · XVII · CAPVT · SOLIS · I · IMAGINES
ARGENTEAS · IIII · CLVPEVM · I · ARAS · AENEAS
DVAS · DELPHICAM · AENEAM · SPONDEVM · I ·
5 ARGENTEVM · ET · PATERA · BASILEVM · ORNATVM
EX GEMMIS · Ñ · I · SISTRVM · ARGENTEVM · INAVRATVM
SPONDEVM · INAVRATVM · PATERA · CVM · FRVGIBVS
COLLAREM · EX · GEMMIS · BERYLLIS · SPATALIA · CVM
GEMMIS · II · COLLAREM · ALTERVM CVM · GEMMIS
10 Ñ · VII INAVRES · EX GEMMIS · Ñ · X NAVPLIA · II
PVRA · CORONA · ANALEMPSIACA · I · CVM · GEMMIS
TOPAZOS N · XXI · ET · CARBVNCVLOS · N · LXXXIIII · CANCELLI
AENEI · CVM · HERMVLIS · Ñ · VIII · INTRO · ET · FORAS
VESTEM · LINIAM · TVNICAM · I · PALLIVM · I · ZONA · I ·
15 CVM · SEGMENTIS · ARGENTEIS · STOLA · I · VESTEM · ALTERA
LINTEA · PVRA · TVNICAM · PALLIVM · STOLA · ZONA
BVBASTO · VESTEM · SIRICAM · PVRPVREAM · ET
CALLAINAM · LABELLVM · MARMOREVM · CVM
COLVMELLA · HYDRIA · HYPSIANA · ET · LENTEA
20 PVRPVREA · CVM · CLAVIS · AVREIS · ET · ZONA
AVREA · TVNICAS · II · PRAECINCTA · ET · DISCINCTA
ET · PALLIOLVM · VESTEM · ALTERA · ALBA · TVNICA
STOLA · ZONA · ET · PALLIVM

Figure 3.12   Transcription of a Latin inscription from Ostia, giving the inventory
of objects in the Temple of Isis and Bubastis. Ostia, early Empire

Chapter 1, there were thought to be no coincidences or accidents in nature.
Thus when a cat's coat color was black, this meant that the cat was sympa-
thetically related to the goddess Isis, whose sacred color was also black. This
is indeed probable with the identification of Isis with Bastet and the notion
that the soul of Isis is incarnate in the sacred cat. Thus in addition to
Artemis and Diana, some black cats may have been regarded as the divine
epiphanies of Isis as well.

Another divinity, Anubis, also accompanied Isis to Europe. Anubis, who
was represented as a dog or a jackal, helped Isis find the pieces of her
departed husband. He represented the qualities of loyalty and devotion,
characteristics many admire in his sacred animal. As in the case of the sacred

cat of Bubastis, the dog was not worshipped *per se*, but the divinity that was supposed to be incarnate in the Temple Animal.

The religious attributes of Isis and Bubastis are critical for the religious history of the West. Like many other goddesses, Isis was also a divinity of marriage, family, motherhood. Unlike Artemis and Diana, however, she herself was a devoted wife and mother who inspired women for millennia. Nevertheless, she also upheld women's vows of chastity. She remained devoted to her husband, even after his death, and was responsible for his resurrection into the afterlife. She is frequently portrayed nursing her son Horus, iconography that will form the basis of the "Madonna and child." Indeed, one of her epithets was "Holy Mother of God," *hagia theotokos*.

She was the goddess of all aspects of womanhood, including the upholder of the marriage contract, and physical love, like Aphrodite. As a wife and mother herself, Isis could claim the loyalty and devotion of women throughout the Mediterranean and Europe. In Chapter 1, we have seen the centrality of motherhood for all ancient and medieval women. They could identify with her travails and those of her husband and son.

Isis was also the goddess of good luck and was already identified with the Roman Fortuna and the Greek Tyche Protogeneia by the first century BC. The great temple of Fortuna Primigenia at Praeneste, Italy built in that era shows the unmistakable association with Isis. This can be seen especially in its great mosaic, depicting Nilotic scenes associated with the life of Isis and other Egyptian divinities.[85]

The religion of Isis demanded that the initiate bathe frequently. This was also true for the priesthood of Isis and of the other Egyptian divinities. All the priests bathed three times during the day and twice at night. They also completely shaved their bodies once every three days. In this context, it is easy to see how the cat could be associated with this form of sacral behavior. The priests lived lives of purity and ascetic simplicity, dressing in white linen with sandals of papyrus.[86]

Isis was also associated with the intellectual achievement of Alexandria, Egypt, especially in medicine, as *Isis Medica*. In the Museum and Great Library of the city, the foundations of Western science were made in all fields – astronomy, geography, physics, geometry, and especially medicine. Indeed, another major library in the city of Alexandria, called "the Daughter Library," was a branch of the Great Library, and was located in the precinct of the Sarapeum. This library contained copies of the books in the large library and already in the time of Callimachus (d. *c*. 240 BC) contained some 42,800 scrolls or volumes. The small library was intended for general public use, and according to the contemporary rhetorician Aphthonius it "gave the whole city an opportunity to philosophize." [87]

Isis was thought to represent wisdom, *sophia*. Philo of Alexandria – who tried to combine the beliefs of Judaism with the philosophical movements of Alexandria, especially Stoicism – believed that Holy Wisdom, *Hagia Sophia*, was the mother of the divine Logos, her son, Horus (or Harpocrates as he was called when young). In the Jewish pseudepigraphical work, "The Wisdom of Solomon," written in the second century BC, Alexandrian science was praised and it was noted that Wisdom had instructed mankind in the natures of living things, the diversity of plants and the usefulness of medicinal herbs. This *Sophia* was undoubtedly Isis herself.[88]

The power of Isis in the field of pharmacology was widely recognized throughout the Mediterranean world and survived into the Renaissance. She supposedly gave the first draught of ambrosia to her son, Horus. A drug that was named for her, "The Universal Lady" (*kore kosmou*), was used to cure all sorts of ailments by the finest doctors of antiquity, including Galen.[89] As "Mistress of the Elements," Isis was thought to control the weather. She could raise storms or cause calm weather on land and sea, as she saw fit according to her holy wisdom.[90]

Isis Pelagia was also the guardian of all sailors at sea. She took a voyage to Byblos to find the pieces of her slain husband and invented the sail when she sought her son, Horus. In the symbolism of her religion, all journeyed over the sea of life and hoped to return safely, after stopping at many ports, to the final haven of rest, symbolized by Alexandria and its great lighthouse, the Pharos. In this context, we note again the statue of Artemis of Ephesus (Fig. 3.11) with the syncretic iconography of Isis and Bubastis. The crown on her head is a lighthouse, indicating that she was the beacon and final home of all those embarked on their voyages through life.

One of the popular names for sailing ships in the Roman world was "Isis." A large Alexandrian grain ship of that name put into Athens in the second century AD and was described by Lucian (d. *c.* 200) who was in the city at that time. The goddess's images were placed on both sides of the prow.[91] Many Roman vessels were named after divinities, especially those of the sea. These divinities and their images were not merely decorative and sentimental but were thought to be the divine protectors of the vessels.

In this context we have the remarkable passage from Martianus Capella (fl. 410–39) telling us that the image of a cat was commonly found on the prows of ships.[92] This we recognize is the image of Bubastis, the incarnation of Isis. The notion of the cat as a guardian spirit of the ship continued in European folk custom until the late twentieth century, as we shall see in the Epilogue. We have already seen that ship's cats were common in the ancient Mediterranean and can be traced back to the sixth millennium BC.

Finally, it is of interest to note that her great festival, the *Navigium Isidis* "The Vessel of Isis," that celebrated the *Ploiaphesia* or "Opening the Sailing Season," occurred on 5 March every year. Lucius Apuleius also provides a vivid description of this celebration and religious procession through the streets of ancient Corinth and Cenchreae.

The crowd of people was walking in a triumphant religious procession, filling the whole world, it seemed, with good spirit and happiness. People were dressed in costumes that represented various occupations in life and also mythological figures. Women in the procession were dressed in white linen and scattered flowers and perfumes along the route. Some women went caressingly through the motions of combing and dressing the sacred image of Isis herself.

Next was a crowd of men and women carrying lamps, torches, and candles in honor of the stars of heaven. Musicians came next, both men and women, who sang hymns composed for the occasion to instrumental accompaniment. There followed the initiates themselves dressed in their white linen vestments, shaking their sistrums in unison. Priests followed carrying the goddess's sacred emblems and symbols, all in gold. Last, the images of the gods were carried, Anubis, a sacred cow, and finally, the golden image of Isis herself.

At this point in the story, a priest carrying the sistrum and Isis' sacred roses redeemed Lucius, the protagonist, back into humanity, "At last Lucius, after long days of disaster and heavy storms of fortune, you have reached the haven of peace and the altar of mercy." [93]

The climax of the procession was at the same beach where Lucius first saw the vision of Isis emerging from the sea. Here, a sacred ship was launched in honor of the goddess. Loaded up with dedications and offerings, it was sent out on its own into the Saronic Gulf.

The enormous popularity of Isis during the Roman Empire cannot be stressed enough: there are vast quantities of dedicatory inscriptions, votive offerings, altars, and temples dedicated to her throughout Europe. In Apuleius' novel concerning Isis in Corinth, we see throngs of laymen, initiates, and priests of both sexes and all stations of life coming together for her sacred procession. It seems half the population of the great city of Corinth was at the event. This depiction is probably accurate; like other talented novelists throughout history, he has honestly depicted the social, economic, and spiritual worlds in which his main protagonist lived.[94]

Women played a prominent leadership role in the religion of Isis as well as in other pagan religions, reflecting the high status women enjoyed in the classical era in general. They owned property, made legally binding contracts, had choice in marriage, and the right to divorce. Upon divorce, women received back their dowries plus a half of what the couple had accumulated during the marriage. In the Hellenistic and Roman eras, women were even elected to the high magistracies of eastern city states when they had performed meritorious service to the community. The important religious roles of women would continue into the early Christian church.[95] The civil status of classical women compares favorably to those living in the West in much later eras.

As will be seen in the Epilogue, the basic religious tenets, practices, and beliefs concerning Isis and the sacred cat of Egypt survived through the Middle Ages and into nineteenth- and even twentieth-century Europe. Some of the most prominent of these survivals are the image of the "cat and the fiddle," that is Bubastis and her sistrum, in religious contexts; the use of cat sacrifice to ensure good fortune and fertility; the general good fortune and fertility granted to those who owned a cat; and above all the notion that the cat can be an incarnation of a spiritual being. There always remained the association with women and the moon. In addition, there are powerful associations with the cat and the afterlife in a non-Christian sense. It is thought that the spiritual power of the cat was so great that they were able to resurrect the dead under certain circumstances. In the context of the afterlife Isis, as we have seen, is probably the operative divinity and not Atum-Ra, the Egyptian solar cat of the underworld. Cats are thought to have healing power, and are frequently used in magical formulas to restore health. Finally, there are the notions that cats can control the weather and are the protectors of sailors on the sea. Black cats are thought to be especially sacred.

So these two, the Queen of the Black Robe and her sacred cat, entered the religious consciousness of Europe. There, after suffering many vicissitudes, they remained together as long as paganism existed.

The Celtic tradition

While Diana, Isis, and Bubastis had the greatest effect on the European religious tradition concerning the cat, there were influences from the Celtic tradition as well. Animal symbolism played an important role in native Celtic religion. Some gods, such as Cernunnos, were portrayed in a semizoomorphic form, in his case as a man with antlers. The goddess Epona was portrayed with a horse and Sequana with a duck.[96] The association of animals with divinities probably made the populations of Romano-Celtic Europe receptive to another religion that included a sacred animal.

Another Celtic influence was the unfortunate tradition of mass sacrifice of the animal, continuing until the early nineteenth century. In both England and France, the cats were placed in large wicker baskets, suspended from a fire and slowly roasted to death. This nasty form of sacrifice had its origins in the Celtic world, as we learn from our ancient sources. Indeed, before the Romans conquered the region, such sacrificial methods were also used for human beings. A second method of cat sacrifice found up to the early nineteenth century, the throwing of the animals from great heights, probably also had its origins in Celtic practice.[97]

The calendar dates of mass cat-killing in medieval and early modern Europe also seem to be based in part on ancient Celtic ritual dates for animal sacrifice. One of the most important was Midsummer's Eve, when huge bonfires were lit throughout northwestern Europe. In the Christian calendar, these festivals correspond to St John's Eve. Up to the seventeenth century, the bonfires were the site of animal sacrifice, especially of cats. Another common date for cat sacrifice was around Mardi Gras or Shrove Tuesday, a date associated with the great festival of Isis.[98]

Although it cannot be proven from ancient sources relating to Celtic religion, it may well be that the practice of sacrificing any cats found in fields after harvest and burying them under trees to ensure fertility also comes from this tradition. Nor was it remarkable to find cats in a wheat field around harvest time, since this is also a time when field mice and other rodents would be plentiful. Although the basic belief of the cat as an embodiment of the divine principle of fertility probably derives from the religion of Diana and Isis, it is possible that Celtic peoples could have also made this connection on their own, before the arrival of these Mediterranean goddesses.

The magical cats

Some of the earliest representations of the cat occur in magical contexts on apotropaic amulets from Egypt dating to about 2000 BC. The magical aspect of the cat is another attribute that continued in Europe through the Middle Ages. There are two main sources of information about the use of the cat in magic rites. The first are the Greek Magical Papyri, a group of volumes devoted to magic found in Egypt dating from the second century BC to the fifth century AD. Second are the references to magical practices found in Pliny the Elder's *Natural History*.

From the first source, the most important ritual concerns the drowning of a cat to make it an *Esies*, a member of the sacred dead with prodigious powers. While the magician drowns the cat, he utters the following formula:

> Come hither to me, you who are in control of the form of Helios, you the cat-faced god, and behold your form being mistreated by your opponents [who are named at this point], so that you may revenge yourself upon them, and accomplish the [named at this point] deed, because I am calling upon you, O sacred spirit. Take on strength and vigor against your enemies [who are now named again], because I am conjuring you by your names ... raise yourself up for me, O cat-faced god and perform the ... deed.[99]

After drowning the unfortunate animal, it was mummified and walled up in a tomb or burial place. When the rituals were complete, the soul of the cat was thought to be united with its spirit, and it became a powerful spiritual force. The cat-faced god who was in control of the form of Helios was undoubtedly Atum-Ra and not Bubastis. As was discussed in Chapter 1, this solar god was depicted in the form of a cat. It is significant that the cat achieves its power through death and the preservation of its body. In the

Epilogue we shall see that a comparable ritual was performed in medieval Spain, France, and Britain.

From this collection we also learn that the black cat is especially efficacious in sending dreams. Unfortunately the animal must be killed first and a scroll containing the desired dream placed in its mouth.[100]

From Pliny the Elder we learn that magical amulets containing (what else?) cat dung and the claw of a horned owl were thought by Magians (priests of Mithra) to be especially efficacious in warding off malaria or quartan fever. Further, the ashes of a cat mixed with seed grain were thought to keep mice away from the fields.[101]

The cats and the early Christians

No hatred of cats, nor of other animals, can be found in the New Testament or among the leaders of the early Apostolic church. "Look at the birds of the air: they neither sow nor reap nor gather into barns, and yet your heavenly Father feeds them" (Matt. 6: 26). "Are not two sparrows sold for a penny? And not one of them will fall to the ground without your Father's knowledge" (Matt. 10: 22). God's concern extends to the fate of even the smallest animals.[102]

The early church remained faithful to the teachings of Christ for about three hundred years. In general, the Christians lived in peace with their pagan neighbors and, miraculously, even with heretical Christian groups. Nor did the Christians, up to the time of Constantine (d. 337), use violence or terror to coerce "conversion" to their religion.

Sometimes as was noted, the Christians were falsely accused of practicing human sacrifice and cannibalism by their pagan neighbors (and unfortunately by some of their fellow Christians), and even treason. If proven, these were capital offenses that demanded the death penalty. Nevertheless, they never responded to these scurrilous attacks with violence or hate against their adversaries.

Moreover, many animals would have benefited by a strong Christian presence in their communities, especially the cats. The Christians refused to sacrifice animals and often refused to eat meat sacrificed to pagan gods.[103] Although some animals, such as sheep and cattle, would have been killed eventually in any event for their meat, especially for celebrations, cats would have been sacrificed without usually being eaten. As we have seen, the animal was only consumed in time of famine. The Christians also tried to suppress magical rites. A Christian presence would therefore have probably reduced the incidence of cat sacrifice in that community.

In general, up until the end of the eighteenth century, Christianity was never more tolerated than it had been during the first three centuries of the Roman era.[104] So the pagans, the Christians, and the cats coexisted in relative peace for some three centuries. The Roman *concordia* of religions included the Christians as well.

When Constantine converted to Christianity, however, the nature of the religion was considerably transformed. That emperor (ruled 305–7 as Caesar, 307–37 as emperor) put military and police power at the disposal of the Catholic church. In return, he was granted the status of *isapostolos*, "equality to an apostle." The notion that the religious power of the emperor is above that of the pope is called Caesaropapism, and would play a profound role in Western history for the next 1,600 years. At the time of Constantine's conversion (*c.* 312), approximately 5 per cent of the Empire's people believed in some form of Christianity, while the remaining 95 per cent preferred other religious traditions, including Judaism.[105]

As early as 319, the heretical Donatists of North Africa began to be persecuted. The persecution of the Jews soon followed and by 391, the emperor Theodosius I banned all heretics (non-Catholic Christians) and pagans throughout the Empire. The penalty for these beliefs was death, the same as for the crime of high treason. Since the emperor was at the head of the church, any dispute concerning its orthodox dogma was considered a capital crime. By 400, more Christians had been killed by other Christians because of their faith than by the pagans; the death toll would continue to mount.[106]

It was often the monks who enforced the new theology upon the unwilling Jews, pagans, and heretics. They were instrumental in destroying the religious and intellectual institutions of the pagans, including the remaining public library at Alexandria. They killed many pagans and heretics as well.[107] The animal fabulists of the late Empire, among them those who wrote the cat fables discussed below, noted their cruelty. Despite persecution, at the time of the end of the western Empire in 476, a majority of the people were still pagans, and remained so for many centuries thereafter.[108]

It is important to discuss briefly the role of women in Christianity, and how it changed over the years. In the early Catholic church, women had major leadership roles as one can easily discern by reading "Acts of the Apostles." In fact, women such as Priscilla (or Prisca), Lydia, and Chloe were leaders of their local churches and had a role comparable to that of ordained priests.[109] They preached, evangelized, and were sent on important missions by the church along with their male counterparts. Of course, the important position of deacon was also open to them as well as holy orders of serving widows and virgins. Women were an integral part of the church, the Body of Christ.

In the Gnostic tradition, in addition to holding the priesthood and diaconate, women were also bishops. Feminine spirituality was an especially important component in this Christian sect (*hairesia*).[110]

By the late third and fourth centuries, however, women had lost their leadership positions in the Catholic church that they had held during the first two centuries and heresies such as Gnosticism were suppressed. Indeed, it seems that the notion of women in positions of high authority was regarded as suspiciously pagan and heretical by many of the church's hierarchy.[111] They were excluded from the church sanctuary as unclean during their menstrual cycle, and were forbidden to hold any office of authority, even the position of deacon. The only way left for them to express their spirituality was to live as hermits in caves in the wilderness, isolated from others. Later, by the sixth century, convents were built for them, especially for noble women, in order to protect their property.

The removal of women from important roles in the Body of Christ during the late Empire probably played an important role in their alienation from Christianity and their continued embrace of paganism, especially their goddesses of motherhood. Indeed, during this era, the church also demeaned the roles of marriage and the family, while rewarding celibacy (or at least those who gave the appearance of celibacy). As one worthy, Gregory of Nyssa (d. 395) expressed it,

> Marriage then, is the last stage of our separation from the life that was led in Paradise; marriage therefore ... is the first thing to be left behind.[112]

Since the vast majority of ancient and medieval women married and had children, the hostility towards these roles further alienated them from the religion. As we shall see in the Epilogue, hundreds of thousands of medieval women were brutally killed and many more risked death because they refused to abandon their ancestral mother goddesses or their beloved cats.[113]

In the post-Nicene church (after 325) through the end of the Roman Empire in the West, there is only one reference to the evil nature of the cat. St Athanasius, the patriarch of Alexandria from 328 to 346, complained about the worship of "hateful" animals such as snakes and cats, but this seems to be the only such reference among Christians of this era.[114]

Almost all of the references to cats made by the early Church Fathers are false accusations concerning the animal's alleged worship, not only by the Egyptians but also by others during the Empire. As early as AD 60 St Paul may allude to the practice in Romans 1: 22–3, "Claiming to be wise, they became fools, and exchanged the glory of the immortal God for images resembling mortal man, or birds, or animals, or reptiles." There are many passages complaining of cat worship, but that by the Christian apologist, Justin Martyr (*c.* 160) is of some interest:[115]

> And although we who do no wrong are put to death as sinners, others elsewhere worship trees, rivers, mice, cats, crocodiles, and many

kinds of irrational animals. And the same animals are not honored by all, but in one place, one is worshipped, and another in another, so that all are impious toward each other, on account of their not worshipping the same objects.

We can see trouble brewing ahead for the animal in the large numbers of these authors ridiculing "cat worship." One author complained that ibises, dogs and cats were worshipped, another added crocodiles, a third added the worship of beetles. But all the complaints concerned the "worship" of cats. The Christian apologist Arnobius (fl. early fourth century) improbably added that not only were cats worshipped but "the loftiest temples have been dedicated to cats, beetles, and heifers."[116]

If the false notion of "cat worship" was so evidently preposterous, then why the vast outpouring of invective against the alleged practice? This must have been because the power of the religion of Isis and Bubastis was seen as a substantial threat to the Christians.

A member of the heretical Monophysite church was named Timotheos Ailouros, "Timothy the Cat" (d. 477), and was actually appointed the Patriarch of Alexandria in the 470s. The Egyptian Monophysites were violently persecuted by the Catholics in the sixth century. They offered little resistance to the Arabs when they invaded the country in the 630s and in fact were grateful to live under Muslim rule. The Muslims did not force people to convert to their religion and they put an end to the horrific sectarian struggles amongst their Christian subjects. Today, the Monophysites are known as Copts and account for about 10 per cent of the Egyptian population.

Cats in the later Aesopic corpus with Christian themes

There are five cat fables (and one variant) from the Aesopic corpus with Christian themes. The first one is in Greek, written by Nicephorus Gregoras in the thirteenth century. All the rest are in Latin. It is possible that in the first story the animal may be a white ferret (*gale*), not a cat. Nevertheless, since a white, albino ferret must have been a rare animal, whereas white cats were probably common at the time this was written, the fable is included amongst the cats. Indeed, Perry has translated *gale* as cat in this fable, and since that may be a distinct possibility, it is discussed here. Although the present fable dates to the thirteenth century, once again, there is little possibility of accurately dating the fable itself, which may have been originally written many centuries earlier. The Latin fables are difficult to date. Two come from Odo of Cheriton and two from the late Codex Bruxellensis, but a *terminus post quem* of about AD 350 would be reasonable, since at this time the religion was well established in both the western and eastern Empires.

THE BLACK CAT

A shoemaker kept a white cat (*gale*) in his house that caught a mouse every day. One day, the cat fell into a pot of blacking and came out black all over. The mice reckoned that the cat would no longer be carnivorous, now that she had taken the aspect of a monk, and so they scattered fearlessly over the house. On finding such an abundance of prey, the cat would have liked to seize them all at once, but that was impossible. As it was, she caught two mice and devoured them. All the others ran away, wondering why the cat had become even more savage after donning the habit of a monk.[117]

THE CAT AS A MONK

In a certain pantry there was a cat (*murilegus*) who had killed all the mice (*mures*) except one big rat (*magno rato*). For the purpose of deceiving and catching this big fellow, he shaved the crown of his head and put on a skull cap, pretending to be a monk, and he sat and ate with the rest of the monks. When the big mouse saw this, he rejoiced in the belief that the cat would no longer want to do him harm. He ran about freely, and the cat (*gatus*) turned his eyes away, pretending to avoid the vanity of all worldly appetites. At last the rat, believing himself to be safe, drew near to the cat; and then the cat seized him in his claws and held them fast. "Why do you act so cruelly?" asked the rat. "Why don't you let me go? Haven't you become a monk?" The cat said, "Brother, you'll never pray so eloquently as to induce me to let you go. I'm a monk when I want to be, but, when I prefer it, I'm an ecclesiastical official, a canon." Thus he spoke and devoured the rat.

Thus many, when they desire illicit things, never give up. [118]

THE BISHOP CAT

A cat (*cattus*) wearing a miter and leaning on a scepter, called the mice (*mures*) together and, declaring that he was a bishop, ordered them to bow before him and be obedient to him. An old mouse spoke up and said to him, "I'd rather die a pagan than become a Christian and be under your power." Then all the mice fled from his benediction and hid themselves in their holes, and the cat, taking off his miter, put aside his episcopacy.

The moral: the mouse is afraid that if the cat put them under his rule, it would not be easy to get free, since other types of subjection are mild, but from this type, it is difficult to escape. [119]

THE MOUSE AND HER DAUGHTER, THE ROOSTER AND THE CAT

A mouse instructed her daughter not to go out from the hole, but the little mouse nevertheless ventured out. She saw a rooster scratching in the straw and crowing at the top of his voice, and was afraid. She also saw a cat (*catus*) approaching quietly on the edge of the path with slow and graceful steps; and because this was so unexpected, she went back into the hole trembling. To her mother's question as to why she was trembling, she said that she had seen a rooster that looked like the devil, and a cat that had the appearance of a pious hermit. "Don't be afraid of the one who seems so bad," said her mother, "but watch out for the one who has the appearance of sanctity."

And this is a warning to hypocrites.[120]

DINNER AT THE LION'S HOUSE

It so happened that the animals were invited by the lion to a great feast. A cat (*murilegus*) was among the invited guests. The lion asked her what she liked to eat the best, wishing to please each one of his guests. "Rats and mice," said the cat. The lion thought that unless all the guests shared of this dish, it would be in poor taste. So, after thinking the matter over, he had a casserole brought in mainly of rat meat, and the cat (*catus*) enjoyed this meal very much. But the others complained, exclaiming, "Fie, what is this stuff we're being served?" Because of this the whole dinner was spoiled. This is the way that most people put on a big banquet. There are always a number of cats (*catti*) present who can't be pleased with anything except a lot of dirty talk and drunkenness, and for their sake all the diners must stay late into the night, so that everybody can get drunk, filling his belly with wine and his mind with the devil (*Diabolo*).[121]

In these fables the cats were compared to monks, who were portrayed as cruel, sanctimonious hypocrites. We have already seen the reasons for this portrayal. The mice and rats were identified with the common people, helpless victims of their cruelty. This perspective of the predatory nature of the post-Nicene (post-325) church was observed by the common people of late Roman and early medieval society who would have written and read these tales. Indeed, it is of some significance that these fables, written for a non-elite audience, display such hostility to Christianity, and especially to the monks. The perspective of common people seldom survives in "official" literature of the church.

Once again, the animals are metaphors for human behavior, and the cat itself is portrayed as sneaky and devious, now using religion to camouflage his predatory intentions. In some ways, this is not very different from the depiction in the earlier part of the Aesopic corpus. The cat is depicted as a realistic character with no sentimentalism. This can be seen as a continuation of the *"feles virginaria,"* "the virgin predator," in Plautus and even Ausonius. In my view, there is no demonization of the cat intended in the first four fables. The symbol of the cat preying on the mouse was simply the best metaphor to use for the predatory church destroying the common people who often remained pagans. This was especially true in the countryside, the *pagus*, where the *pagani*, the country folk lived.

Nevertheless, in the last Latin fable, we note for the first time that the cat is directly associated with the devil. Once again, it is unfortunate that these late fables, including this one, cannot be dated with any accuracy. The late Latin word *catus* is used for the animal, but the fable itself may be much earlier. However, there is also a change in character in the last fable. While the cat was accurately depicted in the earlier fables as a crafty predator, willing to use trickery and deceit to get a meal, it was also portrayed as part of nature, and its behavior as part of its natural role. In the last fable, the cat's behavior is portrayed as evil and immoral, and indeed, diabolical.

The distribution of the cat by AD 500

As we saw in Chapter 2, the cat probably arrived in India during the second century BC. It is likely that the domestic cat increased its numbers in India and spread to China during the Roman Imperial era via Rome's enormous trade with those regions through the Red Sea ports of the province of Egypt. By the time of Augustus (27 BC – AD 14), 120 vessels left Red Sea ports annually on the long voyage across the Indian Ocean to obtain spices, silks, precious stones, exotic animals, and other products from South and Southeast Asia.[122]

Other routes to the East went through Arabia and Mesopotamia to the Persian Gulf. From these regions, Indian and Chinese goods were traded overland to the eastern Roman provinces. There was also direct trade with China through the Silk Route which opened up a vast commerce after Alexander's campaigns, and continued through the late Empire.

Fortunately for us, a cat from the Roman Red Sea port of Quseir el-Qadim dating to the first or second century was found in a remarkable state of preservation.[123] This individual received a proper burial after death. He was laid to rest in a niche of a building which was an administrative and storage center, probably for trade goods. The cat was carefully placed on some woolen striped cloth, one piece with bands of green and purple on a beige background. He was then wrapped with a linen shroud with edges of drawn thread work. The continued Egyptian reverence for the animal can be seen in the care taken in this burial.

The cat himself was domestic but very large, 42 inches (1.07 m) in overall length, and powerfully built. His fur was beige-yellow in color and of a comparable length to that of domestic cats. We recognize the general *libyca* coloration. Remarkably, he had the remains of no fewer than six black rats in his digestive system upon his death. The larger ancient domesticated cats would have needed correspondingly larger numbers of prey animals to eat. The cause of death is unknown. It was precisely such individuals that would have been invaluable to the Roman traders on their voyages to India. We also remember that the black rat originated in that country. Doubtless many eastern cats were descended from such individuals – their progeny (as seen by their *libyca-* or Abyssinian-type coats) still frequent the streets of Southeast Asian cities today.

By the fifth century AD the domesticated cat had arrived in China.[124] One may still discern the route that the animals took to reach these destinations by observing Abyssinian cats today in Bangkok, Thailand.[125]

During the fifth century, the Roman Empire suffered many calamities, especially in the West, where it finally collapsed in 476. Hundreds of cities were violently destroyed, and millions of their inhabitants were probably killed, through destructive invasions of its territory by German barbarians. Doubtless the cats suffered along with their human owners. But once again, they survived into the new era. Indeed, during the early Middle Ages, they continued to be treated with respect and honor because of their role in hunting mice and other rodents. The religious traditions concerning the animal continued among large segments of the population of western Europe, as did paganism itself.

4

THE EARLY MIDDLE AGES:
AD 500–1000

I and Pangur Ban my cat,
'Tis different tasks we're at.
Hunting mice is his delight,
Hunting words, I sit all night.
So in peace our tasks we ply,
Pangur Ban my cat an I.
(Eighth-century Irish
Monastic Poem)[1]

Although the main focus of this book is the classical era of Greece and Rome, the ancient traditions of the cat continued through the Middle Ages and into modern European folklore and customs. In this chapter we shall briefly discuss the history of the cat in western Europe, the Byzantine Empire, and the Islamic Near East during this period. This will help to trace the continuity of ancient cat-lore in western Europe through this era.

The Latin, Celtic, and Germanic West

The barbarian invasions

Western Europe experienced numerous calamities from the late fourth through the sixth centuries. Germanic tribes including the Vandals, Alans, and Suevi invaded and overran the region during the winter of 406–7. Together with other barbarian groups, the Visigoths, Ostrogoths, and Franks, they burned, raped, looted, and killed their way across half the continent, destroying millions of lives during the course of the century. Nor were the calamities restricted to the fifth century. The invasion of Italy, North Africa, and southern Spain by the Byzantines under the emperor Justinian in the 530s to the 560s caused the deaths of thousands more innocent people and a swath of destruction throughout those unfortunate regions. This substantially weakened Italy, so that the peninsula was invaded once again by the primitive tribes of the Lombards in the late 560s. Finally, the Arab invasions of the seventh and eighth centuries oppressed the coastal regions of Italy and France. Spain was conquered by the Arabs starting in 711 and the last Muslim state, Granada, was not recaptured by the Spanish Christians until 1492. Eastern Britain was lost to Christendom during the invasions of the Angles, Saxons, and Jutes. Nevertheless, the remnants of the Romano-British population held out in Cornwall and Wales. Indeed, these regions were the only territories of the former Roman Empire not to be overrun by barbarians. Many Britons living in the eastern regions of the country fled the Anglo-Saxon invaders and settled in Brittany in northern France. It was precisely these regions that were important for preserving ancient lore concerning the cat.

When the Germans overran the Balkan peninsula, Greece, and western Europe in the fifth century, almost every major city was looted, sacked, and burned – over three hundred cities in western Europe alone. In some cities, the few humans left after the devastation resettled the ruins, but in most others, there was little or no attempt to rebuild what had been lost. Many cities were gone forever.

It has long been known that despite these tragedies, the basic cultural traditions of the late Roman Empire survived largely intact among its former subjects – the Gallo-Romans, Italians, Spanish (even after the Arab conquest), and western British – through at least the eleventh century. Nevertheless, much was also lost. Polish traditions and culture also survived from September 1939 through April 1945. The Polish language was still spoken, the church still functioned, and some Polish literature was still produced. The same was also true in France from June 1940 to December 1944. Similarly, Roman traditions survived to 1000 and even beyond. Yet much of value was lost: cultural monuments, literature, schools, libraries, the rule of law, and peace and prosperity. These were now replaced by violence, poverty, mayhem, and continual tribal warfare among the new Germanic invaders that did not cease for centuries.[2]

Worst of all, the state of civilization itself was lost, that is, the ability to live in peace and harmony in a civil society with one's neighbors, without carrying weapons in the city's streets. This, since the time of Thucydides, had always defined the civilized from the barbarous way of life.[3] Weapons in the form of swords continued to be carried in public among the European ruling classes through the end of the eighteenth century.

As always, the cats must have suffered along with their human companions during these calamities. The destruction of their cities and their owners' lives probably had a devastating effect on their own numbers. However, the status of the cat had never been higher than in early medieval western Europe. Indeed, laws concerning cats of this period showed a respect for the animal that bordered on reverence. This was probably related to a decline in their numbers after the invasion era in a society that still understood the value of the animal. A further factor was the bubonic plague of 540–7 which doubtless killed many of the animals. Once again, the cats were the first line of defense against the rats and their dangerous diseases. Thus they are also the first to die off after the rats themselves during a plague. Finally, pagan religious beliefs that honored the animal survived among substantial portions of the population.

The persistence of pagan society and institutions

Notwithstanding irreparable losses, much of the traditional Gallo-Roman peasant life was maintained during the early Middle Ages throughout France despite the repeated disasters that overtook the country. The same was probably true throughout much of western Europe:

> It is at the end of the tenth century that a very ancient social fabric begins to fall apart; and there was an end of the dominance of a very ancient mode of production. Neither the slavery of the Roman estates, nor its Carolingian successor, labor service, had succeeded in suppressing the independent peasant communities ... The crushing but fragile military domination of Rome or Aachen was in the end powerless to overcome the freedom surviving in the countryside.[4]

Indeed, paganism strengthened as Roman control over western Europe waned in the late fourth and fifth centuries. All through the region one finds that churches had been deserted and that pagan temples were rebuilt and refurbished. In sixth-century Visigothic Spain, sources noted that Christianity had virtually vanished from the country.[5]

One reason for this persistence in western Europe was the relative lack of urban centers compared to the Greek East, from which control could be exerted by civil and church authorities. Western Europe was largely rural, especially so after many cities were destroyed during the fifth-century invasions.

During the early Middle Ages throughout much of France, the peasants still attended the regular public assemblies to decide legal disputes based on Roman law. These assemblies were called the *mallum*, or the *tria comitia* in Lorraine, and were still held at the sites of the old Gallo-Roman cities, even though the cities themselves were often ruined. Furthermore, elements of the Roman low-tax, market economy persisted until the eleventh century. The old Roman *tributum* of 10 per cent of the crop was still collected (minus the late Roman accretions) from the peasant allodialists and the *coloni*, or tenant farmers, had to pay an additional 10 per cent as rent to their landlords, plus some other minor services, the *eulogiae*. Indeed, most peasants still owned the land they farmed throughout the era.

It has long been known that pagan religious traditions persisted in the countryside of western Europe through the Middle Ages. Recent research by

Ramsay MacMullen, Jeffrey Burton Russell, Carlo Ginzburg, Jean-Pierre Poly, and Eric Bournazel has reconfirmed this view. These traditions were important for the cat, especially the continued worship of Diana and Isis. It seems that a majority of the French peasantry, and hence the French people, were still practicing pagans through the eleventh century and even beyond:

> Recent research, based chiefly on "missionary" sources, sermons, or penitentials from the ninth and tenth centuries, shows that there was in fact an astonishing permanence among the peasants of a truly pagan religiosity ... Already it seems likely that the true Christianization of the country areas was far from complete in the early eleventh century and that ancestral [pagan] rituals that had continued to be used despite the teachings of the Church had survived among the majority of the "rustics."[6]

The forms of paganism included the survival of numerous small temples in the countryside, the preservation of old images of the gods, and religious rites, rituals, sacrifices, and processions. Female divinities were especially popular among women including Diana, Mater Lucina, and Isis. A statue of Isis continued to be worshipped in the church of St Germain-des-Pres in Paris through the thirteenth century, before it was finally removed and smashed.[7] The cult of Diana was still practiced in Modena, Italy through the sixteenth century, in a much changed form, some 1,200 years after "the conversion of Europe."[8] The survival of female cults was associated with female ownership of land among allodialists, all characteristics of the ancient Gallo-Roman tradition.

The most important divinity among these survivals was Diana, who had become thoroughly assimilated with many female goddesses including Isis and even Bubastis. A Carolingian capitulary, the *Cannon Episcopi* dating to about 900, noted the power of this religion among women of the era:

> It is also not to be omitted that some wicked women perverted by the devil, seduced by illusions and phantasms of demons, believe and profess themselves, in the hours of the night to ride upon certain beasts with Diana, the goddess of the pagans, and an innumerable multitude of women, and in the silence of the dead of night to traverse great spaces of earth, and to obey her commands as of their mistress, and to be summoned to her service on certain nights. But I wish it were they alone who perished in their faithlessness and did not draw many with them into the destruction of infidelity. For an innumerable multitude, deceived by this false opinion, believe this to be true and, so believing, wander from the right faith and are involved in the error of the pagans when they think that there is anything of divinity or power except the one God.[9]

Later editions of this work complained that "Diana, the goddess of the pagans," rode out at night with her band of female companions, often with their cats, on the *wilde Jagd* or wild hunt. This was also the time, it was thought, that the rites of this ancient fertility goddess were performed. Ecclesiastical documents now associate the worship of Diana with the worship of Satan. The women (and cats) who accompany her on the hunt were thought to obey her as their lady (*domina*) as opposed to their true Lord (*Dominus*). Although the goddess is called Diana, it is clear that she was a composite of many Greco-Roman and Germanic divinities, the Valkyries, Holda, as well as Isis and Diana.[10] Despite these bitter invectives, the church still lacked the institutional means to crush the women. The Inquisition only became fully developed during the twelfth and thirteenth centuries.

Remarkably, folk traditions maintained that the worship of Bubastis survived in Ieper (Ypres), Belgium through AD 962 when the cult was finally suppressed. She was worshipped in the form of a bronze cat with kittens, the traditional image of the goddess during the Hellenistic era and Roman Empire (Fig. 1.6, p. 30). The Cat Festival of Ieper that commemorates the cult still continues today (Fig. 4.1).[11] As was noted, there are numerous images of cats playing fiddles in medieval ecclesiastical architecture. In Figure 4.2, the image of a cat playing the fiddle, with kittens, almost replicates the statuette of Bastet and her kittens with a sistrum in Figure 1.6.

The collapse of public health and the bubonic plague of 540–547

As was noted, there has always been a close connection between cats, rats and standards of public health and personal hygiene within a society. Classical traditions of medicine and public health collapsed during the early Middle Ages and were not restored until the nineteenth century. The consequences of this loss for the inhabitants and for the cats of western Europe during the early Middle Ages were tragic, the worst being the "Plague of Justinian," the bubonic plague of 540–7. Religious factors played a major role in this unfortunate development. The collapse was part of a larger phenomenon, the demonizing of nature and the criminalizing of rational thought in general.

As was observed in Chapter 3, some basic principles of Christianity as it developed through the Roman Empire and early Middle Ages were based on its opposition to classical religion and philosophy. Some of these oppositional views had a direct effect on the cat. The first, already discussed, was the elimination of women from positions of authority in the church and, indeed, the addressing of much hateful invective against them. This caused many women to remain pagans through the Middle Ages. The second was the demonizing of pagan religion in general and especially the religion of

Figure 4.1   Cat festival, Ieper (Ypres), Belgium, *c.* 1991

Diana. Third was the destruction of public health facilities and the rejection of the spiritual ideas upon which they were based. This latter development helped the spread of destructive plagues that would have a direct impact on the cat as well as the black rat.

The Judeo-Christian tradition had agreed that the classical nature gods existed but regarded them as evil and demonic spirits.[12]

> Christian people continued to practice ancient superstitions in a more or less disguised form, and pagan and magical elements entered the saints' cults. The infinite resourcefulness with which the Church sought to destroy paganism by ingestion advanced the development of witchcraft, convincing those who remained attached to the old gods that they were really revering demons. By establishing that demons were evil by nature, theology lent an initial practical reality to the worship of evil. The fathers accused the pagans of demonolatry. Medieval writers, taking them literally, found it all the easier to believe that many people in their own day were worshiping Satan and his minions.[13]

Figure 4.2 Cat playing a fiddle, with kittens, from the medieval church of Beverley Minster, Beverley, England

Thus the Latin Christians came to believe that Satan's power pervaded nature and the study of nature was diabolical.[14] The notion of living in harmony with nature was now regarded with intense hostility. In fact, during the late fourth and fifth centuries, the more one rejected nature by practicing celibacy, refusing to bathe, and rejecting the study of science, the higher one's status in the Christian hierarchy.[15] Both the use of reason and the study of nature or science were discouraged by Christian authorities in the fourth century and later.[16]

Furthermore, the ideals of Christian society now stressed the renunciation of the world and focused on one's own personal salvation, especially in the West. The material world, including the human body, was devalued and regarded as an impediment to salvation. The concern for public service, health, and welfare that had characterized Greek and Roman elites for centuries was now abandoned. The revival of these values did not take place until the Enlightenment.[17]

Perhaps the changed ideals towards nature and holiness can best be seen in the numerous saints' lives written from the fourth through the sixth centuries.[18] In these lives, the holiest men and women live in squalid conditions, inhabiting small, rat-infested cells, dressed in filthy rags, and loaded down with heavy chains.[19] Indeed, some monastic orders made it a point of honor to reject bathing. It was thought that such flea-ridden, emaciated creatures, who inhabited all parts of the late Empire but who were especially numerous in the deserts of Syria and Egypt, represented the highest ideals of a truly Christ-like renunciation of the world. The Plague of Justinian struck Syria particularly hard, probably because it had a superabundance of these "Holy Men and Women."[20]

The influence of these changing values was tragic for both science as well as medicine and public health. Although Aristotle had proved that the earth was a sphere in his *De Caelo*, Lactantius, a bishop of the early fourth century AD said that to believe this was to commit a dangerous sin, because the Bible says it is flat.[21] Augustine wrote that a curiosity about the world we live in was one of the three most dangerous sins, along with pride and lust.[22] Zacharias in his life of Severus (late fifth century) wrote that in his day, anyone who was brilliant and cultivated must be consorting with demons and hence a heretic.[23] Indeed, anyone found copying a work of classical antiquity was liable to have their hands cut off. Burning works of classical authors was encouraged by the highest levels of authority through the thirteenth century.[24]

Scientists were also persecuted and killed. The intellectual institutions that were associated with paganism, such as the Museum and Library of Alexandria were destroyed. The last great library in the city, the Daughter Library in the Sarapeum, was burnt down by religious fanatics in 391. The Christians tried to eliminate the power of Isis by the complete destruction of her sanctuaries. The last philosopher-scientist associated with the library, Hypatia, was murdered by rampaging monks in 415. According to contemporary sources, she was murdered because of her "surpassing wisdom." Unfortunately, the persecution of scientists by Western Christian churches through the use of state power was not restricted to the Dark Ages, but has persisted through the twentieth century.[25]

While the loss of the Western scientific tradition during the Late Empire and western European Dark Ages was an intellectual tragedy that set mankind back a millennium or more, the loss of the medical tradition was a human catastrophe. The thoroughgoing rejection of reason and natural law was an especial disaster for cities. The *raison d'être* of public health policies was now regarded as a kind of diabolism. Only in the Byzantine Empire did some of the classical medical tradition survive. Eastern Orthodoxy achieved a synthesis of Christianity and Stoicism thanks to church leaders such as Origen, Gregory of Nyssa, and Basil of Caesarea. During the darkest eras of irrationalism and fanaticism, the connection between God, reason, and humanity was never entirely abandoned. This enabled Eastern Christian physicians to resist the onslaught of religious fanatics.[26] Western Europe was not so fortunate.

St Jerome (d. 420) advised the good Christian to "avoid hot baths," and, "let a squalid garb be the evidence of a clean heart" (*Epist.* 125). Some of the first institutions to be destroyed during the early Middle Ages, along with the temples and libraries, were the public baths.

Indeed, cleanliness was not a virtue that was generally highly regarded during the Middle Ages: "the matter-of-course mention of dirt and vermin, are among the first things that strike us in medieval literature,"[27] comments a leading expert on the Black Death. Rats, of course, have always been associated with filth and now that dirt was related to holiness and renunciation of the world, a connection was soon made between the presence of rats and a life of sanctity.[28] It has also been noted that Christian opposition to bathing was based in part on the demonization of Muslim beliefs which encouraged bathing and cleanliness.[29]

Recent archeological work by Andrew Jones and others have shown that in England, the streets of medieval York were "one third excrement," and one street in the city, known as Shambles, was "an open sewer with workers pushing barrows of offal to dump in the river and women emptying chamber pots from windows." The floors of Viking homes in England "were a mix of dirt and mouse droppings, pigs rooted in the yard, and latrines, if used at all, lay a few feet from wells."[30] As Ziegler notes, the medieval house, "might have been built to specifications approved by a rodent council as eminently suitable for the rat's enjoyment of a healthy and carefree life."[31]

So enamored were the western Europeans with grime that they were still drinking water polluted with sewage through most of the nineteenth century. The residents of culturally advanced London still drank from the polluted Thames through the 1860s.[32]

While Greek and Roman physicians kept scrupulously clean, late nineteenth-century physicians made it a point of honor to refuse to wash their hands before an operation. Often, doctors would dissect bodies of those that had died from cholera, typhoid, tuberculosis, and so on, and then use the same unwashed scalpels for performing operations. When a few voices, enlightened by the discoveries of Pasteur in the 1860s, began to suggest that doctors wash their hands and instruments, they were greeted with ridicule and scorn by the medical establishment. Little wonder that Joseph Lister found that in the 1860s, up to 80 per cent of all operations that ended in death were due to infection.[33]

This opposition to cleanliness cannot be explained simply by the poverty of the medieval and earlier modern European world. In fact, nineteenth-century western Europe was the most prosperous and technologically advanced region of the planet. An ideological opposition to cleanliness must have contributed to the fact that the nineteenth-century European water supply compared poorly with that of the ancient Greeks and Romans. Cleanliness was an essential characteristic of ancient societies and religions, and was rejected along with other religious beliefs.

And so it is not surprising that the first pandemic of the bubonic plague in the West occurred in the reign of the Emperor Justinian from 540 to 547. This plague was pandemic, that is, it affected many regions and was not restricted to a particular area. It afflicted the Byzantine Empire in 540–1, and by 547 it had spread to Italy and France, finally reaching England. As has been observed, it is not coincidental that the pandemic occurred at a time when urban public health systems and a concern for personal hygiene had broken down. Thereafter, there were several serious outbreaks throughout Europe and the Near East. After this pandemic, there was a hiatus of some seven hundred years. One reason for this was the die-off, caused by the plague, of rats in northern and western Europe. Rats, of course, are the first victims of the disease. During this era, their numbers could not be replenished from abroad because of the commercial isolation of western Europe from the East as a result of the Arab invasions. The decline of urban human populations further reduced the numbers of rats. During these outbreaks, there were also large die-offs of cats, who were the first line of defense against the rodent carriers and would have been killed in large numbers. This would thus add to their rarity throughout the region. The reintroduction of the black rat into Europe during the tenth century was due in part to the Viking invasions and increased trade with the East.[34]

The outbreak of the plague shows that cats alone could not have saved a population from that scourge, and that the cooperation of humans was necessary too. The destruction of many cats by the plague was probably one reason for the high legal status they enjoyed during the era.

The role of the cat in the early Middle Ages

Among the many social, economic, and religious aspects of late Roman culture that survived into the early Middle Ages, especially among the peasantry, was a respect for the cat. As will be discussed in the Epilogue, this was especially true in Wales and western Britain where ancient traditions concerning the animal survived the invasion era into modern folklore.[35]

Some of the most significant laws concerning the cat come from the law code promulgated by King Howel Dda, Howel The Good, of Wales during the tenth century. Because of the size and geography of the country, Howel's code was soon interpreted in three separate ways, the Venedotian code, the Dimetian, and the Gwentian.

According to the Venedotian code, a kitten until its eyes open was worth a penny, from that time until it can kill mice, two pennies, and four pennies thereafter. At this time, a lamb, kid, goose, or hen was worth one penny and a grown sheep or goat was worth four. The ability to kill mice was especially valued and for a female, the ability to raise her young. According to the other codes, the worth of a cat was also four pence. If it was killed, that was the price paid to the owner, or the amount of grain that would completely cover the dead animal when it was suspended by its tail with its head on the floor. In case of divorce, if the couple had one cat, it went to the husband, if more than one, the remainder went to the wife. In Saxony, Germany, the culprit who killed an adult cat had to pay sixty bushels of grain or two sheep. The penalty of grain symbolized the cat's role in destroying grain-eating mice.[36]

Just as a ship without its guardian cat was regarded as a derelict, so a Welsh village under Howel's laws could not be a lawful hamlet without a cat. A dog or a horse was not necessary. In Ireland, too, cats were highly regarded during the early Middle Ages. This can be seen not only in the contemporary poem to Pangur Ban, but also in the numerous cats that appear in the Book of Kells and the Lindisfarne Gospels (Fig. 4.3). On the continent, the name Catula still appears among pagan women.[37] There was little to suggest the future tragedy that would befall the animal in western Europe, beginning in the thirteenth century.

The Byzantine East

The Byzantine Empire also suffered greatly from the Plague of Justinian, mostly caused by the collapse of public health systems and poor personal hygiene in that region, especially Syria. It also suffered terrible invasions from Visigoths, who wrecked the ancient cities of mainland Greece during the late fourth century. The worst invaders were the Sassanid Persians, who overran much of Egypt and the Near Eastern territories in the early seventh century. Nevertheless, a high level of civilization was still maintained through the final collapse of the Empire in 1453.

There is no religious opposition to the cat apparent in our Byzantine sources. They were not tortured or massacred, nor were witchcraft hysterias a factor in Eastern Orthodoxy, as in the West.

Preserved in the *Greek Anthology* are two poems by the Byzantine author Agathias (c. 532–82), and a related epigram by his student, Damocharis. The poems concern an unfortunate cat who has made a meal of his master's pet partridge.

> No longer, my poor partridge exiled
> From your rocky roost, does your latticed home hold
> you in its light withes;
> No longer in the light of bright-eyed Dawn
> Do you shake the tips of your sun-warmed wings.
> Your head the cat bit off, but all the rest of you
> I took from her, nor did she satisfy her greedy jaws.
> Now may the dust lie not lightly but heavily,
> lest she drag you from the tomb.[38]

In the next epigram Agathias contemplates the disposition of the miscreant cat: sacrifice on the grave of his beloved partridge.

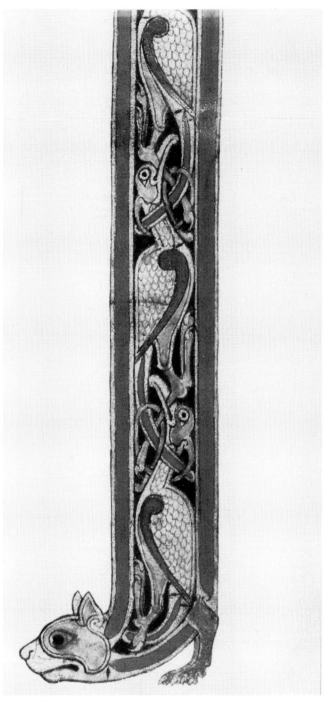

Figure 4.3　Cat on Lindisfarne Gospels, Irish, *c.* 700

Does the house-cat, after eating my partridge,
Expect to live in my halls?
No dear partridge, I will not leave you unhonored in death,
But on your body I will slay your enemy.
For your spirit grows disturbed until I perform
The rites that Pyrrhus performed on the tomb of Achilles.[39]

The last epigram of this series was written by Agathias' pupil Damocharis. The cat's master seems to have relented in his wrath, at least temporarily.

Wickedest of cats, rival of the man-eating hounds,
you are one of Acteon's pack.
By eating the partridge of Agathias,
you wounded him as much as if you had feasted on himself.
Your heart is now set on partridges, but meanwhile the mice
Are dancing, running off with your dainties.[40]

The Muslim world

The Muslims conquered the Byzantine territories of the Near East, Egypt, and North Africa during the mid- and late seventh century, leaving them Greece, Turkey, and the Balkans. By 711 they had reached the Straits of Gibraltar. Indeed, many populations welcomed the Muslims since they put an end to the violent sectarian strife among the Christians of those regions. Nor did the Muslims forcibly impose their religion upon the Jews and Christians. After the conquest, they mostly left them in peace and accepted conversion through free choice.

Fortunately for the cats, they found spiritual protection under the rational and humane principles of Islam and its prophet Muhammad. Islamic control of North Africa and Spain spared the cats there from the hysteria and irrationalism of medieval Western Christianity, that, beginning in the thirteenth century, would slaughter them without mercy.

According to Arabic folklore, the prophet Muhammad so loved his own cat, that when he was asleep on the sleeve of his robe, he cut off the sleeve rather than disturb him when he had to rise. It is said that the parallel lines on the fur of the heads of cats with *libyca* or *sylvestris* markings were put there when Muhammad stroked the animal. Furthermore, the animal's ability to land on its feet when dropped was also a gift given by Muhammad after a cat had saved him from a poisonous snake.

In Islam, the cat is regarded as a clean animal, unlike the dog, and does not compromise man's purity for prayer. Indeed, its drinking water can be used if needed, for ritual ablutions. Cats are welcome in the mosques, dogs are not permitted. Unlike the Western Christians, the Muslims, like the

Jews, emphasized cleanliness, washing, and bathing. Hence they seem to have appreciated the cat, in part, for this reason.

In Muslim folklore cats can foretell the future and can sacrifice themselves to save humans from death. There is a cult of cats among a North African sect called the Heddawa in which the cats are treated as humans. In pre-Islamic Arabia, desert spirits or *ghul* appeared with cat's heads. In Islamic culture, cats can assume the shape of saints or helpers. God's presence, the Sakinah, appeared to Muhammad in the shape of a white cat. Cats appear to people in dreams and teach them music. To some, the cat's purr is interpreted as its prayer.[41]

In the Islamic world, the cat's value in killing rats was always appreciated and their presence helped keep rodent populations in check. While they were being massacred in Europe, charitable organizations to provide homeless cats with food and shelter were funded in Cairo by the Sultan Beybars in 1280.[42] He was also the Muslim leader that drove off the cat-massacring French Crusaders from the Holy Land. Furthermore, the Muslims maintained traditions of bathing and personal hygiene as far as possible, including the maintenance of Roman aqueducts, such as the famous one in Segovia, Spain. These aspects helped to protect the Muslims from plagues but, of course, did not eliminate this scourge.[43]

Thus we leave the Eastern cats in the humane hands of the Muslims and the Eastern Orthodox Christians. As we shall see in the next chapter, their brethren living in western Europe were not so fortunate.

EPILOGUE

Persecution and redemption

> Lat take a cat, and fostre hym wel with milk
> And tendre flessche, and make his couche of silk,
> And lat hym see a mous go by the wal;
> Anon he weyvith milk, and flessche, and al,
> And every deyntee that is in the hous,
> Swich appetyt hath he to ete a mous.
> (Geoffrey Chaucer, *Canterbury Tales*)[1]

In this chapter, the vicissitudes that befell the cats and their owners from approximately 1000 to 1700 will be discussed. During this period, millions of cats and hundreds of thousands of their female owners were brutally tortured and slain throughout western Europe during the Great Cat Massacre and the associated witchcraft hysteria. Mercifully, our story will not end there. We shall continue on to more recent times and show that modern European folklore concerning the cat has preserved the memory of the ancient goddesses, Diana, Bubastis, and Isis. Finally, the restoration of the animal to its rightful place in civil society over the last century will be discussed.

In a work that focuses on the Greek and Roman world, the late Middle Ages can only be an epilogue. Once again, there is no serious study of the cat in the Middle Ages, nor does this brief chapter pretend to be one. There is however, an abundance of literary, artistic, and archeological evidence for the animal during that time. The medieval sources for the Great Cat Massacre need to be collected and the incidence and locations of cat-killing analyzed. This important subject deserves its own study.

The transformation of paganism: AD 1000–1700

Domestic animals depend on a reasonable expectation of decent treatment or at least benign neglect, if not religious adoration, by humans. This expectation was generally fulfilled over the millennia because most have understood the benefits derived from them. However, when a society is overcome by

152

delusion and fanaticism, the unwritten contract between human and animal may be broken. This is unfortunately what happened to the cats in western Europe during the Great Cat Massacre between the thirteenth and seventeenth centuries, especially in the towns and cities.[2]

Lest one feel too sorry for the millions of cats who were tortured and burnt to death over the era, one must remember that hundreds of thousands of innocent women suffered the same fate along with their beloved animals.[3] They were falsely accused of being "witches," worshipping evil, and performing barbaric acts. As J.B. Russell has observed:

> It might be argued that the witch craze must have been initiated by madmen, but this would again be to ignore the relativity of the term madness and, more specifically, to forget that witchcraft arose within the context of a coherent and widespread magical world view and developed in the context of the system of medieval Christianity.[4]

In other words when an entire society adheres to absurd principles, it becomes difficult to blame the individual inquisitors for their own actions. The Great Cat Massacre provides one of the more striking historical examples that a society which encourages the widespread abuse of animals seldom shows much respect for human life either.

As was noted, the cults of many female divinities persisted through the Middle Ages. These survivals were from various pagan traditions, Celtic, German, Greco-Roman, and even Egyptian in the case of Isis. For Diana, Artemis, and Isis, the cat was the sacred animal of divine incarnation. This was also true for the German goddess of fertility and motherhood, Freya. She was pulled in a chariot, not by lions as with Cybele, but by two large cats. Invariably, the various divinities of fertility and motherhood throughout Latin-speaking medieval Europe were called "Diana," both by the women themselves and by the Christian inquisitors who obtained their confessions under torture. It must be remembered, however, that the worship of Diana also includes aspects from other pagan traditions.

To understand the calamity that befell the cats and their women companions in western Europe from the thirteenth through the seventeenth centuries, one must briefly review some salient facts of Christian theology of the era. The Christian practice of demonizing and dehumanizing religious opponents has a long, unfortunate history that still continues today.[5] First the Jews fell victim, then the heretics – that is, those Christians who were not orthodox Catholics – and last, the pagans.

As was observed in Chapter 4, both the Jewish and the Christian traditions agreed that the pagan nature gods existed but regarded them as evil and demonic spirits. This notion remained common through the Middle

Ages.[6] Thus many in the church were persuaded that male and female pagans were worshipping evil.

Another ideological factor that doomed the cats and hundreds of thousands of their female owners was the successionist theology of St Augustine (d. 430) that became accepted by the Latin church during the course of the fifth century. To Augustine, all humans were innately evil, and all were worthy for eternal damnation, regardless of their good works or moral character. Nevertheless, God in his infinite mercy saved some Catholic Christians through his grace given at baptism. All humanity not receiving this baptism was predestined by God for eternal damnation.[7] This meant, of course, that the vast bulk of people living on the planet as well as the numerous pagans and Jews living in Europe were denied their full humanity in the sight of God.

This successionist view of history maintained that those with the misfortune to be born in the eras before the Incarnation of Christ, or who did not know about the event because they lived too far away (or, in the case of the philosophers and pagans, were skeptical), were without God's grace and lived in Godless, un-Christian cultures, unworthy to survive. This notion has always been common among Christian fundamentalists and is increasingly popular among some church historians of late antiquity today.[8]

Catholic church councils rejected Augustine's theology as un-Christian and without scriptural authority. The Greek church of the eastern Empire never accepted it. Since the reign of Constantine, however, it was the emperor, and not the pope or church councils, who was the head of the church. The western Emperor Honorius welcomed the new theology since it gave him justification for the absolute power of the state over people who were naturally depraved and incapable of governing themselves.

Nevertheless, as was noted in Chapter 4, paganism enjoyed a revival in the West during the late Empire. The feeble western emperors were incapable of enforcing these theological views, nor were they enforced by the Merovingians, Carolingians, and the weak successor states in Britain, Spain, and Italy. It was also fortunate that Augustine's ideas were never accepted in the Greek church. This probably prevented a similar catastrophe befalling the cat and its female owners in the Greek East. Of course, cats continued to flourish in the Muslim East.

The eleventh century saw the implementation of successionist ideology. It is not a coincidence that the massacres of pagans, heretics, and Jews began in western Europe with the development of the Inquisition and the imposition of the feudal system with its coercive force over the individual peasant. In 1095, when calling for the First Crusade, Pope Urban II was able to declare that the biblical strictures against killing humans were only applicable to Christians killing other Christians. Christians could kill non-Christians with impunity, however, and this was not a sin, since God had already shown his displeasure towards them by condemning them to eternal damnation since

the beginning of time. And so Augustinian theology came to its full
fruition. The implicit denial of the full humanity of non-Christians was now
made explicit, and acted upon by the secular authorities.[9]

The first actions of the Crusaders after the pope's pronouncement were
the massacre of thousands of Jews throughout Germany, especially in the
ancient cities of Cologne, Mainz, and Worms.[10] On crossing over into Asia,
the Crusaders were able to kill and eat the Muslim, Jewish, and indeed
Greek Christian residents of the region with no hesitation. Since it was
thought they were little better than animals, they could be treated as such
with impunity.

> In the eleventh century, and even more in the twelfth, punishments
> and procedures on the part of both secular and religious courts
> became more severe. Theologically the position of the dissenter was
> weak. To most medieval theologians, no illegitimate violence was
> being done to the Jews, infidels, and heretics put to the sword at
> the behest of the Church: these people had no rights to be violated
> … The infidels by virtue of their deliberate choice of error had cut
> themselves off from humanity. St. Augustine believed that the indi-
> vidual had no right to dissent. He and those who followed him
> insisted that error had no rights and that ignorance of the law of
> God was no excuse.[11]

It is in this context that the massacres of the cats and the women must be
seen.

As was discussed in Chapter 4, the traditional Romano-Celtic peasant life
was maintained in most of western Europe prior to about 900, despite the
numerous disasters that had overtaken the region.[12] Recent historical
research has also confirmed the persistence of pagan traditions through the
High Middle Ages, especially among women. This was especially true for
the female goddesses of motherhood and fertility, Diana, and Isis.

During the course of the tenth century, this traditional system was gradually crushed by the armed, petty thugs, "fist men," who appropriated the
peasants' lands for themselves in return for "protection" against Viking
assaults in their small fortifications. This internal conquest of the countryside was not completed for two centuries, but the old Gallo-Roman
aristocracy in southern France fought the process and protected their *coloni*
and allodialists from the crusade launched against them to the bitter end.
After their final defeat, the free peasants and tenants were turned into slaves,
servi (serfs), owing three days service per week on their lord's lands and innu-
merable other burdensome duties and fees. At this time, the cities were
transformed into centers of fiscal, legal, and military oppression. A similar
process occurred in other parts of western Europe at this time.[13]

It took longer to destroy the peasants' beliefs and religion. This was accomplished by the institution of the Inquisition. As we have seen, the recent work of medievalists has called into question the whole notion of religious "conversion" to Christianity during the era. "Coerced conformity" would be a more accurate term. A majority of the French peasantry, and hence the French people, were still practicing pagan rites through the eleventh century and beyond. Starting in the tenth century, Christianity was imposed on the pagan peasantry with the use of considerable terror and violence by the Inquisition and feudal authorities.

The peasants resisted the Inquisition and the new feudal order, not only on the social, economic, political, and religious levels, but also for moral and ethical reasons. They often rose up in arms against the new order that had stolen their land, their labor, their political and legal institutions, and that now threatened to rob them of their humanity. Their "heresies" were often no more than Apostolic Christianity, the belief in which was now a capital crime, or one of the other diverse Christian beliefs that flourished in ante-Nicene churches.[14] The Cathars or Albigensians of Latin, southern France, who seem to have been the spiritual descendents of the Manichaeans, resisted the crusade that was launched against them for twenty years before they were exterminated.[15] They, like many other heretics were falsely accused of "cat worship." The destruction of so many innocent human beings in the crusades against various heretical groups in southern France (some only representing Apostolic Christianity), may have prevented a Renaissance occurring in that region in the thirteenth century, a full century before it began in Italy.

The survival of the legend of King Arthur in Wales, Cornwall, and Brittany at the lowest levels of peasant society is another example of moral and ethical resistance, in this instance of Romano-British society, to the new order.[16] Whatever the historical truth of Arthur may be, in the transmission of his legend through the Middle Ages the peasants preserved a folk memory of a better age of prosperity and justice, so much in contrast to their own.

By 1200, all European peasants were reduced to serfs, and none owned the lands that most had once possessed. All were now the *servi* of a feudal lord: a count, a duke, an earl, or some other vassal. Now, for the first time in history, the coercive power of the church and state could be brought to bear directly against the peasant and his beliefs.

The fate of Diana and her cat

Women offered the bitterest resistance to the destruction of their old religion. As the Christians themselves well knew, persecution frequently makes the persecuted groups fiercer in their opposition. Thus it was thought that only massacre could successfully overcome their resistance.

It proves difficult to separate the truth from false confessions elicited from pagan women under torture from the Inquisition. We now understand that cats were not possessed by evil demons, nor were their female owners worshipping evil. It was only under torture that such false statements were made. Nevertheless, it is probable that cats were regarded as the incarnations of spiritual beings, especially the goddesses, who were now demonized by the church. Indeed, the general notion is consistent with the religious ideas about cats through the Roman Empire when the pagan traditions concerning the animal in western Europe were formed. They also accord well with the folklore from later Europe that was not obtained under threat of torture and death.

In the thirteenth century, the church leadership believed that evil spiritual beings such as *bonae muliares*, lamias, *strigae*, *incubi*, *sylvani*, and *panes* (plural of Pan) could be embodied in cats. In that enlightened century, French inquisitors tortured women suspected of witchcraft in Clermont, Lyons, and the Auvergne. They confessed that they met at night, held orgies, and had intercourse with the devil. When the women met at a house for a feast, it was said that a black cat appeared on the table. The cat would walk around the table top in a circle and immediately the table would be spread with a glorious feast. The cat was said to be the devil himself.[17]

Both the Templars and the Cathars were thought to both worship cats and to kiss the rear ends of cats during their rituals. Since paganism was officially suppressed, most meetings of the men and women occurred at night. At these assemblies, candles and torches were held, as had been done in earlier centuries for nocturnal celebrations of Isis. When Lucifer was summoned, a large cat entered the assembly.[18]

As early as the twelfth century, the black cat was thought to symbolize satanic power by church authorities. Satan and other demonic spirits were thought to reside in cats, especially the black cat. It was thought that the devil borrowed his black robe from a cat. Indeed, St Dominic (1170–1221) identified the black cat with Satan.[19]

As was discussed, Christian opposition to paganism, its beliefs, practices, and philosophies, helped to form the Christian religion itself.[20] As early as the late fourth and early fifth centuries, the Christian leadership had begun the process of demonizing the color black. Indeed, part of the reason for this may have been a reaction to Isis and her sacred color, especially in Egypt. As recorded by his hagiographer, Sophronius, St Cyril, the Patriarch of Alexandria (412–44) saw a vision of "a dark Egyptian devil accustomed to appear in a female form." We learn later in the text that the devil was Isis and the vision persuaded the devout Cyril to destroy yet another of her sanctuaries, that of *Isis Medicus* in Menouthis.[21]

Another factor that helped doom the cat was the Christian attitude towards Islam. As has been observed, Christian opposition to bathing was based in part on the demonization of Muslim practices that encouraged cleanliness. Similarly, the church's hostility to the cat may have been reinforced by the opposition to Muslim beliefs which respected the animal.

Finally, in 1233, Pope Gregory IX issued his notorious *Vox in Rama* (see

Appendix 3) which gave divine sanction for the extermination of the cat, especially the black ones, and the massacres of their female owners.[22] Once again, the shock troops of the war against women were the monks. Indeed, after centuries of savage inquisitions, tortures, burnings, and hangings, many pagan men and women became convinced that they were indeed worshipping evil. The worship of pagan divinities had finally been transformed, in the eyes of some at least, into the worship of demons.

This is indeed what occurred to the *benandanti*, a local cult of Diana that persisted in northeastern Italy through the seventeenth century. As late as 1610, the women insisted even under torture and the threat of death that they had not been worshipping evil. However, by 1640, they were finally coerced into admitting that they worshipped the devil.[23]

Throughout some areas of France and Germany, so many women were massacred that in many towns and villages not a single adult woman could be found. One reasonable estimate of the number of women who were killed during this tragedy is 200,000, while other estimates run far higher.[24] Those who risked their lives on behalf of their beliefs, who were tortured, imprisoned, fined, falsely accused of practicing human sacrifice or worship of evil, or suffered other indignities, numbered considerably more.

> The poor creatures, writhing on the rack, held in horror by those who had been nearest and dearest to them, anxious only for death to relieve their sufferings, confessed to anything and everything that would satisfy the inquisitors and judges. All that was needed was that the inquisitors should ask leading questions and suggest satisfactory answers: the prisoners, to shorten the torture, were sooner or later to give the answer required, even though they knew that this would send them to the stake or scaffold.[25]

This was especially true of elderly women. As we saw in Chapter 1, numerous studies have shown the emotional and physical value of a cat in the lives of elderly men and women. Such pets have been shown to reduce blood pressure and increase the resistance to diseases as well as to provide emotional well being. Brooms were also suspect, no doubt because of the general suspicion of cleanliness in medieval society. Older women had no doubt learned both the value of cats and brooms through long experience, even if they were not pagans.

Even the possession of a cat by a woman was often enough for her to be accused of diabolism and witchcraft. If she was unfortunate enough to possess a broom as well, her doom was often sealed. As late as the mid-nineteenth century, elderly women with cats were still harassed, persecuted and even killed in some western European societies.[26] The cat and the broom, symbols of good luck and cleanliness for most human cultures, became objects of satanism and witchcraft for medieval man.

Diana and Isis were also moon goddesses, especially the full moon, and so the full moon too became a symbol of witchcraft and evil. Those who were too far under the influence of the moon and the demonic forces it represented were called lunatics (in French, *lunatiques*). Similarly with the number thirteen, which represented the number of lunar cycles in a solar year. Thirteen was also the number of pagan women that made a *coventus* (*conventus*) for the worship of their goddesses, later demonized into the witches' coven.[27]

In the crusade of extermination against the hapless cat, the European folk tradition makes it clear that their complete elimination was a serious goal of the religious authorities. Contemporary evidence and folk traditions from later eras show that the medieval cats were not killed by the swift broken neck of ancient Egyptian sacrifice, but the cruel and brutal sacrificial practice of the Celts. They were placed in wicker baskets, suspended over fires, and slowly roasted alive. Folk traditions from later periods record that in many towns and cities, every single cat was rounded up and tortured and burnt alive for local festivals. "The cat, who represented the Devil could never suffer enough." [28] There are depictions of cats being killed in medieval art, and this evidence remains to be collected and analyzed. The assumption is made, correctly in my opinion, based on artistic representations, folk traditions, and contemporary documents such as the *Vox in Rama*, that the cats were massacred with their female owners in large numbers. The cat population of the continent was probably decimated, especially in the towns where the culprits could be more easily rounded up.

> Cats both black and brave unnumbered
> Have for naught been foully slain.[29]

Displays of cruelty continued through the eighteenth and even the nineteenth century. It probably took every ounce of the animal's intelligence, skill, and reproductive capacity to survive at all in the towns.

In the countryside however, the value of the cat was still recognized through the darkest days of hysteria and persecution. Its great value in destroying rodents – each cat can potentially save the farmer 250 tons (225 tonnes) of grain per year – ensured its survival in rural areas. "It is no wonder that the farmers, millers, and brewers of the Middle Ages managed somehow to keep *their* cats on the side of the angels."[30] The great reverence for the animal among the peasantry of medieval Europe, dating back over a millennium, could never be entirely eradicated by the Inquisition. It is indeed in the farms and villages of France and England that the ancient lore of the cat has been preserved for future ages.

Finally, it must also be acknowledged that in the atrocious slaughter of the cats, there always remained an element of pagan sacrifice in the practice through its last stages in the nineteenth century. The killings were thought to give good luck and the cat's dying screams were thought to frighten away the devil. This was especially true when the cats were killed by the Celtic sacrificial method of burning them alive in large wicker baskets. Nevertheless, the systematic destruction and elimination of the animal from the towns and cities of medieval and early modern Europe went far beyond pagan notions of animal sacrifice.

Hundreds of thousands of women were killed during the witchcraft hysterias from the fourteenth to the seventeenth centuries, and many more risked death simply for possessing a cat and honoring the goddess to whom the cat had been sacred. They would rather be brutally killed, tortured, imprisoned, and falsely accused of performing barbarous acts than abandon the religion that had been central to their lives for a millennium. Despite the false accusations and "confessions" elicited under savage torture, they never worshipped evil, as their accusers claimed, nor was their beloved animal a minion of Satan. Unfortunately, yet more centuries had to pass before these facts were understood. It is indeed difficult to learn about the women's beliefs directly, since they were burnt alive with their beloved cats – only their dying screams still echo across the years.

So, through the Christian process of demonizing opponents, the guardian and protector of the home, the symbol of *Fortuna* among the Romans, was turned into the minion of Satan and massacred by the millions. This development probably had serious public health consequences, especially in urban areas, through the seventeenth century.

The Black Death

Cat predation has played a major role in rodent control. The systematic elimination of the cat from the cities and towns of western Europe would therefore have had a major impact on public health. The Black Death pandemic started in 1346 and continued to 1351 with several outbreaks thereafter. It struck the entire continent of Asia and of Europe, as well as North Africa. In Europe, the death toll was one third to one half of the population, as many as 20,000,000. After the main outbreak, there were numerous smaller ones and a few epidemics through the seventeenth century, one of the worst of which hit Europe in 1665.

For many years, historians of medicine have understood that the virtual elimination of cats in medieval towns, beginning in the thirteenth century, led to an explosion in the black rat population.[31] This in turn increased the virulence of the disease. The pandemic of 540–7 showed that cats by themselves could not prevent the bubonic plague when the humans were unwilling to follow rudimentary procedures of personal hygiene and public health. The Black Death showed what happened when the procedures of personal hygiene and public health were ignored, and the cats were eliminated as well.

160

The black rat was reintroduced into medieval Europe in the tenth century, after an absence of about five hundred years which was probably caused by their die-off in the bubonic plague of 540–7, "The Plague of Justinian." As was seen, the rat was probably reintroduced by the Vikings with their vast trade connections with the eastern Mediterranean and eastern Asia. This is a more likely origin for the reintroduction of the black rat than their transport by Crusaders returning from the Holy Land in the early twelfth century. In the Introduction and in Chapter 3, it was noted that the black rat is the main vector for the transmission of the bubonic plague bacterium, *Yersinia pestis*. Our sources, both literary and archeological, indicate that the Middle Ages was something of a golden age for the rat.

As we saw earlier, three factors in particular are responsible for the spread of the black rat: the provision of a safe, comfortable home; the availability of nourishing, wholesome food available in abundant quantities; and the elimination of his natural predators, especially cats.[32] Fortunately for *Rattus rattus*, medieval man conveniently provided all three.

The lack of elementary sanitation and public health facilities, as well as personal hygiene, during the Middle Ages was discussed in Chapter 4. Even urban homes were constructed with wood and plaster with thatched roofs and dirt floors:

> It was in the medieval, "soft-walled" dwelling-house, with its thatched roof, its dark, unventilated, humid interior, and its earthen floor, that *R. rattus* and *X. cheopis* found mutually congenial conditions for their subsistence and multiplication. Under the floor and in the thickness of the wattle and daub or mud walls, the house-rat could construct burrows in which it could climb to its resting and breeding nests in the thatch, whence it could emerge at any time between sunset and sunrise safely hidden by the gloom which obscured the interior of the dwelling.[33]

Often, flea-ridden farm animals would be kept in the houses, even in cities.

In some medieval animal tales, the rats and mice symbolized good, and dogs and cats evil. Indeed, one common theme of medieval art is a cat being hanged by rats. This portrayal often occurs in ecclesiastical contexts.[34] When the black rat was killed, garments were often made from his pelt, providing another ideal home for *X. cheopis* and other fleas.

Grime, in and of itself, does not cause the plague, but as Ziegler notes, "the plague found its work easier in bodies weakened by dysentery, diarrhoea or the thousand natural shocks that the unclean body is particularly heir to."[35] Furthermore, unwashed people provide comfortable homes for *X. cheopis* and *P. irritans*. Naturally, to the medical profession, "bathing was regarded as a dangerous procedure because baths opened the pores and allowed corrupt air to penetrate."[36]

The Jews were never told by their God that filth and squalid garments were the symbol of a pure heart. On the contrary, their religion demanded frequent bathing and they went to great lengths to obtain clean water from running streams, often at long distances from their homes in the cities. The observant reader will recall that this function was originally fulfilled by the aqueducts of the Greeks and Romans. The Jews even encouraged their Christian neighbors to follow their example and stop drinking the polluted water to which they were accustomed; all to no avail. The Jews were accused of diabolism and well-poisoning; if drinking liquid sewage was good enough for Christians, why not for the Jews? It was obvious to the Christian mind that the Jews' hygienic practices were satanic rituals and clearly showed that they were guilty of causing the Black Death, and so they were massacred without mercy by the hundreds of thousands. They had already suffered terribly during the "First Crusade" in 1095, when more thousands were massacred.[37]

Plenty of nutritious if not always wholesome food was made available to the rat. Garbage is its favorite food and it will also eat excrement, both of which were in abundant supply, as we have seen. Grain was also freely available in mills, warehouses, and private homes constructed of wood, plaster, and thatch.

The rat was never held in higher esteem than by medieval and early modern western Europeans, becoming something of a sacred animal.[38] Despite periodic and half-hearted attempts to remove the rat, it was often an object of veneration. They provided it with abundant food, a safe home, and virtually eliminated its predators. For these reasons, European black rats of the era attained a colossal size, never seen before or since.[39]

The cats were not so fortunate. After the Black Death, the war against the animal was redoubled. Not only were the Jews, women, and cats massacred, but now the dogs as well, some of which are also effective rat-killers. In London during the plague of 1665–6, 200,000 cats and 40,000 dogs were slaughtered.[40] The remaining rats, naturally, were unharmed.[41] The destruction of so many beneficial animals caused the needless suffering and death of millions.

The afterlife of the sacred cat

Many cultures have believed in the spiritual power of the cat, as we saw in Chapter 1. Despite the opposition of religious leaders and continuous massacres, the folklore of early modern and modern Europe confirms that these spiritual aspects have continued to the present day, especially among the rural population.

The eminent folklorist Katharine M. Briggs sagely observed that in post-classical Europe, "the persecution of an animal is often a sign that it had once held the status of a god."[42] This was especially true of the cat, which endured more persecution than any other animal.

The persistence of pagan folklore, customs, and practices concerning the cat is probably the most powerful body of evidence for the survival of pagan traditions in the countryside through the Middle Ages. Fortunately, folklorists such as Frazer, Briggs, and Van Vechten have been collecting this material for two centuries, and it is easily accessible. Moreover, this material was not collected under threat of death or torture from the informants. Its general accuracy is therefore difficult to question. Throughout the continent, this lore shows that ancient, Egyptianized beliefs concerning the cat remained widespread among the peasantry.

Some of the most significant and ancient European cat lore comes from the West Country of England, especially Wales and Cornwall. As has already been discussed, these regions were not overrun in the invasion era and retained many of their ancient institutions and values together with much of their culture and language from the Romano-British times. However, persecution of the black cat also occurred there and almost succeeded in turning it into an unlucky animal by the seventeenth century.

The reason for these ancient survivals in England, especially in the western regions, was that witch hunts and witch killings were relatively rare in that nation, so that older traditions had a chance to survive. Important in this context is the quotation from Chaucer (d. 1390) at the beginning of the Epilogue. What is of interest is not so much that cats are still hunting mice but that the cats are so well cared for. They have beds of silk, and are fed scraps of meat and milk, as well as other "dainties" by their owners. This is in stark contrast to the contemporary situation on the continent. The cats would repay the good treatment at the Battle of Agincourt in 1415, as we have seen, at least according to some accounts.

The most important aspect of the cat in folklore has always been its association with good luck, marriage, fertility, motherhood, and the moon, attributes that can be traced back four thousand years. The folk tradition is replete with such symbolism, especially for women. In nineteenth-century Wales,

> Cats were supposed to be endowed with magical powers, and there-fore granted many privileges and indulgences. It was not considered lucky for the inmates of a house to be without a cat. Girls are told to feed their cats well, so that the sun may shine on their wedding day.[43]

An old Welsh rhyme went,

> Wherever the cat of the house is black
> The lasses o' lovers will have no lack.[44]

This was a view supported by other oral traditions, "No wonder Jock's lasses marry off so fast, ye ken what a braw black cat they've got." If a cat sneezed once near a bride on her wedding morning it was a good omen for a happy married life.[45]

The animal was still sacrificed well into the nineteenth century, to ensure the fertility of the crops and good fortune to the dedicator.[46] The sacrifices often took the cruel and brutal Celtic form. As we noted earlier, this involved placing several of the unfortunate animals in large wicker baskets and suspending them over a fire to be slowly burnt alive. Nevertheless, as mistaken as the idea was, their dying screams were thought to frighten away evil spirits and bring good luck.[47] Cats would also be sacrificed and placed under fruit trees and grain fields to ensure fertility.[48]

Furthermore, in medieval Spain, France and England, cats were walled up in houses and other buildings for good luck. They were placed in the walls and sometimes under floorboards. On occasion, a dead mouse or rat would also be placed with the cat, as an object of sympathetic magic. Apparently it was believed that the spirit of the cat would help to eliminate the rats.[49]

Burying animals under the floors of buildings to ward off evil and provide good luck was an ancient Celtic practice.[50] The walling up of animals, however, is not a known practice in this tradition. Archeological evidence for the practice would not be likely to survive in any event, since most ancient buildings, especially those of wattle and daub construction, scarcely survive above their foundations. However, one notes the similarity of this magical practice to the "immuring" of sacrificial cats discussed in the Egyptian magical papyri. One hopes that the unfortunate animals had already perished before being treated in this manner, and were not walled up while still alive. Still, the Middle Ages were not a period where much value was placed on human, let alone animal, life.[51] Finally, the dates for cat sacrifice were often the same as those of important pagan festivals, May Day Eve, (still called by its ancient Roman name, Calan Mai, that is Calends Maius, in present day Wales), Midsummer's Eve, and Carnival.[52]

Cats were also thought to be the incarnations of spiritual beings, now transformed into evil demons through false accusations and confessions elicited under torture from their female owners. Often, these beings were thought to be witches, but sometimes demons and even Satan himself were alleged to be embodied in the animal.[53] In a related notion, it was thought that some cats were enchanted, that is, they were actually possessed by powerful humans, especially princesses. "Chatte dans le jour, la nuit elle est femme."[54] The notion of divine (now demonic) incarnation can be traced back to Egypt. The related notion of human incarnation, that humans can enter into cats or change into cats or other animals, was a common pagan notion in the Greco-Roman magical tradition as can be seen in the *Golden Ass* of Apuleius. It was also an ancient Celtic magical belief.[55]

It was the black cat that was especially important in this regard. We have seen in Chapter 2 that this coat color probably originated in the eastern Mediterranean in the fifth century BC, and spread to western Europe shortly thereafter. In Chapter 3 we saw that the color black was sacred to Isis, who wore a cloak of that color. Thus it is probable that that black cat was seen as the divine incarnation of Isis, Artemis, or Diana. Throughout the European continent, it was the black cat that was regarded as the most sacred (or demonic by the church).

Gregory IX's *Vox in Rama* decree was leveled especially against the black cats that were often used in "witches' sabbots." Their ferocious persecution and near extermination in continental Europe was enough to transform the black cat there into an unlucky creature and the white cat into a lucky one. Many of their owners were killed as well. The five-hundred-year crusade against the black cat finally served its purpose, at least on the continent. It is said that a pure black cat is almost impossible to find in western Europe today. This is in contrast to the eastern Mediterranean where they are common, since there was no crusade launched against them there. In England, however, the older tradition still survives: the black cat gives good luck and the white cat, with its ghostly appearance, is unlucky.

> Kiss the black cat
> An' 'twill make ye fat:
> Kiss the white ane,
> An' 'twill make ye lean.[56]

Also in Wales, according to Mary Trevelyan,

> It is lucky for a black and strange cat to stray into anybody's house. If a black cat is lost, trouble and sorrow will fall upon the house. [57]

Other folk traditions state that,

> It is good for a black cat to come to your house; on no account should it be driven away. When you flit or move to another house, it is unlucky to bring the cat with you. It is all right if the cat follows you of its own accord.[58]

Black cats were also especially efficacious for treating illness and protecting the household from disease, attributes that can be seen in ancient Egypt. It is probable that this universal belief was based in part on the cat's role in destroying disease-carrying rodents and preventing their predation on food supplies. The limitation of starvation and famine would also reduce the incidence and severity of disease.

A black cat, I've heard it said,

Can charm all ill away,
And keep the house wherein she dwells
From fever's deadly sway.[59]

We have seen the role of the goddess Isis as the protectress of ships and sailors at sea. Furthermore, in many ships, her sacred images were placed near the bow. We learned from Martianus Capella that in the fifth century many vessels also had images of cats near the prow. These images undoubtedly represented Bubastis, or Isis incarnate in the sacred cat.

In fact, cats chosen for ship's cats on British vessels were generally black if possible. This can be seen from surviving photographs (Fig. 0.3, p. 13). Furthermore, the descendents of ship's cats that jumped ship in remote sub-Antarctic islands, once used as whaling stations, are also frequently black.[60] The survival may show the persistence of an ancient Romano-Celtic tradition in Wales, Cornwall and elsewhere where the black cat is especially appreciated.[61]

The institution of the ship's cat also reveals the animal's spiritual character. Over maritime regions throughout the continent, the animal was thought to be the guardian spirit of the ship, warding off evil and misfortune from the vessel and the sailors. This role goes far beyond the animal's ability to destroy ship-borne vermin. When sailors were asked why they refused to sail on vessels without a ship's cat, the inevitable answer was not that the ships would be overrun by rats, but that the ships were unlucky and would sink. The folk tradition is replete with stories of sailors refusing to board a ship without its cat and, in Britain at least, preferably a black one.[62] Furthermore, this is not because the sailors were afraid of a few rats – as we have seen, ship's cats were mandatory in the British navy until 1975.

So strong is this belief that it influenced English law well into the present century. If there is no ship's cat, an owner of goods could sue the shipmaster for damages caused by rodents. In fact, a ship with no cat was considered to be derelict, and could be forfeited to the Admiralty, the finder, or the king. On the other hand, a cat who remained on a vessel, even under adverse conditions, saved the vessel from confiscation. As long as the guardian spirit remained on board, the ship was safe from harm. Once it jumped ship, it was doomed. Some British fishermen also gave an offering of part of their catch to a sea-spirit who had the form of a cat.[63]

In the Introduction, we saw the photograph of the ship's cat that accompanied Scott on his Antarctic expedition (Fig. 0.3). The cat was indeed the first of his species to set foot on that continent. After he was swept overboard in a storm, the entire expedition perished on the trek to the South Pole, facts that could only enhance the belief in the animal's spiritual power amongst superstitious sailors.

Moreover, there are large numbers of ship's terms relating to the cat in the English language: cat boat, cat-head, cat's-paw, cat hook, cat block, cat walk, and the notorious cat-o-nine-tails. In Italian, the term *gatta marina* was invented for the catamaran, a type of vessel, originally only a sailboat, that would "land on its feet," that is, not tip over, in a heavy wind.[64]

The otherwise inexplicable nautical term "cat head" was probably derived originally from the images of cats on the prows of ancient and medieval ships. A cat head is a projecting block of wood or metal near the bow to which the anchor is hoisted and secured. This projection protects the hull of the vessel from the damage the anchors would cause while being lowered and hoisted. What do cats have to do with such a part of nautical architecture? Indeed, pictures of ships' cat heads in earlier eras show that they frequently had images of cat's heads on the ends of the blocks.[65] We may extend the evidence still further and suggest that the tradition of naming vessels for women and calling ships, "she," may in part represent the ancient beliefs of the goddess Isis.

The divine protectress of the sailors may still survive in another European tradition, that of the carnival. R.E. Witt has convincingly argued that the European carnival, especially popular in Catholic Europe, is a direct descendent of the sacred procession of Isis on 5 March, the *Navigium Isidis*. This procession was to celebrate the opening of the sailing season. As we saw, one such procession at Corinth was ably described by Lucius Apuleius in the mid-second century AD. Here, on 5 March, the opening of the sailing season, the celebrants of Isis donned costumes portraying different individuals, mythological figures, and divinities. A small dedicatory ship may have been carried on wheels in the procession, the *carrus navalis*. In any event, once the procession reached Cenchreae, the port of Corinth, a sacred boat, loaded up with dedications, was launched out to sea.

The European folk tradition is full of stories of religious processions with sacred boats. Witt notes that dedicatory boats carried on wheels in processions are a common occurrence in carnivals today in Italy, the Rhineland, and in southern England. Furthermore, the term *carrus navalis*, the "carriage of the ship," makes much more sense for the derivation of the word "carnival" than the traditional etymologies, *carne vale* or "farewell to the flesh," or more improbably, *carne levare* "lift up," or "away with the meat!"

Indeed, if meat consumption was a regular occurrence in pre-industrial societies, then such etymologies might make sense. But since this was manifestly not the case, they are probably mistaken. Meat consumption was rare, and often only occurred during festivals, such as Carnival.[66] So far from being a time of "farewell to meat," Carnival was probably one of the few times during the year in which most people would consume meat! Since Witt wrote his book, much work has been done concerning the survival of paganism throughout Europe, and his ideas now seem even more plausible.[67]

Another linguistic aspect that perhaps indicates an association of the Carnival and the transport of a dedicatory vessel is the word "float," used for a display wheeled along in a procession. This word, originating from Old English *flota* and Middle English *flote*, meant boat or ship.[68]

Once again, one finds cats closely associated with Carnival, especially in France. At this time of year, "witches" congregated at their sabbaths with their animals, under the protection of the devil himself in the form of a great tomcat.[69]

We may also note that the rituals concerning St Agatha in Italy and southern France closely resemble the rituals of Isis.[70] Furthermore, she is called Santa Gata in southern France, or "Saint Cat!" One will also note the closeness in spelling and pronunciation between Santa Agatha and Santa Gata.

Throughout many parts of England and France, cats were also thought to have power over death.[71] It was thought that if a cat jumped over the deceased's coffin, he would rise from the dead. Since this was to be avoided at all costs, care was taken to remove all cats from the home at these times. Often, it was thought that the cat would leave the home of its own accord after a death and not return until the funeral was over. A cat on the sick bed of an individual was thought to be a harbinger of death.[72]

In Wales, the house cat knows whether the soul of its master has gone to heaven or hell. If the cat climbs a tree immediately after death, the individual will ascend to heaven, but if it climbs down, he goes to hell.

> Cats *scent* death, that is they smell the presence of the guiding spirit who has come to take the new soul away. [73]

We have already seen the connections of the animal with the underworld from ancient Egypt and in the Greco-Egyptian cult of Isis.

Surprisingly, cats were thought to control the weather, like the goddess Isis, "Mistress of the Elements," and not merely to predict it. Naturally, this practice was thought to show the close connection between the animal and the Prince of the Air, that is, Satan.[74] Demonic agencies were thought to be responsible for storms, rains, and lightning, through the Middle Ages and well into the Renaissance. It is not surprising that Isis was regarded as one of these demonic powers by St Jerome.[75]

Ship's cats in particular,

> had the power to raise a gale ... Pussy was thought to particularly provoke a storm by playing with any article of wearing apparel, by rubbing her face, or licking the wrong way; she was sheltered from rough usage however by the belief that provoking her would bring a gale, while drowning her would cause a regular tempest.[76]

Some of the most important evidence for the survival of the cat in pagan beliefs are the persistent images of the "cat and the fiddle" that is, Bubastis and her sistrum, in religious contexts during the Middle Ages and beyond (Fig. 4.3, p. 149). These representations are found carved in the wood and stonework of many medieval cathedrals along with other pagan symbols.[77]

Finally, many through the ages have seen in the cat a wisdom beyond human comprehension. This wisdom was usually expressed in a spiritual form and was related especially to motherhood. These sentiments are still expressed, now in a secular form, by many in the twentieth century, as we shall see at the end of this chapter.

What is the explanation for the close connection between the ancient attributes of Isis and Bubastis and those of the cat in modern European folk- lore? Both are manifestations of spiritual power associated with motherhood, fertility, good luck, and the moon. For both there is an association with the cow, and for both there is the image of the "cat and the fiddle." In the lore of both, the cat can be possessed by spiritual beings, Artemis, Diana, or Isis, "the soul of Bastet" in antiquity, or demonic spirits and enchanted princesses in folklore. Black is their sacred color. They are the protectors and guardian spirits of sailors at sea. Both have profound healing powers. Both control the weather and both have power over death. Indeed, for every aspect of Isis in antiquity, there is a direct parallel in modern folklore. This is too much for coincidence. Where did this lore come from?

For the cat, there is little possibility of antiquarian revival, as in the case of Diana. For Diana, it is believed, learned inquisitors, supposedly steeped in the classics, elicited false confessions of worshipping the goddess from their tortured victims. Doubtless this sometimes occurred. Thankfully, however, European folklore is not derived from the torture of informants. At last, the rural population can speak to us directly without the fear of torture or death.

Furthermore, the Egyptianized beliefs concerning the cat scarcely appear at all in the surviving corpus of classical literature. Indeed, in Plutarch's *On Isis and Osiris*, only the fertility of the cat and its connection to the moon is mentioned. It is unlikely that the brilliant minds who sadistically tortured and burnt hundreds of thousands of female pagans alive over three centuries had access to this work. Nor is it likely that their command of Greek was so profound that even if it were accessible, it could have been understood. Nor indeed was respect for classical masterpieces so intense among medieval inquisitors that they were familiar with texts and inscriptions that have no longer survived. On the contrary, as we saw, books written by pagans and philosophers such as Aristotle continued to be burnt through the thirteenth century.

In fact, the recovery of ancient Egyptian beliefs concerning the cat has only occurred during the last century and a half. Indeed, only during the last century have these beliefs been made accessible to the public in translation. Thus we cannot expect a learned revival of Egyptianized lore among the medieval and early modern serfs. Nor is it likely that the European peas- antry and sailors of the last century eagerly purchased works that translated ancient Egyptian literature into European languages and were so impressed with the portrayals of the cat as embodiments of the natural forces of fertility, motherhood, good fortune, and control of the weather that they immediately adopted these views as their own.

The most reasonable explanation for the widespread European lore concerning the cat is the most obvious one: a genuine survival of ancient Greco-Roman and Egyptian traditions concerning the mother goddesses and their sacred animal in the countryside through the Middle Ages.

Renaissance and redemption

We first begin to see changed attitudes towards the cat in the work of numerous Renaissance artists that portray the Holy Family with a cat, now once again a symbol of motherhood, if not fertility. Perhaps the most moving of these representations is Our Lady of the Cat (Madonna del Gatto) by Baroccio (d. 1612). Here the baby John the Baptist plays with a cat while Mary and the infant Jesus look on with a smile. It is also possible that the cats are meant to represent incarnations of Isis or Diana herself. Perhaps it was thought that the goddesses were now revering one greater than themselves.

It is of interest in the context of these representations that the Renaissance was heavily influenced not only by the classical past but also by ancient Egyptian traditions. Pico della Mirandola (d. 1487) and Giordano Bruno (d. 1600) believed in a revival of Alexandrian wisdom, and regarded the Egyptian and Greek myths as being on a par with the Bible. Bruno was executed for his beliefs and della Mirandola barely escaped a similar fate. In a famous passage in his *Oration Concerning the Dignity of Man*, della Mirandola compares the Renaissance's quest for knowledge with the mysteries of Osiris:

> Using philosophy through the steps of the ladder, that is, of nature, and penetrating all things from center to center, we shall sometimes descend, with titanic force rending the unity like Osiris into many parts, and we shall sometimes ascend, with the force of Phoebus collecting the parts like the limbs of Osiris into a unity, until resting at last in the bosom of the Father who is above the ladder, we shall be made perfect with the felicity of theology.[78]

The philosophy of nature is what we call science today; della Mirandola is restating the view shared by many in the Museum and Sarapeum of Alexandria, that the discovery of God's laws leads to an understanding of God himself. It is also notable that when the limbs of Osiris are assembled, perfect, divine knowledge will be obtained. We recall that it was Isis who assembled the parts of her husband and restored his divinity.

170

However, as in the case of many Renaissance innovations, the changes only occurred at the top and had little influence on the masses, who continued to persecute, torture, and kill the animal through the nineteenth century. As Robert Darnton has observed in his essay about a massacre of cats by apprentices in a Paris printing shop in the 1730s:

> Keeping pets was as alien to the workers as torturing animals was to the bourgeois. Trapped between incomprehensible sensitivities, the cats had the worst of both worlds.[79]

The conflict was also between the ancient and medieval belief in ritual sacrifice, and the modern secular view that denied the efficacy of such practices and indeed of religion in general.

During the Enlightenment, cats and dogs began to resume their rightful place in civil society. This process began in France during the seventeenth century; Cardinal Richelieu kept dozens of cats at court. In the early eighteenth century, the French court was won over to the animal, thanks in part to Queen Maria, the wife of Louis XV, and other titled ladies who lavished attention and indulgences on their felines. Medals were struck in their honor and tombs were erected to hold their mortal remains. Numerous paintings of French ladies show them accompanied by their cats.[80]

Again in the eighteenth century, England too stopped its persecutions of women and cats. They now appear in paintings of aristocratic families. For a time, there was even a constellation called "Felis" in the stellar atlas compiled by J.E. Bode in 1795. In England there is an interesting tradition of cats attending race horses, doubtless in part to ensure good luck, as well as the removal of rodents.[81]

The restoration of the cat was combined with a restoration of rational attitudes towards public health and personal hygiene. These changes caused the plague largely to disappear from western Europe during the eighteenth century. Unfortunately, the water supply was not cleaned up and the streets were not paved until the late nineteenth century.

It may seem remarkable that the cause of bubonic plague was not discovered until 1898 by Paul Louis Simond. This is especially true since the plague first spreads among the rats, who die by the tens of thousands in the cities. Even a dead rat can be a mortal danger, for their fleas can go without feeding for up to 125 days. When their host dies, the fleas will wait patiently until another live host approaches, and can jump over a foot onto the next unfortunate victim. Merely approaching a dead rat can be a fatal mistake – only one flea bite transmitting one bacillum is enough to kill. Rat-borne diseases may have killed more than a billion during historical times (an estimated 75 million world-wide during the Black Death alone) including their destruction of food supplies. The reason no one understood the cause of the plague before 1898 is that rats, dead or alive, and flea bites were so common that no one paid them much attention.[82]

It is also of interest that Louis Pasteur admired the cat and held up its habits of cleanliness as an example for humanity to emulate if they wished to avoid getting sick. When, at last, the Europeans learned that dirt was bad and cleanliness was good, not vice versa, the cat began to resume its rightful place as guardian and protector of the house against vermin and misfortune.[83]

The twentieth century has seen the full acceptance of the cat. In 1920, after the devastation caused by the First World War and the Russian Revolution, the distinguished ailourologist Carl Van Vechten made the following shrewd observations:

> Through all the ages, even during the dark epoch of witchcraft and persecution, puss has maintained his supremacy, continued to breed and multiply, defying when convenient, the laws of God and man, now our friend, now our enemy, now wild, now tame, the pet of the hearth or the tiger of the heath, but always free, always independent, always an anarchist who insists upon his rights, whatever the cost. The cat never forms soviets; he works alone ... If men and women would become more feline, indeed it would prove the salvation of the human race. Certainly it would end war, for cats will not fight for an ideal in the mass, having no faith in mass ideals, although a single cat will fight to the death for his own ideals, his freedom of speech and expression.[84]

Van Vechten observed that other domestic animals may perpetuate group thinking, a "herd or pack mentality," and encourage popular beliefs in monstrous political panaceas. He predicted (in 1920) that the next wars would see the bombing of Berlin, Paris, Madrid, and Saigon into oblivion. But the cat will survive, because he follows nature. Man on the other hand may well become extinct because of his misapplication of natural principles to unnatural practices, the cause of our present state of human misery.

> But the great principles are obeyed by all cats to such an extent that twenty, a hundred, a thousand cats will willingly give their lives, which they might easily save, to preserve an instinct, a racial memory, which will serve to perpetuate the feline race. The result will be that, after the cataclysm, out of the mounds of heaped up earth, the piles and wrecks of half-buried cities, the desolated fields of grain, and the tortured orchards, the cat will stalk, confident, self-reliant, capable, imperturbable, and philosophical. He will bridge the gap until man appears again and then he will sit on new

hearths and again will teach his mighty lesson to ears and eyes that again are dumb and blind.[85]

No doubt the natural free spirit of the cat has attracted many to the animal in the twentieth century, a century dominated by powerful and even totalitarian systems of government. As a rebel against authority and "herd mentalities," it has become something of a symbol of resistance to the calamitous mass movements that have caused so much human destruction and bloodshed throughout the world over the last ninety years. So the cat becomes the embodiment of new values for the twentieth century, a symbol of freedom and autonomy in an era sadly lacking in those qualities.

Many also persist in seeing a spiritual element in cats, who seem to preserve the memory of the ancient heritage of their species, when they were revered as incarnate divinities in Egypt. They made their homes in the great temples, slept on purple cushions in the Holy of Holies, and were adored by millions. They remember when they accompanied Diana and her companions on their wild rides through the midnight sky. At present, if no longer revered as divinities, their behavior seems to some to show they still think they possess supernatural powers or that they are really enchanted princes or princesses. While appearing to be mere cats, in reality, they are much more, and, as befits their heritage, are entitled to our complete devotion.

In the end, though, the old symbol persists and fulfills our deepest human needs: the child who never grows up and needs a mother or a father. As such, cats have promoted our instinct to nurture others since the time of the ancient Egyptians.

APPENDIX 1

Portrayals of cats, cheetahs, and pantherines (lions, leopards) in Greek and Roman art

It is sometimes difficult to differentiate various animals portrayed in works of art unless a few basic anatomical features are discussed. Even this will not always help, because of the limitations of the artist and his familiarity with the animal he depicted, his medium, and the preservation of the object.

There are significant differences in the anatomy of cats and their larger cousins, the pantherines and cheetahs. The latter have small, rounded ears, a long narrow, high-bridged nose, ruffled throat (for the pantherines), tufted tail, and bony body, with bone structure, especially the ribs and backbone, visible under the hide. Lion hide is tawny in color, without spots or stripes. Cheetahs and leopards have spotted hides and tails.

Cats, furthermore, sometimes stand and walk with their tails held up vertically with a slight hook at the end, while the pantherines seldom do so. Often, when standing, pantherines' and cats' tails hang downwards from their rears forming a graceful shape like the letter "J." Both kinds of animal sometimes hold their tails upright, forming a letter "C," while walking or running (Figs 2.1, 3.7). Thus for doubtful representations, a vertical tail angle may be a helpful clue. Other angles are not as useful.

Almost all cats portrayed in ancient art whose variety can be discerned are either Libyan wildcats (*Felis sylvestris libyca*) or *miu*-type Egyptian domesticated cats descended from the *libyca* (*Felis sylvestris catus*, Fig. 0.2, p. 6). Cats portrayed in domestic contexts would always be the latter. They have large triangular pointed ears, a short, wide face, large eyes, clean throat, untufted tail, and furred body that gives the impression of a stockier build. The fur however is short. Usually, bone structure is not visible. The fur color and markings of the early domesticated animals are depicted in Egyptian art, Greek vase paintings, Etruscan frescos and Roman mosaics. The fur shows the basic coloration and tabby patterns of the *miu* and the *libyca*, a tawny base with darker transverse broken stripes on the sides. The tail is ringed and not spotted. To the best of my knowledge, the European wildcat (*Felis sylvestris sylvestris*), is not portrayed in ancient art. This individual has grey tabby markings, a long-haired, heavier coat, and a long-furred, bushy tail (Fig. 0.1, p. 5).

Among the difficulties confronting the ailourologist is distinguishing pantherine and cheetah cubs from adult cats portrayed in art. This is especially the case in several small Athenian lekythoi and pelikai that portray cheetah or hunting-leopard cubs. Nevertheless, anatomically, it is clear that the animals are cheetah cubs and not cats. They have rounded ears, traces of spotted coats and, importantly, proportionally larger paws. This is an indication that the animals are immature cheetahs rather than adult cats.

One of the most challenging artistic identifications is the animal that sits beneath the seat of the Cyrenean king Arkesilas depicted on a Laconian kylix dating to about 550 BC (Fig. 2.8, p. 58). This has been identified as a cheetah cub by Ashmead, but it is more likely to be a cat. Most notable is the slender, graceful feline body, typical of a short-haired adult cat. It is not the short, stocky body of a cheetah or pantherine cub. There are also the small paws, well proportioned for a cat but not for a cub. These differences are well depicted in the cheetah cubs on the small Athenian vases. Finally, the ears have flat upper sides and not the rounded shape of cub's ears. Although the ears are flattened somewhat and not in their usual, upright position, cats often flatten their ears to various degrees depending on their mood and circumstances. Finally, there is a long iconographic tradition of cats beneath chairs, both in ancient Egypt and in Greece, as we see in the coinage of the colonies Rhegion and Taras (Tarentum) in Italy.

It is usually easier to tell cats apart from dogs. The latter almost always have long, slender bodies and legs, with long snouts. The tails are usually proportionally shorter than cats' tails, which are generally one third of the combined head and body length. When dogs stand, their tails are often shown with an upright curve, like a letter "C", e.g. in the Cat and Dog Painter, Fig. 2.10 (cf. Fig. 2.9; both on p. 71). When human figures are present for scale, the dogs are always larger than the cats. Hence the probable cat on the right-hand side of the Tomb of the Triclinium at Tarquinia has a tail length of approximately one third of its (missing) head and body (see p. 91).

On occasion it seems that some artists used the cat for a model of the panther or leopard. This can best be seen in the fresco "The Infancy of Dionysos" in the Museo Nazionale in Naples. There is a leopard in the foreground with its spotted fur. Nevertheless, the head is that of a cat with its sharp triangular ears and flattened face. The body is also feline with its heavy fur, not the slender, gracile form of the adult leopard. The poorly rendered tail is without spots. The large paws may indicate that the artist attempted to depict a leopard cub, but it is clear that a cat was the model.

APPENDIX 2

Cat remains from Greek and Roman archeological sites

This appendix lists the cat remains known to me from Greece, the Aegean area, North Africa, and Europe. The numerous studies of Egyptian cat remains are discussed by Malek and Clutton-Brock, and there is no reason to repeat them here. The chronological span is from the Neolithic period (*c.* 6000 BC) through about AD 500. This list of remains is by no means complete or exhaustive. Its aim is to give a general idea of the extent of our knowledge concerning the osteological remains of cats and their approximate dates. At one time, cat remains from classical archeological sites were rare. In recent decades, however, there has been a welcome emphasis on the excavation and publication of faunal remains from these sites. Needless to say, there has also been a corresponding rise in the number of excavated and recorded cat remains. There are numerous archeological excavations being conducted at the present time that are unearthing and recording the remains of cats and other animals. Furthermore, some bones excavated in earlier decades are now being studied for the first time, or restudied and published.

Nevertheless, it has been frequently noted that cat remains are relatively scanty compared to other animals, such as goats, cattle, sheep, and dogs. To understand this, a few salient facts must be considered. First is the nature of the bones themselves. Unlike larger animals, cats have small and fragile bones that do not always survive in acidic or other unfavorable soil conditions. Often it is difficult to tell whether a small bone fragment belongs to a cat, a rabbit, or other small mammal. Furthermore, the large size of early domestic cats, often reaching 42 inches (1.07 m) in length, was comparable to the contemporary *sylvestris* and *libyca*, making it difficult to differentiate the domesticated from the wild varieties.

We must also understand the nature of cats' deaths in order to understand the circumstances for the survival of their bones. To understand their deaths, we must understand their lives. Most cats lived solitary lives in barns, villages, or as feral cats in the fields. Upon their deaths, they were unlikely to have been interred in gardens or adjoining fields or discarded in refuse pits. It has also been noted (by Lentacker and De Cupere), that when death is near, even house cats will often quietly disappear to hidden places outdoors to die alone. Under such circumstances, their bodies were probably scavenged by their ancient enemies the rats and mice, dogs, or foxes. Thus their bones may often have been completely gnawed away or scattered in small fragments in fields. Most cats died alone and unmourned. Hence it is only through chance that such remains are found.

As the excavations of the gardens of Pompeii have shown, some house cats received a proper burial in the family's garden upon their deaths. Yet until the 1970s, when the gardens were excavated beneath the ancient surface, no domestic cat remains had been found at Pompeii. Unless archeologists excavate beneath the surface levels of ancient fields and gardens, they are likely to miss such remains, but such procedures would of course be enormously time-consuming and expensive, well beyond the resources of most excavators.

It is probable that most, if not all, the cat remains that have been found in or near human settlements were of domestic animals. In general, the *sylvestris* shuns human company and settlements. As we have seen, Oppian noted (2. 572) that the *sylvestris* was not generally hunted in classical antiquity. Plutarch observed (959E) that cats in general were not consumed as food except in times of famine. Since they were not generally eaten, cats are not found in refuse pits with the remains of other animal bones that were consumed.

Thus the *sylvestris* would have seldom found its way into a human settlement on its own, nor would it have been brought in as a source of food from hunting. Cat remains found in settlements would therefore usually be those of the *catus*. Many of the specific locations of the cat remains, i.e. deliberate burials in the gardens of Pompeii, also suggest domesticated individuals. As was seen in Chapter 2, it is likely that all cat remains found on Mediterranean islands were from individuals or descendants of individuals who were brought there by man. The most likely candidate for this transport was the *catus*.

Finally, it must be remembered that just as one cat bone means that the entire cat was once present, so one cat usually implies the presence of others. Given their high fertility rates, where there are a few cats, there will soon be many more. While the presence of bones is proof that cats were once present at a site, the absence of bones does not necessarily prove that they were absent, especially given the rudimentary state of our archeological knowledge.

For the remains from Italy and North Africa, I am indebted to Michael MacKinnon. I am also indebted to him for helpful bibliography. See his forthcoming thesis from the University of Alberta, *The Animal Economy of Roman Italy: Integration of Zooarchaeological and Textual Data*, for further source information. For information on Greece and the Aegean region I am indebted to David Reese of the Field Museum of Natural History, and also for his assistance with bibliography. The shortcomings of this list are entirely my own. It is to be hoped that in the future one may be able to obtain more indices of excavated animal bones, listed by site, date, species, and variety, as was provided by Luff for Roman western Europe in 1982. Such works are of great assistance to those interested in the history of animals and their relation to man. I have relied on compendia of archeological data compiled by Luff, Lentacker, de Cupere, and others, as well as the personal communications of the learned authorities, MacKinnon and Reese. I have given the sources used for each region in parentheses.

The listings will be in alphabetical order by region with the approximate dates, if known. The following abbreviations will be used: EB – Early Bronze; EH – Early Helladic; MB – Middle Bronze; MH – Middle Helladic; LB – Late Bronze; LH – Late Helladic. All dates are approximate and become less accurate for earlier eras.

CYPRUS

(DAVIS, MORGAN, REESE PERS. COMM.)

Erimi   Neolithic/Chalcolithic remains.

Khirokitia   *Felis* mandible from Early Neolithic (*c.* 6000 BC).

Pamboula   Remains from Chalcolithic levels (*c.* 3900–3700 BC).

Tenta   Several Late Neolithic remains (*c.* 4500–3900 BC).

Vrysi   Several Late Neolithic remains (*c.* 4500–3900 BC).

GREECE AND THE AEGEAN

(MORGAN, NOBIS, DEMAKOPOULOU AND CROUWEL)

Kalapodi, Lokris   Bronze Age cat remains.

Kastana, Macedonia   Bronze Age cat remains.

Kea   Bronze Age cat remains.

Messene   remains from Late Archaic to Late Classical (*c.* 800–300 BC); 2 remains from Hellenistic era (*c.* 300–100 BC).

Seratse   Late Bronze Age remains.

Sitagroi   Neolithic cat remains.

Thera   Possible cat remains from before 1628 BC.

Tiryns   Bronze Age *Felis* remains.

TROY, TURKEY

(REESE, PERS. COMM.)

Troy I (EB)   One *Felis* ulna.

Troy II (EB)   Three *Felis* remains: 1 mandible; 1 maxilla; 1 proximal ulna.

Troy III (EB)   18 *Felis* remains: 4 mandible fragments; 7 vertebrae; 1 pelvis, 1 pelvis fragment; 1 skull fragment; 1 proximal radius; 1 proximal femur, 1 distal femur; 1 tibia.

Troy IV (EB)   2 *Felis* remains: 1 distal humerus; 1 vertebra.

Troy VI (MH–LH I–III)   1 *Felis* mandible.

Troy IX (Roman)   2 *Felis* mandibles.

ITALY

(MACKINNON PERS. COMM.)

Capaccio, Campania   Several bones for a minimum of three cats from a Hellenistic pit (*c.* 300–30 BC).

Carminiello, near Naples   Semi-complete skeletons from fifth- to sixth-century deposits.

Matrice, Roman villa in the Biferno Valley   Several cat bones from Late Roman levels (*c.* AD 300–500).

Naples, Santa Patrizia   A few undated ancient or medieval remains.

Naples, Via San Paolo   A few undated ancient or medieval remains.

Ostia, bath   2 bones from fifth to third centuries BC from a *F. sylvestris*.

Otranto   A few bones from medieval levels, none from the Roman era.

Pompeii   A few bones found in the gardens and elsewhere from Pompeii dating before AD 79.

Rome Schola Praeconum *on the Palatine Hill*   2 cat bones from late antiquity (*c.* AD 350–500).

Rome: Via Gabinia, late antique site near the city. 1 cat bone fragment (*c.* 350–500 AD).

San Giacomo, central Adriatic coast   Approximately 12 cat bones from the early fifth century AD. Some cuts on one bone may indicate skinning.

San Giovanni di Ruoti   Several domesticated cat remains from Late Roman deposits (AD 350–55).

Settefinestre, Tuscany   9 cat bones from *c.* AD 130–180.

NORTH AFRICA

(MACKINNON, PERS. COMM.)

Berenice, Libya   About 100 cat bones, 42 from late first century to mid-third century; 3 individuals found in Roman cistern.

Carthage, Tunisia   84 cat bones from Vandal–Byzantine levels.

Carthage, Bir Djebbana, Tunisia   Several Roman cat remains.

Setif, Algeria   A few cat bones from the Roman era.

Wadi el-Amud, Libya   1 cat bone from late first to third century.

FRANCE

(LUFF)

Marseilles   2 bone remains, Roman era.

Montmaurin   5 cat remains, Roman era.

BELGIUM

(LENTAKER AND DE CUPERE, LUFF)

Braives   Cat remains from Roman well.

Burst, near Erpe-Mere   Roman tile with cat paw print.

Eprave   Roman remains found in a cave site.

Piringen, near Tongeren   Mandible found in Roman villa site.

St Gilles in Namur   Roman cat remains.

NETHERLANDS

(LUFF)

Rijswijk   Remains from Native farmstead, AD 150–200.

Tritsum   1 cat bone, AD 100.

Valkenburg   1 individual, first to third century.

SWITZERLAND

(LUFF)

Basel   1 individual in Roman pit beneath cathedral.

Gorbelhof   2 remains, Roman era.

Schaan   1 cat bone, fourth century.

GERMANY

(LUFF)

Butzbach   1 remain, AD 130–235.

Hüfingen   3 cat remains, third century.

Kempten (Cambodunum) 2 cat remains, first to third centuries.

Künzing (Quintana) 4 remains, Roman era.

Lorch (Lauriacum) 4 Roman remains, second to third centuries.

Lorenzberg 1 cat bone, late Roman era.

Vemania 3 remains, late Roman era.

AUSTRIA

(LUFF)

Magdalensberg 26 remains, 15 BC – AD 45.

HUNGARY

(BÖKÖNYI)

Tac, Roman villa site Remains of 14 individual cats.

ENGLAND

(LUFF, HARCOURT, CLUTTON-BROCK, TOYNBEE, MARSDEN, BURKE)

Chelmsford (Caesaromagus) Cat remains from votive wells, *c.* AD 150–200.

Chesham Roman cat from Latimer villa.

Gussage All Saints, Dorset 5 kittens, 2 adults from Middle Iron Age, *c.* 250 BC.

London, Southwark Several remains from first to second century AD.

Lullingstone, Kent 1 individual from Roman villa site.

Pevensey (Anderida), Sussex 1 cat skull in fifth-century well.

Silchester Cat paw prints on Roman tile.

Wroxeter Cremation burial of Roman cat.

APPENDIX 3

The *Vox in Rama* of Gregory IX

One of the most significant events in the history of witchcraft and the cat is the promulgation of Pope Gregory IX's first bull of the *Vox in Rama*, on 13 June 1233. This decree urged the German bishops to give all their support to the zealous papal Inquisitor, Conrad of Marburg, who through torture and terror had encouraged some to confess that they worshipped Lucifer and his diabolical black cat. The bull warns the bishops of Mainz and Hildesheim about the satanic cult that Conrad has found in their dioceses.[1]

There are four separate documents in the *Vox in Rama*; only the first and most important one mentions the cat. The three remaining documents encourage greater zeal amongst the inquisitors. It is the first that is translated here.

> To the archbishop of Moguntinum [Mainz, Siegfried III], the bishop of Hildesheim [Conrad II], and Conrad of Marburg: Proclamation of the word of God.
>
> A voice is heard in Ramah [Matthew 2:18], with wailing and loud lamentation. Rachael, namely the holy mother church, weeps for her children, who the devil smites and destroys. She cannot be consoled since, as vipers lacerate the womb of their mother when they are born, so her own children strive to destroy her. Now with many violent pains, since the birth mother still contains them within her, she cries out, "Oh, my anguished womb! Oh, my anguished womb!" like the prophet [Jeremiah] lamented. As, according to the Apostle [Paul] all creatures groan in travail, so the sacred womb of the mother church is wracked with pain, since they dismember her flesh with each bite. If indeed this tortured serpent gives birth by the hand of God in its appropriate hollow, so we certainly ought to ordain instruction for the carnal hearts of men.
>
> He [the devil] fights against men's hearts from without since he does not rule them from within. Because his rule within them has perished, he wages war from without, and renews the persecution of the church, the bride of Christ, the very bride of Christ, through his

183

ministers of iniquity. Indeed, he did not stand in truth from the first, but strives to change truth into lies, so that his venom pours forth in widespread fraud. He labors to destroy pregnant souls, lest a faithful child, conceived from divine love, might from birth prevent the consummation of his works.

Hence we who have care of her fecundity are injured, as if wounded by a perfidious sword's point. Through the evil hearts of these heretics, the womb of the church is torn apart, and we are attacked in silence as if by the hunting arrows of these new and confusing errors. The whole spirit is full of bitterness. Our bile (*iecur*) pours out over the land, our soul is thrown into severe tumult, and our heart is full of suffering. Our eyes have run out of tears from crying. The kidneys (*renes*) tremble at such nefarious abominations and all our flesh is in turmoil. We are not able to suppress our tears or contain our sighs. Nevertheless, although your letters are full of great, unmixed, and terrible pain, they will not restrict us to a meaningless demonstration against these errors.

Among the diverse types of heresy that have corrupted Germany with grievous sins, one is both far more detestable and much more common than the rest. These horrors should not only be brought before us but also be heard by us, since the heresy is already breaking out with intensity among some renowned members of the church. This heresy is discordant to all reason, contrary to all piety, odious to all hearts, inimical to all that is in heaven and earth, and is not only contrary to reasonable humans, but even contrary to those that lack reason. Since this plague of theirs exceeds insanity, the very elements themselves ought to rise up and arm themselves against it.

Now this pestilence arises from the following beginnings. At first, a certain postulant [potential initiate] enters this school of perdition (*scholas perditorum*) and is received. A kind of frog appears, which some are accustomed to call a toad. Some kiss it on its rear end and others give the damnable kiss on the mouth, receiving the tongue and saliva of the beast in their mouth. Along with the frog, sometimes a number of other animals are present, such as geese or ducks. These are often placed in an oven (*furni*) to bake. Then a thin pallid man comes forward to see the postulant. He appears like the skin drawn over bones that is left after some meat is consumed, and has the blackest of eyes. The postulant kisses him and feels cold and frigid. After the kiss, the memory of the Catholic faith completely disappears from his heart. They recline on couches during the banquet and they stand up when the meal is over. At this time, a black cat (*gattus niger*), the size of a small dog, with an upright tail descends backwards down a statue which is usually at the meeting.

The postulant first kisses the cat's rear, then the master of the sect, and then other individuals in order who are worthy of the honor and perfect. Those who are imperfect and those not regarded as worthy, receive a word of peace from the master. Then, each member takes his place and after singing some songs, they face the cat in turn (*ac versus gattum capitibus inclinatis*). The master says, "Save us" (*parce nobis*) to the cat, and the one next to him states this. Then those present respond three times and say, "We know the master," and four times they say, "and we ought to obey you."

When this is done, they extinguish the candle, and proceed to perform the most sordid acts of dissipation; no distinction is made between strangers and family members. If the numbers of men in the meeting exceeds the numbers of females, they are led to ignominious passions. Burning with desire in turn, the men perform shameful acts with men. Similarly, the women change their rightful nature for that which is against nature and perform damnable acts with each other. When these most nefarious sins are completed and the candle is relit, each one returns to his proper place.

Thereupon a man proceeds from an obscure corner of the meeting, for they do not withdraw themselves from the most damnable of men. They say that the upper part of his body shines with rays brighter than the sun [i.e. he is Lucifer, the Lightbearer], the lower part is hairy like a cat (*hispidus sicut gattus*). His light illuminates the whole place. Then the master takes part of the clothing of the postulant and says to the shining one, "Master, I give you this gift from me." The shining man responds, "You have often served me well and may you continue to serve me well. I commit to your care the one whom you have dedicated." Having said this, he straightaway disappears.

They also receive the Body of Christ [the communion wafer] from the priest once a year on Easter and bring it back home while it is still in their mouths. There, they spit it into the latrine with contumely for the Redeemer. In addition, these miserable wretches, blaspheming the rule of heaven with polluted lips, even assert in their ravings that their lord of heaven, Lucifer, was violently, painfully, and unjustly thrown into Hell (*infernos*). The wretches even believe and affirm that their lord was the founder of heaven, and that he will return there in glory as the most high lord. They hope they will obtain eternal bliss from him, and not in spite of him. All that is pleasing to God they do not allow to be done, and that which he hates, they are able to do.

What sorrow! Who would dare to do such things? Who would think such wickedness possible? Who would not be able to abominate such perfidy? Who would not be enraged at such iniquity?

Who would not be inflamed against such perdition and the sons of perdition? Where is the zealous Moses who on one day killed 23,000 [*viginti tria milia*, modern texts say 3,000]? Where is zealous Phineas who killed a Jewish man and a Midianite woman with a single thrust of a spear? Where is zealous Elijah who put 450 prophets of Baal to the sword in the torrent of Kishon? Where is zealous Mattathias who was so inflamed with righteous anger, that he rose up and killed a Jewish man upon the altar as he was sacrificing to an idol? Where is the authority of Peter, who, when Ananias and Sapphira were not afraid to lie to the Holy Ghost, struck them dead? Certainly, he would rise up against such a land and their iniquities, revealing them to the stars of heaven, and make manifest their sins to the entire world.

Not only mankind but also the elements would unite together for their ruin and destruction, blotting them out from the face of the earth. They would spare none on account of their sex or estate, and the wretches would have the eternal opprobrium of all humanity. No vengeance against them is too harsh. Furthermore, it is quite fitting that this pestilence be ground down as if by the pounding of the sea. We also know that the hand of God is not weak, and that it is not possible to smelt or purify this unadulterated dross into an alloy of silver; since they seek to conceal their innermost hearts by strong contrition. Some may think it possible to charge that we have neglected to reform them by the correction of rods and axes (*fasciis*), or by cherishing them with the oil of gentleness. We hope that in your anger, you will not cease to have mercy, and that your pious heart will not always be constrained against them, so that the heat of your wrath will forcibly bring them to the correction that we labor to provide. Although your truth is not the commissioned word of God, he pours out his grace to you in a flood that flows in all things.

We ask that you will have the power of deeds and words at your discretion. We admonish and exhort you in the Lord, so that, thanks to you, we can bring about the redemption of these sinners, mitigating their suffering with a salve and curing their wounds. Hence, by the peace of the angels, you will labor diligently offering a remedy for their wound and correcting them with solicitude. But if it should happen that the wound must be extracted by your threatening sword, do not neglect to use this gift, so that their scars will not putrefy. This wound is like a desperate penitent who is not inclined to return to the lap of the mother church. You must show great caution and perseverance in your conversions, so that by no means may it be feared that they will return to error. In such a grave and serious disease there might be a recurrence and a harsher remedy may be needed when a weaker medication is not sufficient. And you must bring fire and sword against the wounds if the medication of poultices does not work, since putrefying flesh must be cut off from the intact whole. You will be the advocate against them, those who harbor them, their defenders, and partisans, in both spiritual and material matters, and use the power of the sword. You will warn them carefully and induce them efficaciously to turn towards the universal fidelity of Christ. You must rise up and arm yourselves bravely against these heretics in your assistance of Christ.

You shall have complete trust in the omnipotent mercy granted to us by the authority of the blessed apostles Peter and Paul. Since God grants this mercy to us, he has conferred on us the power to bind and release. Therefore, we shall increase the indulgences and privileges of all penitents and confessing Christians who will raise up the sign of the cross and arm themselves for the eradication of these heretics (*ad eorundem hereticorum exterminium se accinxerint*). We shall also provide assistance for them, as is provided for those who journey to the Holy Land.

Given from the Lateran on the Ides of June in the seventh year [of our authority, 13 June 1233].

Here, in microcosm, we see much of the rueful religious and secular history of Europe for the last 1,500 years. First, the victimhood of the perpetrator of evil is established. The heretics, who in this instance were probably pagans, were said to have had the same relation to the church as infant vipers had to their mother, who, it was thought, was torn apart by their offspring during their birth. As Edmund Burke observed about the French Revolution, the worst atrocities are often committed by those that claim to be victims.[2] Next, defamatory lies, the more outrageous the better, are told about the poor wretches who are about to be tortured and killed without mercy. The false accusations of incest and indiscriminate sexual orgies were already an ancient part of the language of defamation when the *Vox in Rama* was written. After de-humanizing them with false and absurd charges, the crescendo of hate mounts: how can such subhumans, variously described as a pestilence, wounds, putrefying flesh, and dross metal, be allowed to survive? Finally, there is the call to eradicate (*exterminium*) the unfortunates if they do not see the light.

Since the heretics are subhuman, anyone who kills them will not only not be punished for killing fellow human beings whose only crime was not to be orthodox Christians (or kissing frogs and cats!), but will actually enjoy expanded privileges and honors. In fact, they will have the same honors as the crusaders who killed and ate the unfortunate inhabitants of the Holy Land. The same story is repeated *ad infinitum*. At other times and places such hateful attacks against other despised and powerless groups have led to

187

their forcible "conversion" or extermination, or have turned them into legitimate targets for the aggression of others.

In the document, the black cat is actually addressed as "master" by the worshippers, indicating he is an incarnation of Satan. The shining man is of course Lucifer himself, the bearer of light. He is in fact half-cat, and may be the same black cat who figures prominently in the initiation ritual in a different guise. This reminds one of the medieval folk saying that the Devil borrows his cloak from a black cat. It is of interest in this context that in the Roman pagan tradition, the epithet Lucifera "Bearer of Light," was sometimes given to Diana.[3] The pallid man with the black eyes is apparently a minion of Satan and not Satan himself. We may recall from the Epilogue the Welsh folk saying:

> Kiss a black cat
> An' 'twill make ye fat:
> Kiss the white ane
> An' 'twill make ye lean.

Now this folk belief or custom has been demonized beyond all recognition. We also note that the kissing of a frog has long remained a European folk belief. As we have seen, there is good evidence that the black cat was still sacred to Isis and Bubastis during this era. It is also possible that the geese and ducks were associated with the Celtic goddess Sequana, to whom these animals were sacred.

The *Vox in Rama* is the first official church document that condemns the black cat as an incarnation of Satan, and consequently it was the death warrant for the animal, which would continue to be slaughtered without mercy until the early nineteenth century. It is said that very few all-black cats survive in western Europe as a result. Pope Innocent VIII officially excommunicated all cats and decreed that any that were found in the possession of "witches" should be burnt along with them.[4]

Of interest in this context is the medieval demon Baphomet, who also embodies many characteristics of Bubastis. Worshippers of this "demon" were thought to enjoy good harvests, good health, and wealth. The demon himself was sometimes portrayed with female breasts, reminiscent of the Egyptian statuettes of Bastet and her images on the garment worn by Diana of Ephesus from the Villa Albani.[5]

NOTES

INTRODUCTION

1 Christopher Smart, "Of Jeoffry, My Cat," written between 1756 and 1763. Quoted by R. Altman, *The Quintessential Cat*, New York, Macmillan, 1994, p. xiii. Because the poem was untitled, it appears under various names.

2 A fact noted as early as Diodorus 20. 58. 2 in connection with the Libyan campaign of Agathocles in 307 BC. In central Libya, at that time forested, native wildcats had killed so many birds in the region, that there were none to be seen. Presumably, they had fled and roosted elsewhere. R. Tabor, *Understanding Cats*, Pleasantville, N.Y., Reader's Digest, 1994, p. 102, shows that cats have been unjustly blamed for declines in bird populations. This is also a conclusion of G.J. Patronek, "Free-roaming and Feral Cats – Their Impact on Wildlife and Human Beings," *Journal of the American Veterinary Medical Association*, 1998, vol. 212, p. 221, discussed below. Indeed, rats will eat eggs and attack fledglings in their nests with impunity. Thus a predator that kills rats will be a benefit to bird populations. R. Hendrickson, *More Cunning than Man: A Social History of Rats and Men*, New York, Stein and Day, 1983, p. 39 for the destruction of bird populations by rats.

3 Of the few works on the topic, we may mention L. Bodson, "Les debuts en Europe du chat domestique," *Ethnozootechnie*, 1987, vol. 40, pp. 13–38; J.M.C. Toynbee, *Animals in Roman Life and Art*, Baltimore, Johns Hopkins University Press, 1996, reprint of 1973, pp. 87–90; *RE*, s.v. Katze; O. Keller, *Die Antike Tierwelt*, vol. 1, Hildesheim, Georg Olms, 1963, reprint of 1909, pp. 67–85; C. Tétrault, "L'histoire des chats à Rome," *Société des Études Anciennes du Québec*, 1995, vol. 2, pp. 69–71; A. Lentaker and B. De Cupere, "Domestication of the Cat and Reflections on the Scarcity of Finds in Archaeological Contexts," in L. Bodson, ed., *Des animaux introduits par l'homme dans la faune de Europe*, Liège, Université de Liège, 1994, pp. 71–8; and short sections in F.E. Zeuner, *A History of Domesticated Animals*, New York, Harper and Row, 1963; J. Clutton-Brock, *Cats, Ancient and Modern*, Cambridge, Mass., Harvard University Press, 1993. In addition to these works, there is a great mass of superficial, often inaccurate, references to classical cats in popular treatments of the animal that are too numerous to mention.

4 For the most recent work on the evolution of the cat see S.J. O'Brien and M. Antón, "The Family Line: The Human–Cat Connection," *National Geographic*, 1997, vol. 191, pp. 77–85, esp. p. 78.

5 E.M. Thomas, *The Tribe of Tiger*, New York, Simon and Schuster, 1994, pp. 18–29 is the basis of this discussion.

6 Ibid., p. 22. My cat Daphne spent her first weeks in an animal shelter with no opportunity to learn hunting from her mother. Nevertheless, she is an accomplished hunter of rodents, birds, and insects, as I am frequently reminded.

7 A former cat of ours, Harvey, a white male tom cat, could jump from the bottom of an empty swimming pool, seven feet to the top.

8 The most famous recent example of this is the cat Scarlet of Brooklyn, N. Y., who on 30 March 1996 rescued five of her kittens from a burning building, and nearly expired herself. Associated Press story appearing on 2 April 1996, *Arkansas Democrat Gazette*, p. 4A: "She ran in and out of that burning building five times, got them all out and then started to move them one by one across the street," reported firefighter David Gianelli. At the time of writing, Scarlet and her surviving kittens have all found good homes. The Greek historian Herodotus, *Histories*, 2. 66. 3–4, also noted this characteristic, however imperfectly.

9 Thomas, op.cit., p. 25.

10 Thomas, op.cit., p. 36.

11 Patronek, op.cit., p. 221, and the sources cited; Beadle, pp. 28, 222–3. This is also the number of kills estimated by the Australians for their own native species by stray cats. Mother cats that must feed their kittens probably kill more.

12 P.B. Churcher and J.H. Lawton, "Beware Well-Fed Felines," *Natural History*, July 1989, p. 46.

13 Tabor, *Understanding*, p. 102.

14 Patronek, op.cit., p. 223.

15 G.J. Patronek, op.cit., p. 221. Furthermore, as Patronek notes (p. 222), rodents are the main element in cats' diets which are also bird predators, especially of their eggs. I have noted my cats Katie, Daphne, and Zsa Zsa taking birds that had already died, probably of natural causes. As Patronek points out, the number of prey eaten by a predator is not necessarily the same number killed by it.

16 Tabor, *Understanding*, p. 62.

17 Tabor, *Understanding*, pp. 32–4; Van Vechten, pp. 64, 110. Cf. Erasmus Darwin's poem, "Signs of Foul Weather":

> Puss on the hearth, with velvet paws,
> Sits wiping o'er his whiskered jaws.

Saki, a female Siamese owned by LeRoy and Helen Middleworth, predicted a tornado that struck Venice, Florida in March 1988. She hid under the bed before the storm and could not be removed until after it had passed.

18 Quoted by Tabor, *Understanding*, p. 32.

19 Van Vechten, p. 108; Briggs, pp. 71–2. See the discussion in the Epilogue.

20 Beadle, p. 122.

21 European female cats generally come into heat twice a year, in January and June, Clutton-Brock, *Cats*, p. 15. I calculated these numbers myself.

22 Beadle, pp. 203–4; Dioscorides, *Materia Medica*, 2. 49, ed. R.T. Gunther, where ingesting the liver of a rabid dog is recommended as protection against hydrophobia. Rabies or hydrophobia is not recorded as an ancient Mediterranean disease in other Greek or Latin literary sources, nor is it apparent in paleopathological studies of animal or human remains recorded by our standard modern works on ancient diseases. JoAnn Scurlock has found references to dog bites causing insanity in humans in Mesopotamian sources dating to about 2000 BC, as I learned from personal communication on 1 May

1998. There are recorded descriptions of the disease in China dating to the sixth century BC, D. Brothwell and A.T. Sandison, *Diseases in Antiquity*, Springfield, Ill., C.C. Thomas, 1967, p. 229. Otherwise, it does not appear in the literary or paleopathological sources discussed in D. Grmek, *Diseases in the Ancient Greek World*, Baltimore, Johns Hopkins University Press, 1989, trans. of 1983 edn; G. Majno, *The Healing Hand: Man and Wound in the Ancient World*, Cambridge, Mass., Harvard University Press, 1975; E.D. Phillips, *Aspects of Greek Medicine*, New York, St. Martins, 1973; J. Baker and D. Brothwell, *Animal Diseases in Archaeology*, London, Academic Press, 1980.

23 Clutton-Brock, *Cats*, esp. pp. 9–13. See also Lentaker and De Cupere, op.cit., pp. 69–78.
24 Clutton-Brock, *Cats*, pp. 12–13; Beadle, pp. 63–5, "*F. Sylvestris {sylvestris}* is quite untamable; even if raised from kittenhood by human beings, it remains fierce and intractable. It is hard to imagine any European wild cat developing the docility which must be a preamble to domestication. Its African cousin, on the other hand, tames easily."
25 *Webster's Collegiate Dictionary*, 5th edn, Springfield, Mass., Merriam, 1936, s.v. feline. Today, the large cats such as lions, leopards, jaguars, and tigers are placed in the genus Panthera. S.J. O'Brien and M. Antón, op.cit., pp. 77–85.
26 This is indeed the topic of Elizabeth Marshall Thomas' excellent book.
27 Diodorus 20. 58. 2.
28 See the discussion in Chapter 2.
29 In fact, one of the world's most famous ship's cats (unnamed) went on Scott's expedition to the South Pole in 1912, and was the first recorded cat to land and overwinter on that continent, Tabor, *Cats*, pp. 86–8. Cats may therefore have a wider distribution than rats or mice.
30 H. Silvester, *Cats in the Sun*, San Francisco, Chronicle Books, 1994, pp. 5–7.
31 A. Burford, *Land and Labor in the Greek World*, Baltimore, Johns Hopkins University Press, 1993, pp. 56–7; R. Osborne, *Classical Landscape with Figures: The Ancient Greek City and its Countryside*, Dobbs Ferry, N. Y., Sheridan House, 1987, pp. 53–61;
32 Thomas, op.cit., pp. 100–1.
33 Sylvester, op.cit.
34 Ibid., p. 6.
35 Ibid., p. 5.
36 E. Topsell, *The History of Four-Footed Beasts*, London, 1607, quoted by Clutton-Brock, *Cats*, p. 19.
37 Quoted in Tabor, *Cats*, p. 88.
38 Beadle, p. 94.
39 Hendrickson, op.cit., p. 18. The following discussion of mice and rats will be based on Hendrickson.
40 S.J.M. Davis, *The Archeology of Animals*, New Haven, Yale University Press, 1987, p. 182; R.A. Harcourt, "The Animal Bones," in G.J. Wainwright, *Gussage All Saints: An Iron Age Settlement in Dorset*, London, HMSO, 1979, p. 155.
41 Hendrickson, op.cit., p. 180–1.
42 J. Scarborough, *Medical Terminologies: Classical Origins*, Norman, Okla., University of Oklahoma Press, 1992, pp. 158–60.
43 P.L. Armitage, "Unwelcome Companions, Ancient Rats Reviewed," *Antiquity*, 1994, vol. 68, pp. 231–40.
44 Hendrikson, op.cit., pp. 102–3.

45 In contrast, brown rats average between 10 and 17 oz (280–480 gm) in weight, total length 13–18 inches (330–460 mm), body length 7–10 inches (180–250 mm), tail length 6–8 inches (160–200 mm). The largest brown rats weigh in at 3½ lbs (1.5 kg) and have a total length of nearly 2 feet (610 mm), Hendrickson, op.cit., pp. 70–1.

46 Hendrickson, op.cit., pp. 40–1, lists thirty-five diseases borne by mice and rats at present. Of these, typhus, bubonic plague, Salmonellosis, Rickettsia in the Roman but not in the Greek era, leptospirosis and possibly trichinosis existed in antiquity and are discussed by Grmek, op.cit. and Brothwell and Sandison, op.cit.

47 Hendrickson, op.cit., pp. 36, 84, 180.

48 Toynbee, op.cit., pp. 102–24; Hendrickson, op.cit., p. 99. There were also dogs trained to do tricks.

49 Hendrikson, op.cit., pp. 97–9. 200,000 cats were also killed in 1665–6 according to Daniel Defoe, *Journal of the Plague Year*, cited by Hendrickson, op.cit., p. 101.

50 H. Zinsser, *Rats, Lice, and History*, Boston, Little Brown, 1935, pp. 153–65. He also noted that high explosives have less destructive power than rodents.

1 EGYPT

1 "The Address to the Gods," from *The Book of the Dead* in M. Lichtheim, *Ancient Egyptian Literature*, vol. 2, Berkeley, University of California Press, 1976, pp. 128; substituting the term "eternity" for "the Open-mouthed" since the ceremony of opening the mouth of the deceased is necessary for a blessed life after death (p. 120).

2 British Museum Press, 1993.

3 Malek, pp. 24–5.

4 Diodorus 20. 58. 2. See now the Ph.D. dissertation of Donald Taylor, *The Logistics of the Roman Army in Africa*, University of Arkansas, 1997, pp. 47–78.

5 *NA* 4. 44.

6 *NA* 5. 7.

7 *NA* 5. 30, 10. 29.

8 Malek, p. 47.

9 F.J. Yurco, "The Cat and Ancient Egypt," *Field Museum of Natural History Bulletin*, 1990, vol. 61, pp. 15–23, esp. p. 17. He has personally observed Egyptian cats killing venomous snakes.

10 Malek, pp. 45–51.

11 Ibid., pp. 59–62.

12 Ibid., pp. 57–65.

13 Ibid., pp. 65–9.

14 A.B. Lloyd, *Herodotus Book II: Commentary 1–98*, Leiden, Brill, 1976, p. 293.

15 Ibid., pp. 73–6.

16 Here I respectfully disagree with Malek's contention (p. 75) that Herodotus misrepresented the sacral nature of animals in Egypt. Neither Herodotus nor Diodorus show any malice towards the Egyptians and their religion. In fact, Herodotus refrains from mentioning many aspects of Egyptian religion out of respect for their traditions. Diodorus is a fair observer and historian, not without errors indeed, as with the rest of us. Furthermore, Herodotus gains much of his information from native informants, who must have been well aware of their own traditions. That the information provided by these informants may not always be to our liking, is no reason to reject it. Diodorus also,

like a good historian, gains his evidence from questioning the priests themselves and from his own personal observations. There is sufficient evidence
from these and other late sources to show that many animals were sacred in
Egypt from the fifth century BC to the early Empire. However, our good
sources also make it clear that the animals themselves were not worshipped.
This notion is indeed a fallacy, but is not repeated by Herodotus, Diodorus, or
other honest sources.

17 Lloyd, *Commentary 1–98*, p. 293.
18 Ibid., p. 294.
19 Malek, p. 78.
20 Ibid., p. 79.
21 Christopher Smart, "Of his Cat Jeoffrey," quoted by R. Altman, *The
 Quintessential Cat*, New York, Macmillan, 1994, p. xiii.
22 The sense of death possessed by cats and its associations with the underworld
 will be discussed further in Chapter 3.
23 Smart in Altman, op.cit., p. xiii.
24 Smart in Altman, op.cit., p. xiii.
25 Quoted by F. Gettings, *The Secret Lore of the Cat*, New York, Carol Publishing,
 1989, p. 25.
26 R. Tabor, *Understanding Cats*, Pleasantville, N. Y., Reader's Digest, 1994,
 p. 27.
27 Malek, pp. 93–9.
28 R. Bagnall and B. Frier, *The Demography of Roman Egypt*, Cambridge,
 Cambridge University Press, 1993, esp. p. 139; N. Demand, *Childbirth, Death,
 and Motherhood in Classical Greece*, Baltimore, Johns Hopkins University Press,
 1994.
29 There are many excellent works devoted to the ancient family written by historians such as Lacy, Treggiari, Dixon, and Bradley, to name but a few. However,
 it was only recently with the publication of works such as Demand's (above
 note 28) in 1994 that demographic factors have finally been taken seriously for
 the lives of ancient women. The situation is different in the study of the classics, however. Here one seldom encounters the fact that motherhood, family,
 childbirth, and childrearing were central to the lives of nearly all women. One
 recent book written by several classicists, purportedly on women in the classical world, devotes approximately five pages to these important aspects out of
 250. One section indeed pertains to "childrearing by Amazon men"! It is not
 stated how infants would have been nursed under such circumstances. But such
 is the delusional view of women when they are seen as "texts" and "images"
 rather than flesh-and-blood human beings. Fortunately, the constraints on
 women in pre- and non-industrial societies are well known in other fields. See
 for example, L.T. Ulrich, *A Midwife's Tale: The Life of Martha Ballard, Based on
 Her Diary, 1785–1812*, New York, Knopf, 1990. This excellent book studies
 the diary of Martha Ballard, who lived in Massachusetts and Kennebec, Maine.
 Of surprise to no one, even during the early industrial era, her life centered on
 marriage, family, childbirth, childrearing, suffering, illness, and death. Her
 main economic concerns and those of her daughters and other women in her
 life were taking care of their households, together with the carding, spinning,
 weaving, sewing, and mending of cloth.
30 R. Tabor, *Cats: The Rise of the Cat*, London, BBC Books, 1991, p. 80.
31 Ibid., p. 182.
32 If we give the population of Egypt as three million, approximately one half, or
 1.5 million, will be over the age of 18 or 19 in a country with a low life

expectancy at birth. Hence about half of the adult population may have been in attendance. However, Herodotus' numbers are often inaccurate, whether misrepresented by his sources, or misrecorded by later scribes copying his work over 2,000 years before the printing press.

33 Malek, p. 100.

34 I am grateful to Dr Elias Saad for this suggestion. In general, colloquial Arabic words may be of greater antiquity than those in classical Arabic. The word *bast* has a hard "t." Beadle, p. 75, asserts this common etymology with Pasht. The *OED*, s.v. Puss, notes that the word is confined to Germanic languages as a call-word for cats.

35 Malek, pp. 123–34.

36 P. Cairo Zen. 59. 451, cited in M. Austin, *The Hellenistic World From Alexander to the Roman Conquest*, Cambridge, Cambridge University Press, 1981, p. 419.

37 U. Wilcken, *Urkunden der Ptolemaerzeit*, vol. 2, Berlin, 1957, p. 157, cols 2–4 cited in Austin, ibid., p. 424.

38 Malek, p. 133; P.L. Armitage and J. Clutton-Brock, "An Investigation of the Mummified Cats Held by the British Museum (Natural History)," *MASCA Journal*, 1980, vol. 1, pp. 185–8; J. Clutton-Brock, *Cats, Ancient and Modern*, Cambridge, Mass., Harvard University Press, 1993, p. 38. They believe that some of the cats who had died of natural causes and others that were sacrificed were mummified and buried in sacred ground as votive offerings on behalf of pious pilgrims who visited the sacred sites.

39 Furthermore, religious rites concerning marriage, the family, motherhood, and childrearing, were central among ancient pagan women, but seem to be absent among modern neo-pagans. Nor were ancient pagan cults gender-specific, that is, female goddesses solely worshipped by females and so on, the way we see among modern American neo-pagans. Of course, there were secret rites restricted to women, but the worship of Athena, Artemis, or Isis was in no way restricted solely to women.

40 The Timocles fragment (1. 4) is preserved in Athenaeus, *Deipnosophistae*, 7. 55. (7. 300): "Well then, what help could an ibis or a dog render? When in fact, people who sin against the gods whom all people share don't pay the penalty right away, who will be undone by a mere cat's altar (*ailourou bomos*)?" This passage once again mocks Egyptian religious beliefs concerning animals, as indeed does this whole section of Athenaeus in which the passage appears. Therefore the altar of the cat probably refers to an altar of Bastet (Bubastis), in which case it would mean an altar for sacrificial victims to that goddess and not necessarily an altar for the sacrifice of cats. In other words, just as the ibis (Thoth) and dog (Anubis) cannot render aid in our prayers, so we should not fear the cat (Bastet). Sextus Empiricus, *Pyrrh.* 3. 221. 2, however, writes about cat sacrifice in Alexandria. For those who feel sorry for the Egyptian cats that died, may I suggest trying to do something about the cats in our own country that over-reproduce and have to be put down by the millions each year rather than face a life of starvation, neglect, abuse, and predation.

41 Clement, *Pedagogus*, 3. 2.

42 Celsus, *On the True Word*, 3. 17 (Origen, *Contra Celsus*, 3. 17–21).

43 R. De Larouche and J.-M. Labat, *The Secret Life of Cats*, Hauppauge, N. Y., Barrons, 1995, p. 43.

44 Ibid.

45 Malek, p. 102.

46 Tabor, *Cats*, p. 31.

47 M. Oldfield Howey, *The Cat in the Mysteries of Religion and Magic*, New York, Castle Books, 1956, p. 28.

48 Aristotle, *Historia Animalium*, 580 A. This and other important passages by Aristotle will be discussed in Chapter 2. The remaining stanzas of the rhyme are enigmatic:

> The little dog laughed
> To see such sport
> And the dish ran away with the spoon.

The dog could possibly be a reference to Anubis, the Egyptian dog-faced god. But it is also possible that the passages are meaningless additions to the first three lines, as is indeed the first line itself.

49 Illustrated in Howey, op.cit., p. 125. This comes from the south side, lower row choir stall.

50 Beadle, p. 80. Cf. Gettings, op.cit., p. 43.

51 Lloyd, *Commentary 1–98*, pp. 99–105, who notes the essential folkloric aspect of the story, with perhaps a kernel of truth. The Assyrian army seems to have been decimated by disease during this campaigning season, but as Lloyd says, the Egyptians did not yet make the connection between mice and disease during this era.

52 H. Silvester, *Cats in the Sun*, San Francisco, Chronicle Books, 1994, p. 4, citing André Malraux. Whether this incident belongs to folklore or history, I will allow others to determine.

53 *Strat.* 7. 9.

54 Yurco, op.cit., p. 22.

55 Yurco, op.cit., p. 15.

56 *Reallexikon der Assyriologie*, Berlin, Walter de Gruyter, 1976–1980, s.v. Katze; *The Chicago Assyrian Dictionary*, Chicago, University of Chicago Press, 1992, s.v. *suranu*; H. Limet, "Les chats, les poules et les autres: le relais mésopotamien," in L. Bodson, *Des animaux introduits par l'homme dans la faune de Europe*, Liège, Université de Liège, 1994, pp. 39–54. I am grateful to Richard Beal of the Oriental Institute for his help in this section.

57 Perry, pp. xxvi–xxx.

58 Smart, cited in Altman, op.cit., pp. xiii–xiv.

2 GREECE

1 S.J.M. Davis, *The Archaeology of Animals*, New Haven, Yale University Press, 1987, pp. 133–4. See also Appendix 2 for other early cats from Cyprus.

2 For the desertification of the Mediterranean Basin during the Pliocene, 6.5–5.2 mya see S.J. Gould, *The Book of Life: An Illustrated History of Life on Earth*, New York, Norton, 1993, p. 208; K.J. Hsu, *The Mediterranean Was A Desert: A Voyage of the Glomar Challenger*, Princeton, Princeton University Press, 1983. The terrain was much like the region around the Dead Sea today.

3 Conveniently compiled by L. Morgan, *The Miniature Wall Paintings of Thera: A Study in Aegean Culture and Iconography*, Cambridge, Cambridge University Press, 1988, esp. pp. 41–4.

4 Malek, pp. 27–8.

5 J. Clutton-Brock, *Cats, Ancient and Modern*, Cambridge, Mass., Harvard University Press, 1993, pp. 39–40, F.E. Zeuner, *A History of Domesticated Animals*, New York, Harper and Row, 1963, p. 392. O. Keller, *Die Antike Tierwelt*, vol. 1, Hildesheim, Georg Olms, 1963, reprint of 1909, p. 66 has

suggested that the Hagia Triada cat is a serval, but this is unlikely as we have seen.

6 Morgan, op.cit., pp. 42–3.

7 Ibid., pp. 41–3. There is a dispute as to whether the daggers were made in Crete or mainland Greece. See E. Vermeule, *Greece in the Bronze Age*, Chicago, University of Chicago Press, 1964, pp. 98–9.

8 P.A. Clayton, *Chronicle of the Pharaohs*, London, Thames and Hudson, 1995, pp. 94–5; M. Beitak, *Avaris: The Capital of the Hyksos*, London, British Museum Press, 1996; S. Burstein, "Greek Contact with Egypt and the Levant: Ca. 1600–500 BC. An Overview," *Ancient World*, 1996, vol. 27, pp. 20–8, esp. pp. 22–5.

9 J.M.C. Toynbee, *Animals in Roman Life and Art*, Baltimore, Johns Hopkins University Press, 1996, reprint of 1973, p. 87; British Museum, *Catalogue of Greek Coins in the British Museum: Italy*, London, British Museum, 1873, p. 171, nos. 81, 84.; N. Davis, *Greek Coins and Cities*, London, Spink, 1967, p. 170; C. Kraay, *Greek Coins*, New York, H. N. Abrams, 1966, pl. 99; Keller, op.cit., pl. 2, no. 4. Other coins from Rhegium depicting Iokastos show him with a duck or a dog under his seat. There must have been an interesting story to tell about him and his animals. For later knowledge of the founding of colonies, see J. Boardman, *The Greeks Overseas*, Baltimore, Penguin, 1964, esp. pp. 35–8.

10 Found in U. Jantzen, *Ägyptische und Orientalische Bronzen aus dem Heraion von Samos*, vol. 8, Bonn, Deutsches Archäologisches Institut, 1972.

11 The animal has been identified as a young cheetah or hunting leopard by A. Ashmead, "Greek Cats," *Expedition*, 1978, vol. 20, no. 3, p. 45. Nevertheless, the animal has a thicker tail than the comparatively thin one of the cheetah, while its ears, although flattened and not upright, have a straight top edge, rather than a curved one as a larger cat, and lastly although the animal's head is turned in a three-quarters towards the viewer, it seems flatter than a cheetah's. It has small cat-sized paws, not the larger paws of a young cheetah, that are well depicted on several small vases. The animal is also under a chair, not a position in which the cheetah is shown on surviving representations. Finally, there is the size of the animal itself. Surely not all cat-sized, cat-like animals are young cheetahs; sometimes they are cats.

12 *Etymologicum Genuinum*, 1571.6, "*ailouros, para to aiollein kai kinein ten ouron*" (two lambdas in aiollein); *Etymologicum Magnum*, 492.2, "*Ailouros, to zoon, para to aiolein kai anagein ten ouron kai kinein.*" Thus the *Etymologicum Gudainum* and the *Etymologicum Parvum*, s.v. *ailouros*. See L. Bodson, "Les debuts en Europe du chat domestique," *Ethnozootechnie*, 1987, vol. 40, pp. 17–19.

13 Frag. 314. 303. 6.

14 Ashmead, op.cit., pp. 38–47. This valuable article deals only with cheetahs and so the title, "Greek Cats," is somewhat misleading. A useful study could be done on this animal, combining the artistic representations with the literary evidence. See also J. Clutton-Brock, *Domesticated Animals from Early Times*, Austin, University of Texas Press, 1981, pp. 178–80.

15 Perry, pp. xi–xix.

16 Ibid., p. xvi.

17 Perry, *Aesopica*, pp. viii–x.

18 Babrius, Perry, no. 17. The animal is called an *ailouros*. In the Augustana Recension, Perry no. 79, there is an analogous story where the role of the cat is taken by a weasel and the chickens are mice.

19 Babrius, Halm, no. 16; Perry, no. 121; S.A. Handford, ed. and trans., *Fables of Aesop*, Harmondsworth, Penguin Books, 1964, no. 95. The cat is called an *ailouros*. In the Augustana Recension mice appear instead of chickens.
20 The Augustana Recension, Perry, no. 16; Halm, no. 14; Handford, op.cit., no. 93.
21 Perotti's Appendix of Phaedrus, Perry, no. 18. The animal is a *feles*.
22 La Fontaine 4. 6. The cat in the French tale is a *chat*. The Augustana Recension, Perry no. 165, Halm, no. 291, Phaedrus (4.6), and Babrius (31) record similar stories with weasels in place of cats.
23 Fables excerpted from the writings of Odo of Cheriton, Perry no. 594. It is possible that the *murilegus* is a ferret.
24 From Odo of Cheriton, Perry no. 613. The cat is called *catus*.
25 From Odo of Cheriton, Perry no. 615. The cat is called *catus*. It is of interest that this fable is regarded by the Irish as a native Irish folktale, with a cask of whiskey substituted for the jar of wine; Briggs, p. 45.
26 Pseudo-Dositheus, *Hermeneumata*, Perry, no. 389. The cat is called *ailouros*.
27 Phaedrus 2. 4 in Perry. The cat is a *feles*.
28 Supplementary fable from Phaedrus in the Codex Ademari (eleventh century) 25, in Perry, *Aesopica*, no. 561. The word *cattus* is used.
29 Fable from Odo of Cheriton, recorded by La Fontaine 9. 14. in Perry, *Aesopica*, no. 605. The word *catus* is used.
30 A. Burford, *Land and Labor in the Greek World*, Baltimore, Johns Hopkins University Press, 1993, pp. 117–19, 141–2. Despite the overall excellence of the work, the author omitted references to Aesop's fables concerning cats, mice, and ferrets in farm life and so in general underrated the importance of these animals. I am indebted to my informants Susan Smith and Anita Bukey for the following information about barn cats.
31 Strabo 3. 2. 6. A. Mayor, "Grecian Weasels," *The Athenian*, February 1989, pp. 22–4.
32 Clutton-Brock, *Domesticated Animals*, p. 148, citing the ninth edition of the *Encyclopaedia Britannica*. See also F.E. Zeuner, op.cit., pp. 401–3.
33 In California for example, ferrets are banned as pets because of the damage they do to wildlife and their threat to small children, *Sarasota Herald Tribune*, 3 January 1998, p. 3A.
34 Clutton-Brock, *Domesticated Animals*, p. 148; Zeuner, op.cit., pp. 401–3.
35 See the useful discussion by Bodson, "chat," "Les debuts," pp. 21–2. There is another Greek word for weasel, *iktis*, which rarely occurs. See also Mayor, op.cit.
36 Babrius, in Perry, no. 27.
37 Phaedrus, in Perry, 1. 22.
38 Augustana Recension, in Perry, no. 197.
39 Babrius, in Perry, no. 32.
40 Recension IA, in Halm, no. 423. Babrius, in Perry, no. 135, has a similar story with a ferret and a partridge.
41 Toynbee, op.cit., pp. 102–24.
42 Our former white tom, Harvey, regularly provoked and intimidated a neighbor's much larger Labrador mix dog with impunity.
43 H. Silvester, *Cats in the Sun*, San Francisco, Chronicle Books, 1994, pp. 5, 6.
44 Zeuner, op.cit., pp. 443–55, 466–70. Dioscorides, *Materia Medica*, 3. 45. 5 recommends that digestive juice (*chulon*, not *cholos* or bile) be sprinkled on chickens to prevent their predation by (wild)cats.
45 R. Sorabji, *Animal Minds and Human Morals*, Ithaca, N. Y., Cornell University Press, 1993.

46 Iamblichus, *Life of Pythagoras*, 3. 25. To support the notion that animals were capable of reason, the following story was told by Poseidonius about a hunting dog following the scent of its prey. When the dog came to a crossroads, it sniffed up one trail and did not find the scent. It immediately set off along the other trail without smelling for the scent. That is, it knew from the process of elimination that the prey had taken the other path.

An example from my two cats Daphne and Katie may also be appropriate. Katie had just come indoors after it had begun to rain. Daphne also wished to go out, but I told her it was raining. Then she went over to Katie and sniffed her. On sensing her moist fur, she was no longer interested in going out. She understands the word "raining" and rather than check herself with the risk of getting wet, she sniffed her sister's fur.

47 *Problemata*, 1. 68. Alexander lived in the sixth century AD, and like other late medical authors, his work is based heavily on earlier scholars.

48 Plutarch, *On Isis and Osiris*, 376f; Frag. 145.

49 Plutarch, *On Isis and Osiris*, 376e.

50 *Iatricorum*, 6. 55. He then discusses various remedies used to counteract these conditions.

51 Alexander Trallianus, *Theraputica*, 1. 445; Pliny the Elder has many "cures" based on the substance: for head sores mixed with mustard! (28. 165). It was also recommended for taking orally for objects stuck in the throat, "It will bring it up or pass it down" 28. 190). It was a help in extracting thorns (28. 245), and when mixed with fox fat was good for an ulcerated uterus (28. 254). Other cures can be found in Paul of Aegina, *Epitome*, 7. 25. 10; Galen, *De compositione medicamentorum temperamentis ac facultatibus*, 1. 12. 321, *De compositione medicamentorum secundum*, 10. 12. 408–801.

52 Plutarch, 959 E.

53 Alexandrides, *Poleis*, cited by Athenaeus, *Deipnosophistae*, 7. 55 (7. 300): "You [Egyptians] worship the female dog, I beat her when I catch her eating my best food. Here in our country it is the custom to have our priests whole, but with you it appears it is the custom to cut off their best parts. If you see a cat in any trouble, you mourn, but I am very glad to kill and skin it."

54 Herodotus, *Histories*, 2. 59–60.

55 There are numerous sources that record that the cat was sacred to Artemis: Antoninus Liberalis, 28. 3; Ovid, *Metamorphoses*, 5. 330.

56 Georgius Paroemigraphus, 2. 28. 1; Macarius Chrysocephalus Paroemigraphus, 1. 47. 1; Michael Apostolius Paroemigraphus, 1. 55. 1–3; Zenobius Sophista, 2. 25; Suda, Lexicon s.v. *Athena ton ailouron*; Diogenianus Paroemigraphus, 1. 2. 37. 1, 2. 1. 63. 1–2; Eutechnius 29. 15.

57 Oppian, *Cynegetica*, 2. 572; Xenophon, *Cynegetica* 5. 14. For the character of Artemis, see W.K.C. Guthrie, *The Greeks and Their Gods*, Boston, Beacon, 1955, pp. 99–106, and the other works listed immediately below.

58 R. Bagnall and B. Frier, *The Demography of Roman Egypt*, Cambridge, Cambridge University Press, 1994, esp. p. 139; N. Demand, *Childbirth, Death, and Motherhood in Classical Greece*, Baltimore, Johns Hopkins University Press, 1994. See the discussion in Chapter 1.

59 One way to assess the importance of Artemis is to check the massive numbers of references to her in the index in Pausanias' description of Greece and the dedicatory inscriptions in *IG*.

60 E.g. by Guthrie, op.cit., p. 101.

61 *Metamorphoses*, 5. 325–331; Lucian, *Imag.* 11. 27, "If you seek out the god within (*endon de en zetes tou theou*), it is either a monkey, an ibis, a goat, or a cat."

Antoninus Liberalis (fl. second century AD), 2. 28, tells a similar story, but here, the preposition *eis* "in" is clearly used, *Artemis eis ailouron, Dionysos eis tragon*, and so on.

62 M.P. Nilsson, *A History of Greek Religion*, New York, Norton, 1964, p. 302; M.P. Nilsson, *Greek Folk Religion*, Philadelphia, University of Pennsylvania Press, 1972, reprint of 1940, pp. 15–18; H.J. Rose, *Religion in Greece and Rome*, New York, Harper and Row, 1959, reprint of 1946, 1948, pp. 142–3; T.E. Gregory, "The Survival of Paganism in Christian Greece: A Critical Essay," *AJP*, 1986, vol. 107, pp. 229–42.

63 R. De Larouche and J.-M. Labat, *The Secret Life of Cats*, Hauppauge, N. Y., Barrons, 1995, p. 30.

64 *RE*. s.v. Katze, cols. 52–3; R. Tabor, *Cats: The Rise of the Cat*, London, BBC Books, 1991, p. 31.

65 R.A. Harcourt , "The Animal Bones," in G.J. Wainwright, *Gussage All Saints: An Iron Age Settlement in Dorset*, London, HMSO, 1979, pp. 150–60; S.J.M. Davis, op.cit., p. 182.

66 N.B. Todd, "Cats and Commerce," *Scientific American*, 1977, vol. 237, pp. 100–7. The following discussion is based on his work.

67 Our present cats, Katie and Daphne, are female grey tabbies. In general, their behavior is civil (except for an occasional piddle on the rug when under stress). Daphne is a superb hunter, who was never taught by her mother.

68 R. Tabor, *Understanding Cats*, Pleasantville, N. Y., Reader's Digest, 1994, pp. 21–3, has noted that the domestic cat continues to interbreed with the *sylvestris* where it still exists in Scotland, northern England, and rarely elsewhere in Europe. Indeed, modern examples of the European *sylvestris* seem to be genetically about 66% *sylvestris* and about 33% *catus*.

69 This means that the orange mutation is carried on the female or X chromosome. Since the female has two such chromosomes, she can carry and display both orange and nonorange at the same time. Males have only one X chromosome, the other being Y, and so a male can either be orange or nonorange, but not both simultaneously.

70 Todd, op.cit., p. 106.

71 Beadle, p. 70.

72 Van Vechten, p. 86, citing an unidentified Hindu poem.

3 ROME

1 R. Tabor, *Cats: The Rise of the Cat*, London, BBC Books, 1991, p. 31; *RE* s.v. Katze, cols 52–3. There are many popular and scholarly works that have maintained this view.

2 R. Sallares, *The Ecology of the Ancient Greek World*, Ithaca, N. Y., Cornell University Press, 1991, pp. 32–3, 92.

3 His forthcoming thesis, *The Animal Economy of Roman Italy: Integration of Zooarcheological and Textual Data*, will be of great value to archeologists and historians.

4 It is possible that another cat from the same tomb fresco may be seen among the dancers to the right of the main scene, walking to the right. Unfortunately, the head is missing, but the tail length, color, and body proportions suit a small cat. There is a cat on an Etruscan tomb fresco depicting a banqueting scene from Veii dating to about 440 BC, and yet another in a banqueting scene said to be in the Tomba Golini in Orvieto. See Appendix 2.

5 K. Raaflaub, *Zum Freiheitsbegriff der Griechen*, Berlin, Akademie Verlag, 1981. Indeed, many works that treat the cat in the Roman era maintain that the statue of Libertas in the temple of that goddess in Rome, constructed by Tiberius Gracchus in 238 BC, is accompanied by a small cat, the symbol of freedom. I have not been able to find a single literary or artistic reference to this cat image. The Republican numismatic evidence depicting the goddess shows her without cat.

6 J.M.C. Toynbee, *Animals in Roman Life and Art*, Baltimore, Johns Hopkins University Press, 1996, reprint of 1973, pp. 112–24. Furthermore, the Greco-Egyptian god Anubis, who was represented as a dog or a jackal, was thought to be a guide who led the deceased into the underworld.

7 *Persa*, 751; *Rudens*, 748.

8 Ausonius, *Epigrams* 70 (77).

9 *De Natura Deorum* 1. 81–2; *De Legibus* 1. 32. Indeed, these two passages are the earliest that refer to the misinterpreted "animal worship" of the Egyptians.

10 5. 78–81.

11 Varro, *De Re Rustica* 3. 11. 3; 3. 12. 3; Columella, *De Re Rustica* 8. 3. 6. Columella recommends that the outside of chicken houses be smoothed with plaster so that, "cats, snakes, and other harmful beasts" are kept away. Seneca, *Epist.* 121. 19, notes that instinct plays an important role in the life of animals, and that young chicks, just hatched, will know to flee a cat but not a dog. Presumably, once again, this would have been the *sylvestris*.

12 E. Gibbon, *The Decline and Fall of the Roman Empire*, ed. J. B. Bury, vol. 1, New York, AMS Press, 1974, reprint of 1909, p. 31. In Gibbon's own lifetime, women were still being falsely accused of worshipping evil and were burnt alive as witches. Within the living memory of many during his age were the disastrous religious wars that destroyed the lives of millions of innocent Europeans.

13 For the false charges of cannibalism leveled against the Christians by both pagans and other Christians see, J.B. Russell, *Witchcraft in the Middle Ages*, Ithaca, N. Y., Cornell University Press, 1972, pp. 90–1. It is also true that the Romans killed large numbers of dangerous carnivores in the arena, especially members of the pantherine family. Today, the pantherines are justly admired for their beauty, grace, strength, courage, dignity, and hunting prowess. However, in earlier periods, and in some regions of the world today, groups of large carnivorous predators are regarded with considerable dread by neighboring populations of domesticated animals, and by humans armed only with edged weapons. Thus when the Romans cleared out such animals from a region, the response of these populations, however mistaken in our view, was probably one of considerable relief.

14 Toynbee, op.cit., pp. 89–90, *CIL* 6, 14223. The tombstone is now in Palermo, although it came from Rome.

15 R. De Larouche and J.-M. Labat, *The Secret Life of Cats*, Hauppaugue, N. Y., Barrons, 1995, p. 30.

16 R. Altman, *The Quintessential Cat*, New York, Macmillan, 1994, p. 108 for a picture; see also Toynbee, op.cit., p. 90.

17 For Vincentius, Toynbee, op.cit., p. 90; for the ornament, *CIL* 8, 22658. Under the same number, there is a lead weight with the inscription C . IVL . CA, and a figure of a cat.

18 There is no doubt that the terms Felicula and Felicla mean "Little Cat." Feli- is the root for *felis* and *-culus -a* is the common diminutive ending in Roman names. The *-clus -a* ending is a shortened form. Nevertheless, several dictio-

naries, including the *Thesaurus Linguae Latinae* itself, give an incorrect definition of the words. When one looks up *felicula* in these works, one is referred to
the word *filicula*, which means "little rock fern." In my opinion, this mistake
was made because the indices for the *CIL* were not complete when the
Thesaurus was compiled in 1915. Indeed, the indices for volume 6 of the *CIL*
were not compiled until the 1970s. There is no doubt that Toynbee, op.cit., p.
89, was correct when she identified the cognomen on the tombstone of
Calpurnia Felicla as "Little Cat." This is proven by the bas relief of a small cat
on the tombstone. We can conclude either that for hundreds of years, hundreds
and indeed thousands of Romans (since only a small fraction of all tombstones
has been recovered and recorded) from all regions of the Empire misspelled
their daughters' names and gave them the hilarious nickname of "Little Rock
Fern" or that the Romans actually spelled the word correctly and called their
daughters "Kitten" or "Little Cat." This makes sense to Professor Susan
Treggiari, as I learned from personal communication on 2 May 1998.

19 These can be found in the pages and indices of the *Corpus Inscriptionum
Latinarum* (*CIL*). Volume 6 covers the city of Rome while other volumes cover
the Latin inscriptions found throughout the entire Empire. There are far too
many references to record each one individually.

20 L. Keppie, *Understanding Roman Inscriptions*, Baltimore, Johns Hopkins
University Press, 1991, p. 10.

21 *CIL* 3, 3586, 4263, 14219; 5, 5709; 9, 6083; 3, 4228. Also, Appuleia Catta
from Noricum, 3, 11592.

22 *CIL* 12, 2012.

23 *CIL* 6, 1058, 26121, 34803; 10, 3380; *TLL* s.v. Cattius.

24 *CIL* 9, 2778; 3, 5069.

25 *CIL* 6, 2702; 6, 32520.

26 *CIL* 8, 2494. This is the only individual with a cognomen containing the root
aelur listed in the indices of *CIL*. The Latinized term *aelurus* also occurs a few
times in Latin literature. The fifth-century Egyptian Monophysite patriarch of
Alexandria, Timothy Aelurus (Timotheos Ailouros), will be discussed below.

27 *CIL* 6, 32520, among the most significant inscriptions concerning the animal.

28 For the change in abbreviations see L. Keppie, op.cit., p. 28. *CIL* 8, 18753,
20167. These two contain references to both H. S. E and D. M. together so
unfortunately they are of only limited value for dating. It is also probable that
the word *cattae*, used in Martial, *Epigrams* 13. 69, does not refer to the cat.
Book 13 of the *Epigrams* deals with *xenia* or guest-gifts and the section of the
book containing the word, numbers 65–77, refers to different types of birds as
gifts to prepare for dinner.

29 *RE* s.v. Katze, col. 52. In some Arabic dialects, the word *quttah* is used, O.
Keller, *Die Antike Tierwelt*, vol. 1, Hildesheim, Georg Olms, 1963, reprint of
1909, pp. 74–5; F.E. Zeuner, *A History of Domestic Animals*, New York, Harper
and Row, 1963, p. 390.

30 *Encyclopedia Britannica* (1944), s.v. Berbers. See the *OED* s.v. cat, and *RE* s.v.
Katze for the history and distribution of the name.

31 *Ecc. Hist.* 239. 13.

32 I have not been able to find the Greek word *kattos -a* in the corpus of Greek
inscriptions, *Inscriptiones Graecae*; Boubastis is mentioned occasionally and Isis
frequently. Another name of interest occurs in a cluster of inscriptions found
around Cologne, *CIL* 13, 4435, 8341, 8342, 8409. They all seem to refer to
the same individual, a certain Gatus. Several inscriptions were erected to his
sons, Tippausus and Bienus, who named him as their father. In later Spanish

and Italian, the word for cat is *gato* and *gatto*. Nevertheless, it is difficult to make that connection with this man's name.

33 I am grateful to Dr Fawwaz H.F. Al Khraysheh of Yarmouk University, Jordan for referring me to this inscription from Nemara, found in A. Poidebard, *La Trace de Rome dans le désert de Syrie*, Paris, Librairie Orientaliste Paul Geuthner, 1934. The inscriber may have intended to represent a lion, but it portrays a distinctive cat with upraised tail and cat features. As far as I can determine, the symbol for this legion remains unknown. See Appendix 1.

34 Van Vechten, pp. 143–4. He cites the author, Palliot, *Le vraye et parfaicte science des armoires*, Paris, 1664, who mentions several units of the Roman army with cat emblems. The *ordines Augusti* bore a green cat on their shields and another unit called the *felices seniores* bore a red cat, according to that seventeenth-century author. While it is wrong to reject out of hand Palliot's observations, which cannot be substantiated with any surviving evidence, it is sometimes the case that ancient evidence, such as inscriptions and artistic representations, was available in earlier centuries but has not survived into modern times. R. De Larouche and J.-M. Labat, *The Secret Life of Cats*, Hauppaugue, N. Y., Barrons, 1995, p. 66, maintain that the Felix Legion of the Roman imperial army had a cat on its standard. But the Legio IV Flavia Firma, later named Felix, and Legio XVI Flavia Firma had lions on their standards and not cats, H.M.D. Parker, *The Roman Legions*, Oxford, Oxford University Press, 1928, p. 107.

35 R. Harcourt, "The Animal Bones," in G.J. Wainwright, *Gussage All Saints: An Iron Age Settlement in Dorset*, London, HMSO, 1979, p. 154. As we have seen, these individuals were certainly domesticated.

36 P. Marsden, *Roman London*, London, Thames and Hudson, 1980, p. 66.

37 Toynbee, op.cit., p. 90.

38 This neglect is now being remedied by such works as A. Scobie, "Slums, Sanitation, and Mortality in the Roman World," *Klio*, 1986, vol. 68, pp. 399–433; D.P. Crouch, *Water Management in Greek Cities*, Oxford, Oxford University Press, 1993; D.P. Crouch, "Modern Insights from the Study of Ancient Greek Water Management," in A. Trevor Hodge, ed., *Future Currents in Aqueduct Studies*, Leeds, Francis Cairns, 1991, pp. 93–103. See also M.N. Cohen, *Health and the Rise of Civilization*, New Haven, Yale University Press, 1989.

39 S.L. Carter, *The Culture of Disbelief: How American Law and Politics Trivialize Religious Devotion*, New York, Anchor Books, 1993; G.M. Marsden, *The Soul of the American University: From Protestant Establishment to Established Nonbelief*, Oxford, Oxford University Press, 1994. The study of public health is also something of a taboo among Marxist historians as well. M.I. Finley, "The Ancient City: From Fustel de Coulanges to Max Weber and Beyond," *Comparative Studies in Society and History*, 1977, vol. 19, p. 310, disparaged the empirical study of town planning and specifically drains. But the drains may have been connected to sewers and part of a waste disposal system that kept the inhabitants free from disease spread by contaminated water. These empirical facts may reveal much more about classical cities and civilization than Marxist theory. The primitivists, who believe that rational thought was impossible before René Descartes, may also find it difficult to believe, despite all the medical evidence to the contrary, that drinking clean water delivered by an aqueduct was safer than drinking from a polluted river.

40 Quoted by G. Himmelfarb, *On Looking into the Abyss*, New York, Knopf, 1994, p. 50. A sentiment, originally expressed by Hegel, that deserves to be repeated.

41 Proclus, *Euclid* I, p. 84, 13, concerning Pythagorean belief.

42 Stobaeus, *Ecl. phys*. 1. 21. 7d (Diels and Kranz, 44 B 6).

43 Stobaeus, *Florilegium* 1. 179 (Diels and Kranz 22 B 114).

44 Francis Bacon, *Novum Organum* 51.

45 G. Majno, *The Healing Hand*, Cambridge, Mass., Harvard University Press, 1975, pp. 186–8, 362–8, for ancient antiseptics and hemostasis; Dioscorides, *De Materia Medica* 4. 75, for ancient anesthetics. See S.F. Mason, *A History of the Sciences*, New York, Macmillan, 1977, pp. 518–19, L.N. Magner, *A History of Medicine*, New York, Marcel Dekker, 1992, pp. 258–311, for deaths through the 1860s attributable to a lack of elementary hygiene and antiseptics. Many major operations that were conducted during the Hellenistic and Roman eras are mentioned in Celsus, *De Medicina*, especially books 5–8. Although some cures are admittedly ineffective and even humorous, the contempt for folk medicine in general, such as found in Pliny's *Natural History*, held by some is unwarranted and ought to have disappeared long ago. Over a half of our modern pharmacopoeia is derived from plants, many originally used as folk remedies. In addition to effective antiseptics and anesthetics, Pliny mentions ephedrine, salicin (the major component of aspirin) and digitalis, Magner, op.cit. pp. 12, 83. Fortunately, some are well aware of the potential value of classical pharmacopoeias. It has been estimated that approximately 40 per cent of the remedies in ancient sources were beneficial if used as directed. Other remedies may be effective for other uses; R. Jackson, *Doctors and Diseases in the Roman Empire*, Norman, Okla., University of Oklahoma Press, 1988, pp, 75–85. B.K. Holland, a physician in preventive medicine and community health, is putting together a consortium of historians of medicine, pharmacologists, and botanists to study ancient pharmacological literature. Many substances, in addition to those mentioned above, are showing promise; B.K. Holland, "Prospecting for Drugs in Ancient Texts," *Nature*, 30 June 1994, vol. 369, p. 702.

46 D. Engels, *Roman Corinth: An Alternative Model for the Classical City*, Chicago, University of Chicago Press, 1990, pp. 74–8, for a collection of the evidence.

47 Hippocrates, *Airs, Waters, and Places*; Aristotle, *Politics* 1327a–b; Plato, *Laws* 4. 704–7.

48 J.F.D. Shrewsbury, *A History of the Bubonic Plague in the British Isles*, Cambridge, Cambridge University Press, 1970, p. 21.

49 R. Hendrickson, *More Cunning Than Man: A Social History of Rats and Men*, New York, Stein and Day, 1983, p. 72; P.L. Armitage, "Unwelcome Companions, Ancient Rats Reviewed," *Antiquity*, 1994, vol. 68, pp. 231–40.

50 L. Casson, *Travel in the Ancient World*, Baltimore, Johns Hopkins University Press, 1994, pp. 118–26.

51 Hendrickson, op.cit., p. 47. The references to plagues of mice or rats associated with tumors near the groin (Greek *boubon*) make the identification with the plague likely. The Greeks also understood that the plagues of mice that frequently preceded human plagues were associated with disease. Apollo's epithet Smintheus (from *sminthos*, mouse) referred to his reputed ability to kill mice and avert disease. There is also a possible reference to the plague in Hipp. *Aph*. 55. The symbol of the healing god Asklepios was two intertwined snakes of the species *elaphe longissima*, which are effective rodent killers.

52 Quoted and discussed by Shrewsbury, op.cit., pp. 11, 17. Subsequent epidemics after the time of Rufus (*c*. AD 50) did not include the bubonic plague, see Shrewsbury, op.cit., note 58. See W.H. McNeill, *Plagues and Peoples*, New York, Anchor Press, 1976, p. 123, who also accepts the outbreak

described by Rufus as bubonic. D. Grmek, *Diseases in the Ancient Greek World*, Baltimore, Johns Hopkins University Press, 1989, restricts his scope to the Aegean region and classical, Hippocratic evidence from the mid-fifth to late fourth centuries BC. Since the bubonic plague is not mentioned in Hippocratic works (with the possible exception of *Aph.* 55), it is not mentioned by him.

53 Shrewsbury, op.cit., p. 21.

54 A. Patrick, "Diseases in Antiquity: Ancient Greece and Rome," in D.R. Brothwell and A.T. Sandison, eds, *Diseases in Antiquity*, Springfield, Ill., C.C. Thomas, 1967, p. 225, argues that the plagues of AD 251–66 and that of 312 were smallpox. The cause of the great plague of 166 remains unknown, but its symptoms were not those of bubonic plague.

55 H.E. Sigerist, *On the History of Medicine*, New York, MD Publications, 1960, p. 19, from an article originally published in 1933.

56 G. Rickman, *Roman Granaries and Store Buildings*, Cambridge, Cambridge University Press, 1971; G. Rickman, *The Corn Supply of Ancient Rome*, Oxford, Oxford University Press, 1980, pp. 132–9.

57 Aristotle, *Ath. Pol.* 50. 2 for Athens; *CIL* 1 (2nd edn), 593 for Rome. Sallares, op.cit., p. 382; Scobie, op.cit., pp. 407–17, reluctantly admits that Rome's public sanitation was superior to that of London through the 1840s.

58 *OGIS* 483 for Pergamon; Crouch, "Modern Insights," pp. 99–100; Scobie, op.cit., p. 411. There would always be some danger from contamination of well water, but such contamination would be reduced if the above policies were rigorously put into practice.

59 *OGIS* 483 for Pergamon; Frontinus, *Aq.* 2. 97 for Rome, records fines of up to 10,000 sesterces.

60 All these diseases existed in antiquity: Grmek, op.cit., pp. 89, 348, 354 for typhoid and dysentery; Celsus, *De Medicina* 4. 18. l; Shrewsbury, op.cit., p. 18 for cholera; Brothwell and Sandison, op.cit., pp. 115–90, for parasites. For the value of ancient aqueducts and water supply systems in the reduction of these water-borne diseases see R. Jackson, op.cit., pp. 45f. See Magner, op.cit., p. 336, for the importance of similar public health measures that finally eradicated these and other diseases during the nineteenth and twentieth centuries.

61 Shrewsbury, op.cit., p. 35. The brown rat did not begin to biologically replace the black rat until about 1800, Armitage, op.cit., p. 236.

62 Marsden, op.cit., pp. 46, 108.

63 Rickman, *Corn Supply*, pp. 132–9; A. Burford, *Land and Labor in the Greek World*, Baltimore, Johns Hopkins University Press, 1993, pp. 141–2. Proper grain storage is difficult, for the wrong temperature or humidity can destroy the crop. The grain often needs to be dried out before storage and so is placed in open bins. At this time rodent depredation is likely.

64 Palladius, 4. 9. 4 remarks on the superiority of the cat over the ferret in general.

65 Hendrickson, op.cit., p. 98.

66 Pliny, *Natural History* 10. 202, Palladius, 4. 9. 4.

67 Varro, *De Re Rustica* 1. 12. 2; Columella, *De Re Rustica* 1. 5. 6: marshland, "breeds insects armed with annoying stings, which attack in dense swarms ... from which mysterious diseases are often contracted."

68 Andrew Jones cited by T. Horowitz, "Endangered Feces: Paleoscatologist Plumbs Old Privies," *Wall Street Journal*, 9 September 1991, vol. 95, pp. A1, A7.

69 Augustine, *De utilitate ieiunii* 7. 9.

70 R. MacMullen, *Christianity and Paganism in the Fourth to Eighth Centuries*, New Haven, Yale University Press, 1997, p. 14.

71 M. Bernal, *Black Athena: The Afro-asiatic Roots of Western Civilization*, 2 vols, New Brunswick, N. J., Rutgers University Press, 1987, 1991. Another obstacle to appreciating the role of Isis, and indeed of other goddesses in the religion of Europe, is the unfortunate attempt made to denigrate and indeed ignore the prominent role of women in religion during the classical era by some church historians who study "late antiquity." See the cogent remarks made by R. MacMullen, *Christianity and Paganism*, esp. pp. 7–8, 163–4, n. 13; p. 168, n. 27.

72 R.E. Witt, *Isis in the Ancient World*, Baltimore, Johns Hopkins University Press, 1997, reprint of 1971; S.K. Heyob, *The Cult of Isis Among Women in the Graeco-Roman World*, Leiden, Brill, 1975, esp. pp. 38–44.

73 Apuleius, *Met.* 11. 5, cited from Apuleius, *The Golden Ass*, trans. J. Lindsay, Bloomington, Ind., Indiana University Press, 1971, pp. 236–7.

74 Apuleius, *Met.* 11. 6, cited in Apuleius, op.cit., pp. 237–8.

75 Apuleius, *Met.* 11. 6, cited in Apuleius, op.cit., pp. 238–9.

76 Apuleius, *Met.* 11. 23, cited in Apuleius, op.cit., p. 249.

77 Indeed, the protuberances on her chest have been described, improbably, as bull testicles. There are human-like breasts on the birds, there are human-like breasts on the lions, there are human-like breasts on the goats, there are human-like breasts on the cats. What could Artemis possibly have: human-like breasts? They do not resemble testicles, and to borrow a phrase, "sometimes a cigar is just a cigar."

78 Plutarch, *Plutarch's de Iside et Osiride*, ed. and trans. J.G. Griffiths, Cardiff, University of Wales Press, 1970, pp. 526–7.

79 Witt, op.cit., p. 30.

80 R. Meiggs, *Roman Ostia*, Oxford, Oxford University Press, 1973, pp. 368–88. He has however omitted the important temple inventory discussed below. This is probably because the inventory mentions Bubastis but not Isis, even though it is clear that the inscription refers to both.

81 *CIL* 14, 21, for Caltilia Diodora; *CIL* 6, 2249 for Ostoria Successa; *CIL* 3, 4231 for Isis Augusta and Bubastis.

82 *CIL* 14, 2215.

83 *CIL* 6, 32464, 26980; *IG Sic. et Ital.* 1453.

84 *Imag.* 11. 27; cf. Juvenal 15. 7, who used the word *aelurus*.

85 Witt, op.cit., p. 86.

86 Witt, op.cit., pp. 89–95. This was noted by the Neoplatonic Eunapius as a contrast to Christian monks of the fourth century with their "swinish way of life," who were enslaving the world with "a fabulous and formless darkness."

87 L. Canfora, *The Vanished Library: A Wonder of the Ancient World*, Berkeley, University of California Press, 1990, p. 63.

88 Witt, op.cit., pp. 194–5.

89 Ibid.

90 Ibid., p. 107.

91 L. Casson, *The Ancient Mariners*, New York, Minerva Press, 1959, pp. 214, 235. The vessel was some 180 feet (55 m) long, 45 feet (14 m) wide, and probably carried 1,200 to 1,300 tons (1,100 to 1,180 tonnes) of grain.

92 2. 170, *in prora navis felis forma depicta videbatur*.

93 Apuleius, *Met.*, 11. 15, cited in Apuleius, op.cit., p. 243.

94 For the general accuracy of Apuleius' description of Corinth and its people during the Roman Empire, see Engels, op.cit., esp. pp. 102–7.

95 See the sources in M.R. Lefkowitz and M. Fant, *Women's Life in Greece and Rome*, Baltimore, Johns Hopkins University Press, 1982. Also D. Schaps, *The Economic Rights of Women in Ancient Greece*, Edinburgh, University of Edinburgh Press, 1979; L. Foxhall, "Household, Gender, and Property in Classical Athens," *Classical Quarterly*, 1989, vol. 39, pp. 22–44; B. Witherington, *Women in the Earliest Churches*, Cambridge, Cambridge University Press, 1988.

96 M.J. Green, "The Gods and the Supernatural," in M.J. Green, ed., *The Celtic World*, London, Routledge, 1995, pp. 478–81.

97 A. King, *Roman Gaul and Germany*, Berkeley, University of California Press, 1990, pp. 132–8. In the past, before archeology revealed the mass graves, Roman accounts of Celtic sacrifice were thought only to reveal the bias of the Romans against the Celts. For the ancient sources on sacrifice by burning of individuals in large wicker containers see Caesar, *Bellum Gallicum* 6. 17; A. Ross, "Ritual and the Druids," in Green, op.cit., pp. 423–41. The finding of human remains in ritual pits from Caesaromagus (Chelmsford) in Roman Britain with the remains of sacrificed animals (including cats) dating from AD 150–200 leads one to suspect (although not prove) that human sacrifice may have continued in Britain for some time after Roman rule began. R.-M. Luff, *A Zooarchaeological Study of the Roman Northwestern Provinces*, Oxford, British Archaeological Reports, International Series, 1982, vol. 137, pp. 175–88. For throwing animals off heights see Ross, op.cit., and Van Vechten, p. 69. There are also medieval representations of the latter practice which continued until the nineteenth century.

98 Van Vechten, p. 69.

99 H.D. Betz, *The Greek Magical Papyri in Translation*, Chicago, University of Chicago Press, 1992, p. 18, no. 3. 1–161.

100 Ibid., no. 12. 108.

101 *Natural History* 28. 228, 18. 160.

102 Matthew 10:29 literally reads, "not one of them will fall to the ground without the father (*aneu tou patros humon*)." Indeed, this is the translation of the King James' version. Since this passage occurs in the context of God's knowledge and concern for his people, "knowledge" seems to be a better translation than the "will" of the Revised Standard Version.

103 I Corinthians: 8.

104 MacMullen, *Christianity and Paganism*, p. 14. Cf. Gibbon, op.cit., vol. 2, p. 14.

105 R. Lane-Fox, *Pagans and Christians*, New York, Knopf, 1987, pp. 268–9, 317, 592. John Gager has shown that the proportion of Jews in the Roman Empire by around 300 was about 10 per cent, *The Origins of Anti-Semitism: Attitudes Towards Judaism in Pagan and Christian Antiquity*, Oxford, Oxford University Press, 1983.

106 MacMullen, *Christianity and Paganism*, p. 14; Gibbon, op.cit., vol. 2, p. 14.

107 MacMullen, *Paganism and Christianity*, pp. 15–18; they were the shock troops of the new religion and acted accordingly.

108 R. MacMullen, *Christianizing the Roman Empire: AD 100–400*, New Haven, Yale University Press, 1984, pp. 80–3.

109 Witherington, op.cit., pp. 219–20.

110 E. Pagels, *The Gnostic Gospels*, New York, Random House, 1989, reprint of 1979, esp. pp. 48–69.

111 Witherington, op.cit., pp. 197, 209–10. Indeed, Neoplatonic philosophy also played a major role in eliminating women from positions of authority and in their later persecution. According to this distortion of Plato's teaching, the material world of creation was evil and the spiritual world was good. Men were

spiritual and good, women were material and evil. Indeed, when William of Ockham (d. *c.* 1350) suggested women might have souls and thus should attend church councils, the idea was denounced as heresy.

112 Quoted by E. Pagels, *Adam, Eve, and the Serpent*, New York, Random House, 1988, pp. 79–80. She also discusses the rejection of marriage, family, and nature in general. The hateful invectives of the post-Nicene church leveled against women are well known and have been analyzed, i.e. by V.L. Bullough, *The Subordinate Sex*, Champaign, Ill., University of Illinois Press, 1973; W. Lederer, *The Fear of Women*, New York, Harcourt, Brace, Jovanovich, 1968.

113 Some church historians who study late antiquity maintain that the exclusion of women from leadership roles in the church was actually beneficial to their spiritual development. This is funny. See MacMullen, *Christianity and Paganism*, p. 7.

114 *Apologia Contra Arianos* 78. 7.

115 *Apologia* 24. 1.

116 1. 28.

117 Nicephoras Gregoras, *Hist. Byz.* 8. 1; Perry, no. 435; Halm, no. 87.

118 From Odo of Cheriton in Perry, no. 592.

119 Codex Bruxellensis 536, in Perry, no. 692.

120 Codex Bernensis 679, in Perry, no. 716. 716a in Perry is the same story as in 716 but better told with more descriptive detail.

121 Latin fables supplementary to Phaedrus and his paraphrasers, in Perry, no. 602.

122 Casson, *Ancient Mariners*, pp. 227–33.

123 A. von den Driesch and J. Boessneck, "A Roman Cat Skeleton from Quseir on the Red Sea Coast," *Journal of Archaeological Science*, 1983, vol. 10, pp. 205–11.

124 Van Vechten, p. 91.

125 Tabor, *Understanding*, p. 23.

4 THE EARLY MIDDLE AGES: AD 500–1000

1 Traditional Irish monastic poem written in the eighth century. Cited in R. Tabor, *Cats: The Rise of the Cat*, London, BBC Books, 1991, p. 40.

2 Those who wish to see the fifth century as an era of peaceful transition must ignore the destruction of hundreds of cities in western Europe, well documented from both the literary and archeological records, and the likely deaths of millions of their inhabitants, thus denying them their humanity. This view of history was popular in Germany and Austria in the 1920s through 1945, as seen in the early work of the Austrian Nazi Fritz Schachermeyr for example. Indeed, some historians are now associating Christian successionist theology with German racial and ethnic successionist theories from the 1920s, '30s and '40s. Many hoped that after 7 May 1945, the world had seen the end of such apologias for German aggression.

3 Thucydides 1.6: "Among these people [northwestern Greeks] the custom of carrying arms still survives from the old days of robbery; for at one time, since houses were unprotected and communications unsafe, this was a general custom throughout the whole of Greece and it was the normal thing to carry arms on all occasions, as it is now among the barbarians."

4 J.P. Poly and E. Bournazel, *The Feudal Transformation: 900–1200*, New York, Holmes and Meier, 1991, p. 352.

5 R. MacMullen, *Christianity and Paganism in the Fourth to Eighth Centuries*, New Haven, Yale University Press, 1997, esp. pp. 36–76; J. Burke, *Roman England*,

New York, Norton, 1984, pp. 143–5; T.W. Potter and C. Johns, *Roman Britain*, Berkeley, University of California Press, 1992, p. 209.

6 Poly and Bournazel, op.cit., pp. 310, 314.

7 Ibid., p. 333; R. Witt, *Isis in the Ancient World*, Baltimore, Johns Hopkins University Press, 1997, reprint of 1971, p. 274.

8 C. Ginzburg, *The Night Battles: Witchcraft and Agrarian Cults in the Sixteenth and Seventeenth Centuries*, Baltimore, Johns Hopkins University Press, 1983, pp. xv, 40, 42.

9 J.B. Russell, *Witchcraft in the Middle Ages*, Ithaca, N. Y., Cornell University Press, 1972, p. 76.

10 Ibid., pp. 76–86.

11 Tabor, *Cats*, pp. 43–5.

12 Psalm 96:5 (95:5) mistranslated in Jerome's Vulgate as, *Quoniam omnes dii gentium daemonia*, "all the gods of the heathen are devils." I Corinthians 10:14–22; Augustine, *City of God* 1. 33 and *passim*. To the author of Revelation (2:13) the altar of Zeus at Pergamon was "the throne of Satan." Cf. E. Pagels, *The Origin of Satan*, New York, Random House, 1995, pp. 112–48. The identification of pagan gods with evil demons began with Judaism and continued through the Middle Ages into the Renaissance, Russell, op.cit., pp. 101–16.

13 Russell, op.cit., p. 46. This demonization of pagan divinities especially affected Diana.

14 Ibid., pp. 107–16. Tertullian was among the first to associate the study of nature and philosophy with heresy. In general see, G.E.R. Lloyd, *Greek Science After Aristotle*, New York, Norton, 1973, pp. 167–74. The demonizing of nature was also a principle of Augustine's theological system. E. Pagels, *Adam, Eve, and the Serpent*, New York, Random House, 1988, pp. 127ff.

15 Pagels, *Adam, Eve*, pp. 78–150; P. Chuvin, *Chronicle of the Last Pagans*, Cambridge, Mass., Harvard University Press, 1990, p. 105; W.H.C. Frend, *The Rise of Christianity*, Philadelphia, Fortress, 1985, pp. 717–19, 877.

16 Lloyd, op.cit., pp. 167–78. Origen, who supported learning Greek philosophy, was declared a heretic posthumously, at the Fifth Ecumenical Council of Constantinople in 553. See L.D. Davis, *The First Seven Ecumenical Councils*, Collegeville, Minn., Liturgical Press, 1990, pp. 245–7.

17 Frend, op.cit., pp. 710–29, 877. As was noted, Neoplatonic philosophy also played a role in this development.

18 There is a vast literature on these lives, but Gibbon's judgement is still sound:

> These extravagant tales, which display the fiction, without the genius, of poetry, have seriously affected the reason, the faith, and the morals of the Christians. Their credulity debased and vitiated the faculties of the mind, they corrupted the evidence of history; and superstition gradually extinguished the hostile light of philosophy and science. Every mode of religious worship which had been practiced by the saints, every mysterious doctrine which they believed, was fortified by the sanction of divine revelation, and all the manly virtues were oppressed by the servile and pusillanimous reign of the monks. If it is possible to measure the interval between the philosophic writings of Cicero and the sacred legend of Theodoret, between the character of Cato and that of Simeon, we may appreciate the memorable revolution which was accomplished in the Roman empire within a period of five hundred years.
>
> (E. Gibbon, *The History of The Decline and Fall of the Roman Empire*, ed. J.B. Bury, vol. 4, p. 81)

19 Theodoret of Cyrrhus, *History of the Monks of Syria*, trans. R.M. Price, Kalamazoo, Mich., Cistercian Press, 1985, p. 184.

20 H.I. MacAdam, "Cities, Villages, and Veteran Settlements: Roman Administration in the Syrian Hawran," in D. Panzac, ed., *Histoire économique et sociale de L'Empire Ottoman et de la Turquie*, Paris, Peeters, 1995, pp. 641–52, esp. p. 649.

21 Lactantius, *Inst. Div.* 3. 3. Other "intellectuals" who taught the earth was flat included Eusebius of Nicomedia, Basil of Caesarea, and St John Chrysostom.

22 P.G. Walsh, "The Rights and Wrongs of Curiosity," *Greece and Rome*, 1988, vol. 35, pp. 73–85.

23 Cited by Chuvin, op.cit., p. 105.

24 MacMullen, *Christianity and Paganism*, p. 4, on laws mandating the cutting off of hands. For the destruction of the works of Aristotle in Paris in 1210, see *The Oxford Dictionary of the Christian Church*, ed. F.L. Cross, New York, Oxford University Press, 1997, s.v. Gregory IX. There was also the destruction of the library at Constantinople in 1204 perpetrated by the Fourth "Crusade."

25 Hypatia (d. 415) was not the first, nor Giordano Bruno (d. 1600) the last, scientist to be murdered by the church. The Spanish Inquisition was not shut down until 1834 and only then were some sciences permitted to be taught in Spain. The teaching of Newtonian physics was not permitted there until much later. In the United States, some college professors could still be fired for teaching Newtonian physics until 1900. It was illegal to teach evolution in some states until 1981, and mandatory creationism was required until 1987 when it was overturned in a famous Supreme Court case. For the killing of philosophers and the destruction of scientific institutions by so-called Christians through the end of the nineteenth century see A.D. White, *A History of the Warfare of Science with Theology in Christendom*, vols 1 and 2, New York, Dover, 1960, reprint of 1895. As many readers know, hostility towards reason and logic, "logocentric discourse," still pervades some institutions of higher learning today in my own country.

26 T. Miller, *The Birth of the Hospital in the Byzantine Empire*, Baltimore, Johns Hopkins University Press, 1985, pp. 54–76; L.N. Magner, *A History of Medicine*, New York, Marcel Dekker, 1992, pp. 100–3; Frend, op.cit., pp. 742–52.

27 J.F.D. Shrewsbury, *A History of the Bubonic Plague in the British Isles*, Cambridge, Cambridge University Press, 1970, p. 35; Frend, op.cit., p. 877, for the notion of filth as a symbol of renunciation of the world and its evils. The aversion of Christians to bathing, especially in the Latin West, is also discussed in detail by F. Yegül, *Baths and Bathing in Classical Antiquity*, Cambridge, Mass., MIT Press, 1992, pp. 314–20.

28 Frend, op.cit., pp. 717–18, 877: "Then there was Zoilus the reader, who renounced all family ties to practice the art of calligraphy in a rat-infested cell. Ascetics such as he represented the ideals of rulers and ruled alike in the Byzantine world. [The Byzantine Emperor] Maurice was ... a friend of Theodore of Sykeon, who owed his repute for sanctity to his ability to live in conditions of unbelievable squalor."

29 Yegül, op.cit., pp. 315–20.

30 Andrew Jones, cited by T. Horowitz, "Endangered Feces: Paleoscatologist Plumbs Old Privies," *Wall Street Journal*, 9 September 1991, vol. 95, pp. A1, A7.

31 P. Ziegler, *The Black Death*, New York, John Day, 1969, p. 152.

32 A. Daley and B. Benjamin, "London as a Case Study," *Population Studies*, 1964, vol. 17, p. 251. In comparison, Boston, Massachusetts and neighboring communities still dumped untreated and barely treated sewage into the Charles River through the 1950s and into Boston harbor through the 1980s. These communities drew much of their water from the Charles and related wells through the 1870s.

33 S.F. Mason, *A History of the Sciences*, New York, Macmillan, pp. 518–19; Magner, op.cit., pp. 258–67. Cf. the Greek or Roman physician who was required to be scrupulously clean and whose instruments were sterilized in fire before their reuse. Hippocrates, *The Physician, passim*; R. Jackson, *Doctors and Diseases in the Roman Empire*, Norman, Okla., University of Oklahoma Press, 1988, p. 135.

34 P.L. Armitage, "Unwelcome Companions, Ancient Rats Reviewed," *Antiquity*, 1994, vol. 68, pp. 234–6.

35 For the survival of ancient traditions in Wales in general, see T. Charles-Edwards, "Language and Society Among the Insular Celts: AD 400–1000," in M.J. Green, ed., *The Celtic World*, London, Routledge, 1995, pp. 703–36.

36 Van Vechten, pp. 161–3; Beadle, p. 78.

37 Poly and Bournazel, op.cit., p. 333.

38 *Anthologia Graeca*, 7. 204. An anonymous poem from the Anthology, 11. 359, speaks of a prince who is compared to a cat-like gold-grabber and plunderer of the poor.

39 *Anth. Graec.* 7. 205.

40 *Anth. Graec.* 7. 206.

41 A. Schimmel, "Cats," in M. Eliade, ed., *Encyclopedia of Religion*, vol. 3, New York, Macmillan, 1987, pp. 121–3.

42 Van Vechten, p. 168.

43 M.W. Dols, *The Black Death in the Middle East*, Princeton, Princeton University Press, 1971, pp. 155–9; Yegül, op.cit., pp. 316–19. Islamic peoples understood the danger of rats and mice and destroyed them when they could. They also understood that a rat die-off would precede the plague, but they did not make a causal connection.

EPILOGUE

1 Quoted by Beadle, p. 76.

2 The term "Great Cat Massacre" was, as far as I know, first used by Robert Darnton, *The Great Cat Massacre and Other Episodes in French Cultural History*, Harmondsworth, Penguin, 1984, especially chapter 2. However, in his work, the massacre only referred to the killing of a dozen or so cats in mid-eighteenth-century Paris by an apprentice in a printing shop. I would here like to extend the term to include the general massacre of cats from the thirteenth to the seventeenth centuries.

3 The lowest estimate for the number of "witches" killed from about 1200 to 1700 is 60,000; J.B. Russell, *Witchcraft in the Middle Ages*, Ithaca, N. Y., Cornell University Press, 1972, p. 39, believes 200,000 is probably accurate. If a mere 10,000 cats were killed per year during the 500-year-period of the cat massacre, also between 1200 and 1700, one would have five million cats killed. However, it is not difficult to see that the actual numbers killed were far higher, easily in the tens of millions and perhaps more during the era. It has been noted that in one city in one year alone, London in 1666, 200,000 cats were massacred. As we have seen, the loss of one cat will allow the potential

destruction of 250 tons (225 tonnes) of food by black rats as well as the potential spread of dangerous diseases.

4 Russell, op.cit., p. 265.

5 E. Pagels, *The Origin of Satan*, New York, Random House, 1995.

6 Psalm 96:5 (95:5) mistranslated in Jerome's Vulgate as, *Quoniam omnes dii gentium daemonia*, "all the gods of the heathen are devils." I Corinthians 10:14–22; Augustine, *City of God* 1. 33 and *passim*. To the author of Revelation (2:13) the Altar of Zeus at Pergamon was "the throne of Satan." See Pagels, *Origin*, pp. 112–48. The identification of pagan gods with evil demons began with Judaism and continued through the Middle Ages and early modern era, Russell, op.cit., pp. 101–16.

7 The best discussion of this is in E. Pagels, *Adam, Eve, and the Serpent*, New York, Random House, 1988.

8 Nevertheless, the idea has caused great harm to millions of Christian "heretics," non-Christians, Jews, Muslims, Black Africans, and Amerindians for the last millennium and a half.

9 There are numerous works that discuss Urban II's speech to the Council of Clermont, held in 1095, that launched the First Crusade. Four accounts survive of the speech, the most important by Robert the Monk, who claimed to be present. In Robert's account, Urban calls the Turks Persians and claims that they "are an accursed race, a race utterly alienated from God." He further notes that the Franks had been involved in genocidal tribal warfare in their own kingdom, probably associated with the imposition of the feudal system on their Latin subjects. He suggests that this fury be transferred to the Turks. In Fulcher of Chartres' account, Urban fulminates against "the despised, degenerate race of the Persians who are the slaves of demons." "Christ commands the extermination of this vile race" from the lands of the Byzantines. Naturally, performing such an extermination will win eternal salvation for the crusader. War and conquest are always brutal and cruel, but when such wars have been given religious sanction, they have proven to be especially vicious.

10 S. Runciman, *A History of the Crusades*, vol. 1, New York, Harper and Row, 1964, reprint of 1951, pp. 134–41.

11 Russell, op.cit., p. 148.

12 J.P. Poly and E. Bournazel, *The Feudal Transformation: 900–1200*, New York, Holmes and Meier, 1991, p. 352. This is a book that should be read by all ancient historians and provides a welcome anecdote to the perspectives of revisionists.

13 Ibid., pp. 119–80 ; T.N. Bisson, "The Feudal Revolution," *Past and Present*, 1994, vol. 142, pp. 6–42.

14 Apostolic Christianity was already regarded as heretical in the late fourth century, "As such [Priscillianism] could claim precedents from the early apostolic church, which had in fact been more concerned with ethics and the idea of community than with the development of sophisticated theology or of a precise hierarchy of authority; but in the later fourth century when the Christian church had already elaborated a more complex structure and ideology, it would be perceived as opposition to orthodoxy" R. Van Dam, *Leadership and Community in Late Antique Gaul*, Berkeley, University of California Press, 1985, p. 99.

15 Poly and Bournazel, op.cit., pp. 288–9; H. Smith, *Man and His Gods*, Boston, Little, Brown, 1952, p. 257. As many as one million may have been killed.

16 G. Ashe, *The Discovery of King Arthur*, London, Anchor Press, 1985.

17 Russell, op.cit., pp. 156–8.

18 Russell, op.cit., pp. 154–5, 162–3.
19 Russell, op.cit., pp. 131, 147, 157–63, 196, 216–18, 236–7, 246–7; Van Vechten, p. 98.
20 R.L. Wilken, *The Christians as the Romans Saw Them*, New Haven, Yale University Press, 1984, pp. xv–xvii; 200–5.
21 R.E. Witt, *Isis in the Ancient World*, Baltimore, Johns Hopkins University Press, 1997, reprint of 1971, p. 186; Russell, op.cit., pp. 113–14. Unfortunately for the history of Christianity, it was not only the color black that was demonized but, lamentably, dark-skinned individuals too. "Born of the Devil, we are black," fulminated St Jerome (died 420), cited by Russell, op.cit., p.114. Although Manichean beliefs may have influenced this notion, another contributing factor was undoubtedly the development of "heretical" Monophysite movements in the Near East and especially Egypt from the mid-fifth century till the Arab conquest. The violent suppression of Egyptian Monophysite Christians in Alexandria by the Catholic Patriarchs in the fifth and sixth centuries would seem to go far beyond mere religious lunacy.
22 Russell, op.cit., pp. 160–3.
23 C. Ginzburg, *The Night Battles: Witchcraft and Agrarian Cults in the Sixteenth and Seventeenth Centuries*, Baltimore, Johns Hopkins University Press, 1983, pp. 99–145.
24 Russell, op.cit., p. 39.
25 A. D. White, *A History of the Warfare of Science with Theology in Christendom*, New York, Dover, 1960, reprint of 1895, pp. 352–3.
26 Briggs, p. 97. This particular atrocity occurred in East Anglia. The elderly woman also wore black, probably because she was a widow.
27 It is somewhat ironic that the word "coven" was descended from the Latin *conventus*, via the term "convent", *OED* s.v. Coven. Indeed, the latter institution shows many pagan influences, especially in its earlier stages.
28 Van Vechten, pp. 68–9; A. Lentaker and B. De Cupere, "Domestication of the Cat and Reflections on the Scarcity of Finds in Archaeological Contexts," in L. Bodson, ed., *Des animaux introduits par l'homme dans la faune de Europe*, Liège, Université de Liège, 1994, p. 73; Beadle, pp. 82–4; R. Tabor, *Cats: The Rise of the Cat*, London, BBC Books, 1991, p. 40; J.G. Frazer, *The Golden Bough: A Study of Magic and Religion*, vol. 11, London, Macmillan, 1920, reprint of 1915, p. 40.
29 A folk saying cited by Van Vechten, p. 68.
30 Beadle, p. 92.
31 L.N. Magner, *A History of Medicine*, New York, Marcel Dekker, 1992, p. 121.
32 J.F.D. Shrewsbury, *A History of the Bubonic Plague in the British Isles*, Cambridge, Cambridge University Press, 1970, p. 21.
33 Shrewsbury, op.cit., pp. 35–6.
34 M. Oldfield Howey, *The Cat in the Mysteries of Religion and Magic*, New York, Castle Books, 1956, p. 226. This illustration is from a pew carving in Great Malvern Abby, stall no. 3, fourth block.
35 P. Ziegler, *The Black Death*, New York, John Day, 1969, p. 152.
36 Magner, op.cit., p. 121.
37 Ziegler, op.cit., pp. 100–8.
38 Howey, op.cit., p. 224 (quoting from S. Baring Gould, *Curious Myths of the Middle Ages*): during the Middle Ages, "rats and mice have generally been considered to be sacred animals ... Among the Scandinavian and Teutonic peoples they were regarded as souls of the dead." This citation is based on Germanic folklore.

39 P.L. Armitage, "Unwelcome Companions, Ancient Rats Reviewed," *Antiquity*, 1994, vol. 68, p. 236.

40 R. Hendrickson, *More Cunning than Man: A Social History of Rats and Men*, New York, Stein and Day, 1983, p. 101, citing Daniel Defoe, *Journal of the Plague Year*.

41 Ibid., pp. 98–100; Magner, op.cit., 121.

42 Briggs, p. 10. I have also found Darnton, op. cit., esp. pp. 9–104 of great value in understanding the transmission of folklore.

43 Briggs, pp. 68–9, citing Mary Trevelyan.

44 Briggs, p. 70.

45 Briggs, pp. 70–1.

46 Frazer, op.cit., vol. 1, p. 291: black cats were efficacious in causing rain; vol. 7, pp. 280–1: cats as "Corn Spirits," who were sometimes killed after the harvest; vol. 11, p. 40, in France, "cats represented the devil and could never suffer enough," when they were being burnt at midsummer and Lenten festivals in the nineteenth century; vol. 11, pp. 39–40: cats in Metz, the Ardennes and elsewhere in France were burnt in large wicker baskets to ward off sickness and witchcraft. Frazer also noted (vol. 11, p. 40) that these traditions preserved ancient Celtic practices. T.H. Gaster, *The New Golden Bough*, New York, Criterion Books, 1964, reprint of 1959, pp. 522, 736–8; Briggs, p. 73; Beadle, p. 81. Indeed, Frazer often regarded cat sacrifices as examples of the savage persecution of the animal because of its association with witchcraft. However, as Gaster notes, the sacrifices were often to promote good fortune and fertility and therefore the cats were not always seen as agents of evil.

47 Beadle, p. 83.

48 Briggs, p. 73; Beadle, p. 81.

49 J. Clutton-Brock, *Cats, Ancient and Modern*, Cambridge, Mass., Harvard University Press, 1993, p. 57; Van Vechten, p. 69; F.E. Zeuner, *A History of Domestic Animals*, New York, Harper and Row, 1963, p. 398.

50 R.-M. Luff, *A Zooarchaeological Study of the Roman Northwestern Provinces*, Oxford, British Archaeological Reports, International Series, 1982, vol. 137, pp. 190–3.

51 Van Vechten, p. 69; Darnton, op.cit., pp. 94–5. According to the research of both authors, the cats were walled up alive at least in medieval France.

52 Van Vechten, p. 69; A. Ross, "Ritual and the Druids," in M.J. Green, ed., *The Celtic World*, London, Routledge, 1995, pp. 436–41.

53 Briggs, p. 66; Beadle, p. 80–3; Darnton, op.cit., p. 92.

54 Anonymous poem cited by Van Vechten, p. 97.

55 Ross, op.cit., p. 425.

56 Briggs, p. 69.

57 Briggs, p. 69.

58 Briggs, p. 70. To flit means to change one's habitation.

59 Briggs, p. 72.

60 In the United States, colonized by Britain in the seventeenth and eighteenth centuries, the black cat is generally regarded as unlucky. There may be several explanations for this fact. Our country was originally settled by Puritans and other Protestant dissenters in the seventeenth century, near the end of the witch craze in Europe. At this time black cats may have been thought to be evil by those particular religious groups, and so the tradition has continued. In England however, Puritanism was never dominant over the country and when it was suppressed in the late seventeenth century, the black cat resumed its

proper role as a bringer of good luck, a role that it had probably never lost in many regions of the country.

61 Briggs, pp. 66–7.
62 Briggs, pp. 66–7.
63 Briggs, p. 68.
64 Van Vechten, pp. 132–3.
65 *New Century Dictionary*, New York, Appleton Century, 1938, s.v. Cat-head. Pictures in such works show generic images, not the exceptional or unusual.
66 Darnton, op.cit., pp. 33–8. The lack of meat in the diets of pre-industrial populations should be well known to historians, if not etymologists.
67 Witt, op.cit., p. 183.
68 *OED*, s.v. Float.
69 Darnton, op.cit., pp. 83, 92.
70 Witt, op.cit., p. 183; Van Vechten, pp. 89–91.
71 This power was also thought to exist in China, Van Vechten, p. 114; cf. Darnton, op.cit., p. 94; Briggs, p. 72.
72 Van Vechten, pp. 114–15; Briggs, p. 72.
73 Van Vechten, p. 115. When our cat Zsa Zsa died, the other two, Katie and Daphne, knew of her death as soon as she was brought home in her travel box, although she had not died more than five minutes earlier. Both hid under the bed for many hours.
74 Van Vechten, p. 111; Briggs, p. 67. Beadle, p. 81 notes this view in Indonesia.
75 Jerome, *Com. in Isaiam* 13. 50. In general see White, op.cit., vol. 1, pp. 336–50.
76 Briggs, p. 71.
77 Beadle, pp. 79–80.
78 Pico della Mirandola, "Oration on the Dignity of Man," in K.F. Thompson, *Classics of Western Thought: Middle Ages, Renaissance, and Reformation*, New York, Harcourt, Brace, Jovanovich, 1980, p. 281.
79 Darnton, op.cit., p. 100.
80 Beadle, pp. 84–5.
81 Beadle, p. 85.
82 Magner, op.cit., p. 117. In the United States we are now witnessing the spread of another rat-borne disease, Korean Hemorrhagic (or Hanta) Fever, which has a high mortality rate.
83 These changed attitudes towards the cat were first publicly demonstrated in the London Cat Show of 1871.
84 Van Vechten, p. 302, originally written in 1920.
85 Van Vechten, p. 303.

APPENDIX 3

1 This document is translated from the *Monumenta Germaniae Historica Epistolae Seculi XIII e Registris Pontificum Romanorum Selectae*, vol. 1, Munich, 1982, number 537, part 1, pp. 432–4. Despite the significance of this document for the history of witchcraft, it remains virtually inaccessible for research. I am very grateful to Patricia Dintrone at San Diego State University, for tracking this document down for me after all else had failed. This is my own translation. For the context of this papal bull, see J.B. Russell, *Witchcraft in the Middle Ages*, Ithaca, N. Y., Cornell University Press, 1972, pp. 159–65.
2 "Respecting your forefathers, you would have been taught to respect yourselves. You would not have chosen to consider the French people of yesterday,

as a nation of low-born servile wretches until the emancipating year of 1789. In order to furnish, at the expense of your honor an excuse to your apologists here for several enormities of yours, you would not have been content to be represented as a gang of slaves, suddenly broke loose from the house of bondage, and therefore to be pardoned for your abuse of the liberty to which you were not accustomed and ill fitted."

In Hitler's *Mein Kampf* the victimhood of the German people is a notion often repeated.

3 D. Engels, *Roman Corinth: An Alternative Model for the Classical City*, Chicago, University of Chicago Press, 1990, p. 227, note 33: in Roman Corinth, a dedicatory inscription survives in honor of Diana Pacilucifera Augusta – August Diana, the bearer of peace and light.

4 A. Lentaker and B. De Cupere, "Domestication of the Cat and Reflections on the Scarcity of Finds in Archaeological Contexts," in L. Bodson, ed., *Des animaux introduits par l'homme dans la faune de Europe*, Liège, Université de Liège, 1994, p. 73.

5 R. De Larouche and J.-M. Labat, *The Secret Life of Cats*, Hauppauge, N. Y., Barrons, 1995, p. 72, for a medieval image.

BIBLIOGRAPHY

Aesop, *Fables of Aesop*, trans. S.A. Handford, Harmondsworth, Penguin, 1964.

Altman, R., *The Quintessential Cat*, New York, Macmillan, 1994.

Apuleius, *The Golden Ass*, trans. J. Lindsay, Bloomington, Ind., Indiana University Press, 1971.

Armitage, P.L., "Unwelcome Companions, Ancient Rats Reviewed," *Antiquity*, 1994, vol. 68, pp. 231–40.

Armitage, P.L. and Clutton-Brock, J., "An Investigation of the Mummified Cats Held by the British Museum (Natural History)," *MASCA Journal*, 1980, vol. 1, pp. 185–96.

Ashe, G., *The Discovery of King Arthur*, London, Anchor Press, 1985.

Ashmead, A., "Greek Cats," *Expedition*, 1978, vol. 20, no. 3, pp. 38–47.

Austin, M., *The Hellenistic World From Alexander to the Roman Conquest*, Cambridge, Cambridge University Press, 1981.

Bagnall, R. and Frier, B., *The Demography of Roman Egypt*, Cambridge, Cambridge University Press, 1994.

Baker, J. and Brothwell, D., *Animal Diseases in Archaeology*, London, Academic Press, 1980.

Baring-Gould, S. *Curious Myths of the Middle Ages*, London, Blandford, 1996 (originally published 1868).

Beadle, M., *The Cat: History, Biology, Behavior*, New York, Simon and Schuster, 1977.

Beitak, M., *Avaris: The Capital of the Hyksos*, London, British Museum Press, 1996.

Bernal, M., *Black Athena: The Afroasiatic Roots of Classical Civilization*, New Brunswick, N. J., Rutgers University Press, 1987.

Betz, H.D., *The Greek Magical Papyri in Translation*, Chicago, University of Chicago Press, 1992.

Bisson, T.N., "The Feudal Revolution," *Past and Present*, 1994, vol. 142, pp. 6–42.

Boardman, J., *The Greeks Overseas*, Baltimore, Penguin, 1964.

Bodson, L., ed., *Des animaux introduits par l'homme dans la faune de Europe*, Liège, Université de Liège, 1994.

Bodson, L., "Les debuts en Europe du chat domestique," *Ethnozootechnie*, 1987, vol. 40, pp. 13–38.

Bökönyi, S., *History of Domestic Mammals in Central and Eastern Europe*, Budapest, Académiai Kiadó, 1974.

Briggs, K.M., *Nine Lives: The Folklore of the Cat*, New York, Pantheon Books, 1980.

Brothwell, D. and Sandison, A.T., eds, *Diseases in Antiquity*, Springfield, Ill., C.C. Thomas, 1967.

Bullough, V.L., *The Subordinate Sex*, Champaign, Ill., University of Illinois Press, 1973.

Burford, A., *Land and Labor in the Greek World*, Baltimore, Johns Hopkins University Press, 1993.

Burke, J., *Roman England*, New York, Norton, 1984.

Burstein, S., "Greek Contact with Egypt and the Levant: Ca. 1600–500 BC. An Overview," *Ancient World*, 1996, vol. 27, pp. 20–8.

Canfora, L., *The Vanished Library: A Wonder of the Ancient World*, Berkeley, University of California Press, 1990.

Carter, S.L., *The Culture of Disbelief: How American Law and Politics Trivialize Religious Devotion*, New York, Anchor Press, 1993.

Casson, L., *The Ancient Mariners*, New York, Minerva Press, 1959.

——*Travel in the Ancient World*, Baltimore, Johns Hopkins University Press, 1994.

Charles-Edwards, T., "Language and Society Among the Insular Celts, 400–1000," in M.J. Green, ed., *The Celtic World*, London, Routledge, pp. 703–36.

Chicago Assyrian Dictionary, Chicago, University of Chicago Press, 1992.

Churcher, P. B. and Lawton, J. H., "Beware Well-Fed Felines," *Natural History*, July 1989, pp. 40–6.

Chuvin, P., *Chronicle of the Last Pagans*, Cambridge, Mass., Harvard University Press, 1990.

Clayton, P.A., *Chronicle of the Pharaohs*, London, Thames and Hudson, 1995.

Clutton-Brock, J., *Domesticated Animals from Early Times*, Austin, University of Texas Press, 1981.

——*Cats, Ancient and Modern*, Cambridge, Mass., Harvard University Press, 1993.

Cohen, M.N., *Health and the Rise of Civilization*, New Haven, Yale University Press, 1989.

Crouch, D.P., "Modern Insights from the Study of Ancient Greek Water Management," in A. Trevor Hodge, ed., *Future Currents in Aqueduct Studies*, Leeds, Francis Cairns, 1991, pp. 93–103.

——*Water Management in Greek Cities*, Oxford, Oxford University Press, 1993.

Daley, A. and Benjamin, B., "London as a Case Study," *Population Studies*, 1964, vol. 17, pp. 249–62.

Darnton, R., *The Great Cat Massacre and Other Episodes in French Cultural History*, Harmondsworth, Penguin, 1984.

Davis, L.D., *The First Seven Ecumenical Councils*, Collegeville, Minn., Liturgical Press, 1990.

Davis, N., *Greek Coins and Cities*, London, Spink, 1967,

Davis, S.J.M., *The Archaeology of Animals*, New Haven, Yale University Press, 1987.

De Larouche, R. and Labat, J.-M., *The Secret Life of Cats*, Hauppauge, N. Y., Barrons, 1995.

Delia, D., " Isis or the Moon," in W. Clarysse *et al.* eds., *Egyptian Religion: The Last Thousand Years*, part I, *Studies Dedicated to the Memory of Jan Quaegebeur*, Leuven, Uttgeverij Peeters, 1998, pp. 549–50.

Demakopoulou, K. and Crouwel, J.H., "More Cats or Lions from Thera?" *Archaiologike Ephemeris*, 1993, vol. 132, pp. 1–11.

Demand, N., *Childbirth, Death, and Motherhood in Classical Greece*, Baltimore, Johns Hopkins University Press, 1994.

Dols, M.W., *The Black Death in the Middle East*, Princeton, Princeton University Press, 1971.

Engels, D., *Roman Corinth: An Alternative Model for the Classical City*, Chicago, University of Chicago Press, 1990.

Finley, M.I., "The Ancient City: From Fustel de Coulanges to Max Weber and Beyond," *Comparative Studies in Society and History*, 1977, vol. 19, pp. 3–23.

Foxhall, L., "Household, Gender, and Property in Classical Athens," *Classical Quarterly*, 1989, vol. 39, pp. 22–44.

Frazer, J.G., *The Golden Bough: A Study of Magic and Religion*, 12 vols, London, Macmillan, 1920 (reprint of 1907–15).

Frend, W.H.C., *The Rise of Christianity*, Philadelphia, Fortress, 1985.

Gager, J., *The Origins of Anti-Semitism: Attitudes Towards Judaism in Pagan and Christian Antiquity*, Oxford, Oxford University Press, 1983.

Garnsey, P. and Saller, R., *The Roman Empire: Economy, Society, and Culture*, Berkeley, University of California Press, 1987.

Gaster, T.H., *The New Golden Bough*, New York, Criterion Books, 1964 (reprint of 1959).

Gettings, F., *The Secret Lore of the Cat*, New York, Carol Publishing, 1989.

Gibbon, E., *The History of the Decline and Fall of the Roman Empire*, 7 vols, ed. J.B. Bury, New York, AMS Press, 1974 (reprint of 1909–14).

Ginzburg, C., *The Night Battles: Witchcraft and Agrarian Cults in the Sixteenth and Seventeenth Centuries*, Baltimore, Johns Hopkins University Press, 1983.

Gould, S., *The Book of Life*, New York, Norton, 1993.

Green, M.J., ed., *The Celtic World*, London, Routledge, 1995.

Green, M.J., "The Gods and the Supernatural," in M.J. Green, ed., *The Celtic World*, London, Routledge, pp. 465–88.

Gregory, T.E., "The Survival of Paganism in Christian Greece: A Critical Essay," *American Journal of Philology*, 1986, vol. 107, pp. 229–42.

Griffiths, J.G., *Plutarch's de Iside et Osiride*, Cardiff, University of Wales Press, 1970.

Grmek, D., *Diseases in the Ancient Greek World*, Baltimore, Johns Hopkins University Press, 1989.

Guthrie, W.K.C., *The Greeks and Their Gods*, Boston, Beacon, 1955 (reprint of 1950).

Halm, C., ed., *Fabulae Aesopicae*, Leipzig, Teubner, 1901.

Harcourt, R.A., "The Animal Bones," in G.J. Wainwright, *Gussage All Saints: An Iron Age Settlement in Dorset*, London, HMSO, 1979, pp. 150–60.

Hendrickson, R., *More Cunning than Man: A Social History of Rats and Men*, New York, Stein and Day, 1983.

Heyob, S.K., *The Cult of Isis Among Women in the Graeco-Roman World*, Leiden, Brill, 1975.

Himmelfarb, G., *On Looking into the Abyss*, New York, Knopf, 1994.

Holland, B.K., "Prospecting for Drugs in Ancient Texts," *Nature*, 1994, vol. 369, p. 702.

Horowitz, T., "Endangered Feces: Paleoscatologist Plumbs Old Privies," *Wall Street Journal*, 9 September 1991, vol. 95, pp. A1, A7.

Howey, M. Oldfield, *The Cat in the Mysteries of Religion and Magic*, New York, Castle Books, 1956.

Hsu, K.J., *The Mediterranean Was a Desert: A Voyage of the Glomar Challenger*, Princeton, Princeton University Press, 1983.

Jackson, R., *Doctors and Diseases in the Roman Empire*, Norman, Okla., University of Oklahoma Press, 1988.

Jantzen, U., *Äegyptische und Orientalische Bronzen aus dem Heraion von Samos*, vol. 8, Bonn, Deutsches Archäologisches Institut, 1972.

Keller, O., *Die Antike Tierwelt*, 2 vols, Hildesheim, Georg Olms, 1963 (reprint of 1909, 1913).

Keppie, L., *Understanding Roman Inscriptions*, Baltimore, Johns Hopkins University Press, 1991.

King, A., *Roman Gaul and Germany*, Berkeley, University of California Press, 1990.

Kraay, C., *Greek Coins*, New York, H.N. Abrams, 1966.

Lane-Fox, R., *Pagans and Christians*, New York, Knopf, 1987.

Langton, N. and Langton, B., *The Cat in Ancient Egypt: Illustrated from the Collection of Cat and other Egyptian Figures*, Cambridge, Cambridge University Press, 1940.

Lederer, W., *The Fear of Women*, New York, Harcourt, Brace, Jovanovich, 1968.

Lefkowitz, M. and Fant, M., *Women's Life in Greece and Rome*, Baltimore, Johns Hopkins University Press, 1982.

Lentaker, A. and De Cupere, B., "Domestication of the Cat and Reflections on the Scarcity of Finds in Archaeological Contexts," in L. Bodson, ed., *Des animaux introduits par l'homme dans la faune de Europe*, Liège, Université de Liège, 1994, pp. 71–8.

Lichtheim, M., *Ancient Egyptian Literature*, 3 vols, Berkeley, University of California Press, 1976.

Liebowitz, H. and Dehnisch, A.M., "A Mould-Made Terracotta Cat from Beth Gan," *Israel Exploration Journal*, vol. 48, 1998, pp. 174–82.

Limet, H., "Les chats, les poules et les autres: le relais mésopotamien," in L. Bodson, ed., *Des animaux introduits par l'homme dans la faune de Europe*, Liège, Université de Liège, 1994, pp. 39–54.

Lloyd, A.B., *Herodotus Book II, Commentary 1–98*, Leiden, Brill, 1976.

——*Herodotus Book II, Commentary 99–182*, Leiden, Brill, 1988.

Lloyd, G.E.R., *Greek Science After Aristotle*, New York, Norton, 1973.

Luff, R.-M., *A Zooarchaeological Study of the Roman Northwestern Provinces*, Oxford, British Archaeological Reports, International Series, 1982, vol. 137.

MacAdam, H.I., "Cities, Villages, and Veteran Settlements: Roman Administration in the Syrian Hawran," in D. Panzac, ed., *Histoire économique et sociale de L'Empire Ottoman et de la Turquie*, Paris, Peeters, 1995, pp. 641–52.

MacMullen, R., *Christianity and Paganism in the Fourth to Eighth Centuries*, New Haven, Yale University Press, 1997.

——*Christianizing the Roman Empire: AD 100–400*, New Haven, Yale University Press, 1984.

McNeill, W., *Plagues and Peoples*, New York, Anchor Press, 1976.

Magner, L.N., *A History of Medicine*, New York, Marcel Dekker, 1992.

Majno, G., *The Healing Hand: Man and Wound in the Ancient World*, Cambridge, Mass., Harvard University Press, 1975.

Malek, J., *The Cat in Ancient Egypt*, London, British Museum Press, 1993.

Marsden, G.M., *The Soul of the American University: From Protestant Establishment to Established Nonbelief*, Oxford, Oxford University Press, 1994.

Marsden, P., *Roman London*, London, Thames and Hudson, 1980.

Mason, S.F., *A History of the Sciences*, New York, Macmillan, 1977.

Mayor, A., "Grecian Weasels," *The Athenian*, February 1989, pp. 22–4.

Meiggs, R., *Roman Ostia*, Oxford, Oxford University Press, 1973.

Miller, T., *The Birth of the Hospital in the Byzantine Empire*, Baltimore, Johns Hopkins University Press, 1985.

Morgan, L., *The Miniature Wall Paintings of Thera: A Study of Aegean Culture and Iconography*, Cambridge, Cambridge University Press, 1988.

Nilsson, M.P., *A History of Greek Religion*, New York, Norton, 1964.

——*Greek Folk Relgion*, Philadelphia, University of Pennsylvania Press, 1972 (reprint of 1940).

Nobis, G., "Tieropfer aus einem Heroen-und Demeterheiligtum des antiken Messene (SW-Peloponnes, Griechenland)-Grabungen 1992 bis 1996," *Tier und Museum*, 1997, vol. 5, pp. 97–111.

O'Brien, S.J. and Antón, M., "The Family Line: The Human–Cat Connection," *National Geographic*, 1997, vol. 191, pp. 77–85.

Osborne, R., *Classical Landscape with Figures: The Ancient Greek City and its Countryside*, Dobbs Ferry, N. Y., Sheridan House, 1987.

Oxford Dictionary of the Christian Church, ed. F.L. Cross, New York, Oxford University Press, 1997.

Pagels, E., *Adam, Eve, and the Serpent*, New York, Random House, 1988.

——*The Gnostic Gospels*, New York, Random House, 1989 (reprint of 1979).

——*The Origin of Satan*, New York, Random House, 1995.

Parker, H.M.D., *The Roman Legions*, Oxford, Oxford University Press, 1928.

Patrick, A., "Diseases in Antiquity: Ancient Greece and Rome," in D.R. Brothwell and A.T. Sandison, eds, *Diseases in Antiquity*, Springfield, Ill., C.C. Thomas, 1967, pp. 220–30.

Patronek, G.J., "Free-roaming and Feral Cats – Their Impact on Wildlife and Human Beings," *Journal of the American Veterinary Medical Association*, 1998, vol. 212, pp. 218–26.

Perry, B.E., *Aesopica*, ed. B.E. Perry, vol. 1, Urbana, Ill., University of Illinois Press, 1952.

——*Babrius and Phaedrus*, ed. and trans. B.E. Perry, Cambridge, Mass., Harvard University Press, 1965.

Phillips, E.D., *Aspects of Greek Medicine*, New York, St Martins, 1973.

Poidebard, A., *La Trace de Rome dans le désert de Syrie*, Paris, Librairie Orientaliste Paul Geuthner, 1934.

Poly, J.P. and Bournazel, E., *The Feudal Transformation: 900–1200*, New York, Holmes and Meier, 1991.

Potter, T.W. and Johns, C., *Roman Britain*, Berkeley, University of California Press, 1992.

Raaflaub, K., *Zum Freiheitsbegriff der Griechen*, Berlin, Akademie Verlag, 1981.

Reallexikon der Assyriologie, Berlin, Walter de Gruyter, 1976–80.

Rickman, G., *The Corn Supply of Ancient Rome*, Oxford, Oxford University Press, 1980.

——*Roman Granaries and Store Buildings*, Cambridge, Cambridge University Press, 1971.

Rose, H.J., *Religion in Greece and Rome*, New York, Harper and Row, 1959 (reprint of 1946, 1948).

Ross, A., "Ritual and the Druids," in M.J. Green, ed., *The Celtic World*, London, Routledge, pp. 423–44.

Runciman, S., *A History of the Crusades*, 2 vols, New York, Harper and Row, 1964 (reprint of 1951).

Russell, J.B., *Witchcraft in the Middle Ages*, Ithaca, N. Y., Cornell University Press, 1972.

Sallares, R., *The Ecology of the Ancient Greek World*, Ithaca, N. Y., Cornell University Press, 1991.

Scarborough, J., *Medical Terminologies: Classical Origins*, Norman, Okla., University of Oklahoma Press, 1992.

Schaps, D.M., *Economic Rights of Women in Ancient Greece*, Edinburgh, Edinburgh University Press, 1979.

Schimmel, A., "Cats," in M. Eliade, ed., *Encyclopedia of Religion*, vol. 3, London, Macmillan, 1987, pp. 121–3.

Scobie, A., "Slums, Sanitation, and Mortality in the Roman World," *Klio*, 1986, vol. 68, pp. 399–433.

Shrewsbury, J.F.D., *A History of the Bubonic Plague in the British Isles*, Cambridge, Cambridge University Press, 1970.

Sigerist, H.E., *On the History of Medicine*, New York, MD Publications, 1960.

Silvester, H., *Cats in the Sun*, San Francisco, Chronicle Books, 1994.

Smith, H., *Man and His Gods*, Boston, Little, Brown, 1952.

Sorabji, R., *Animal Minds and Human Morals*, Ithaca, N. Y., Cornell University Press, 1993.

Thompson, K.F., *Classics of Western Thought: Middle Ages, Renaissance, and Reformation*, New York, Harcourt, Brace, Jovanovich, 1980, p. 281.

Tabor, R., *Cats: The Rise of the Cat*, London, BBC Books, 1991.

——*Understanding Cats*, Pleasantville, N. Y., Reader's Digest, 1994.

Taylor, D., *The Logistics of the Roman Army in Africa*, Ph.D. Dissertation, University of Arkansas at Fayetteville, 1997.

Tétrault, C., "L'histoire des chats à Rome," *Société des Études Anciennes du Québec*, 1995, vol. 2, pp. 69–71.

Theodoret, *History of the Monks of Syria*, trans. R.M. Price, Kalamazoo, Mich., Cistercian Press, 1985.

Thomas, E.M., *The Tribe of Tiger*, New York, Simon and Schuster, 1994.

Todd, N.B., "Cats and Commerce," *Scientific American*, 1977, vol. 237, no. 5, pp. 100–7.

Toynbee, J.M.C., *Animals in Roman Life and Art*, Baltimore, Johns Hopkins University Press, 1996 (reprint of 1973).

Ulrich, L.T., *A Midwife's Tale: The Life of Martha Ballard, Based on Her Diary, 1785–1812*, New York, Knopf, 1990.

Van Dam, R., *Leadership and Community in Late Antique Gaul*, Berkeley, University of California Press, 1985.

Van Vechten, C., *The Tiger in the House*, New York, Knopf, 1936.

Vermeule, E., *Greece in the Bronze Age*, Chicago, University of Chicago Press, 1964.

Von den Dreisch, A. and Boessneck, J., "A Roman Cat Skeleton from Quseir on the Red Sea Coast," *Journal of Archaeological Science*, 1983, vol. 10, pp. 205–11.

——*Tiryns XI*, Mainz am Rhein, von Zabern, 1990.

Walsh, P.G., "The Rights and Wrongs of Curiosity," *Greece and Rome*, 1988, vol. 35, pp. 73–85.

White, A.D., *A History of the Warfare of Science with Theology in Christendom*, 2 vols, New York, Dover, 1960 (reprint of 1895).

Wilken, R.L., *The Christians as the Romans Saw Them*, New Haven, Yale University Press, 1984.

Witherington, B., *Women in the Earliest Churches*, Cambridge, Cambridge University Press, 1988.

Witt, R.E., *Isis in the Ancient World*, Baltimore, Johns Hopkins University Press, 1997 (reprint of 1971).

Yegül, F., *Baths and Bathing in Classical Antiquity*, Cambridge, Mass., MIT Press, 1992.

Yurco, F.J., "The Cat and Ancient Egypt," *Field Museum of Natural History Bulletin*, 1990, vol. 61, pp. 15–23.

Zeuner, F.E., *A History of Domesticated Animals*, New York, Harper and Row, 1963.

Ziegler, P., *The Black Death*, New York, John Day, 1969.

Zinsser, H., *Rats, Lice, and History*, Boston, Little, Brown, 1935.

INDEX

Aelian *see* Claudius Aelian
Aesop: cat fables with Christian themes
  133–6; cat fables of Greek and
  Roman eras 59–73; mentioned 15,
  46
afterlife: cats and 115, 128, 162, 168,
  169; Greek 79–80; Isis and 118–19,
  125, 128, 169
agouti (non-agouti) 83, 84–5, 86
aielouros, ailouros (Greek words for cat)
  10, 19, 27, 57–8, 60
Alexander the Great 86, 136
Alexandria: cat sacrifice in 37–8; center
  for worship of Isis and Sarapis
  115–16, 125; Museum and Library
  of 125, 145, 170; patriarchs of 132,
  133; trade of 122; wisdom of 126,
  170
Anubis 125, 127
Apuleius 116–19, 126, 167
Aristotle: books burnt in thirteenth
  century 169; thoughts on cats 74,
  77, 145
Artemis: and Bastet 2, 29–31, 32,
  53–4, 77, 123; in Greece 77–9, 124,
  165, 169; incarnate in a cat 79; and
  Isis 119–21, 125, 126, 153; *see also*
  Diana
Atum-Ra 7, 26–8, 41, 79, 130
Augustine: attitudes to nature 208 n.
  14; curiosity a sin 145; pagans
  maintain religious *concordia* 115;
  successionist theology of 154, 155

Babrius 59–60, 66
Baphomet 188
barn cats: in animal fables 60–1, 65;

behavior 11, 176; in Greece 80; kill
  rodents 1, 6, 10; and roosters 72
Bastet, Egyptian cat goddess 2, 21, 25,
  26, 29–30, 32–3, 35, 37, 38, 42–3,
  142; Greek era 53, 77; Roman era
  89, 104, 106, 115, 120, 122, 123,
  124, 126, 130, 142, 188; *see also*
  Bubastis
bathing: Christian attitudes towards
  144, 145, 146, 151, 157, 161; by
  priests of Isis 125
birds: cats prey on 7, 19, 88, 97; in
  Egypt 22–3, 37; in Greece 49, 63,
  80, 81; rodents prey on 15, 16; in
  Roman era 88, 91, 97, 98, 120
black cat: brings bad luck 165; brings
  good luck 100, 165; earliest
  references to 75–6; especially sacred
  123, 124, 128, 164–5, 169; in
  folklore 163–70; guardian spirits of
  ships 166; incarnations or symbols of
  Satan or the devil 157, 183–8; in
  magic 130; massacres of 158–9;
  origin and spread of 84–5, 86; wards
  off disease 165–6
Black Death 146, 160–2, 172; *see also*
  bubonic plague
black rat *see* rat, black
brooms 158
Bubastis (Per-Bastet), Egyptian city 29,
  32–3, 37, 38, 133
Bubastis, Greco-Roman cat goddess: in
  Hellenistic Egypt 37; in the Middle
  Ages 141, 142, 152, 168–9, 188; in
  Ostia 89, 122–3; in Roman era 89,
  104, 106, 115, 120, 121, 122–8,
  133; *see also* Bastet
bubonic plague: caused by rodents 1,